# The Colour Box

Barbara Anne Waite

For Rita
With a Heart
full of memories
of years
with you
in Antigua!
Barbara Anne
Waite

*Other books by Barbara Anne Waite*

*Elsie—Adventures of an Arizona Schoolteacher 1913-1916*
ISBN 978-0-9839452-0-8
Copyright 2011
Palomar Mountain Bookworks

*Elsie's Mountain—Memories of Palomar & Southern California 1897-1987*
ISBN 978-0-9839452-1-5
Copyright 2015



Cover art: *Green Castle Estate Antigua* by Nicholas Pocock from the Beinecke Lesser Antilles Collection of Hamilton College, and *Free Women of Color* by Augustino Brunias (c.1770-1796) from the Brooklyn Museum collection. Used by permission.

Cover and text design by Diane King, dkingdesigner.com

Scripture taken from the King James Version. Public domain.

Published by Palomar Mountain Bookworks
BarbaraWaiteBooks.com

ISBN 978 09839452-3-9

Library of Congress Control Number: 2021902706

Printed in the United States of America.

*This book is dedicated to committed teachers around the world and to the memory of Anne and Elizabeth Hart who inspired me to visualize their story. As teachers, these undaunted sisters were willing to cross the lines of culture and color to bring education to the disadvantaged, lighting the way to the future for countless lives.*

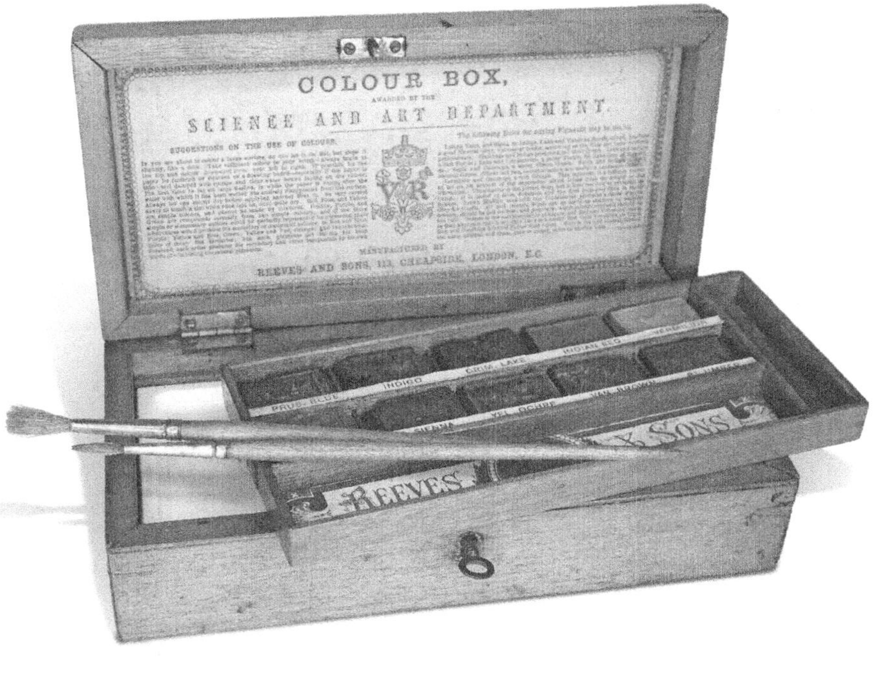

# *Antigua*

French 1725 map with place names added

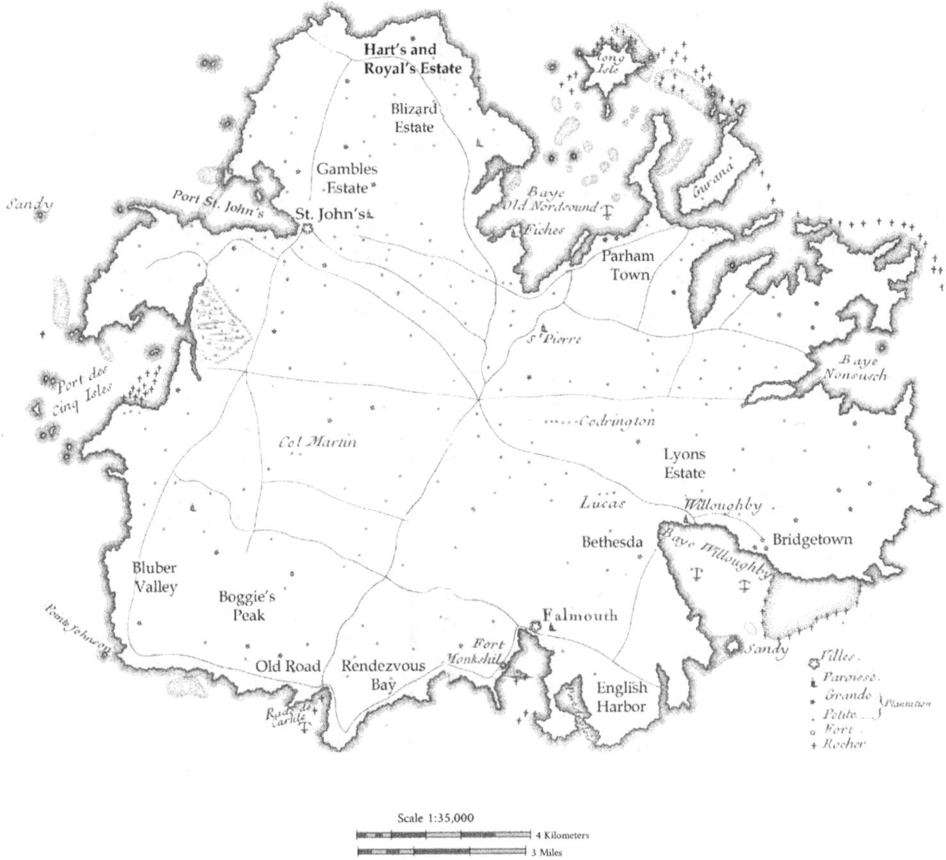

# The Leeward Islands

# Contents

*Individuals in Order of Appearance* . . . . . . . . . . . . . . . . . . . 9
1 *Father and Son* . . . . . . . . . . . . . . . . . . . . . . . . . . 11
2 *Of Books and Bonds* . . . . . . . . . . . . . . . . . . . . . . . 19
3 *Changes and Chance Encounter* . . . . . . . . . . . . . . . . . 25
4 *Courtship Conversations* . . . . . . . . . . . . . . . . . . . . 33
5 *Family, Faith and the Fourth of July* . . . . . . . . . . . . . . 41
6 *Upheavals* . . . . . . . . . . . . . . . . . . . . . . . . . . . . 49
7 *An Answer Named Esther* . . . . . . . . . . . . . . . . . . . . 57
8 *Harsh Realities* . . . . . . . . . . . . . . . . . . . . . . . . . 64
9 *Easing Sorrows* . . . . . . . . . . . . . . . . . . . . . . . . . 72
10 *Becoming Proper Methodists* . . . . . . . . . . . . . . . . . . 80
11 *Blessed to Be Free Blacks* . . . . . . . . . . . . . . . . . . . 88
12 *Tales of Men of Character* . . . . . . . . . . . . . . . . . . . 97
13 *Spider Web of Slavery* . . . . . . . . . . . . . . . . . . . . . 106
14 *Shop Girls Don't Read Milton* . . . . . . . . . . . . . . . . . 115
15 *An Unlikely Setting for Love* . . . . . . . . . . . . . . . . . 121
16 *Changes* . . . . . . . . . . . . . . . . . . . . . . . . . . . . 130
17 *Finding New Purpose* . . . . . . . . . . . . . . . . . . . . . . 136

18 *Sisters Still Bonding* ........ 143

19 *An End to Plantation Life* ........ 151

20 *Grace Bestowed* ........ 161

21 *Elizabeth's Painting* ........ 165

22 *The Move to English Harbour* ........ 171

23 *A Lesson in Love* ........ 182

24 *Plans to Prosper* ........ 192

25 *Dealing with Prejudice* ........ 202

26 *The King's Men* ........ 212

27 *Loss and Gain* ........ 218

28 *The Birth of Sunday School* ........ 223

29 *A New Ministry* ........ 231

30 *A Refuge for Gloria* ........ 241

31 *The Gilberts Move to Town* ........ 250

32 *Sinking of the* Maria ........ 263

33 *The Summons* ........ 267

34 *Great Loss* ........ 276

35 *Emancipation Dawn* ........ 282

*Author's Notes* ........ 287

*Acknowledgements* ........ 295

# Individuals in Order of Appearance

** Fictional characters*

John Hart – white plantation owner (from Ireland).

Barry Conyers Hart – son of John Hart and Fanny Conyers; inherited Hart plantation.

Fanny Conyers – mother of Barry, slave of Conyers, who was previous owner of Hart plantation (Fanny is Conyers' illegitimate mixed-race daughter).

Gratianus Hart – legitimate son of John Hart and his second wife, Elizabeth Hillhouse Moore.

Annie Clearkley – mixed-race, married Barry Hart.

Frances Clearkley – free black, mother to Annie, married to Timothy Clearkley (Annie's father).

Annie's sisters – Grace, Lydia, and "Margaret" (another Elizabeth, for clarity renamed Margaret).

Barry & Annie's children – Anne, Elizabeth, Jacob, Gratianus, Charles.

Dr. Thomas Coke – Methodist Bishop.

*Esther Rosenthal – Jewish girl.

*Old Molly – slave that cooked for Hart plantation.

Elizabeth (Liza) Sharp – Barry's 2nd wife; children Sarah, Francis, George, Joseph, Daniel, Thomas, Mary, Ruth.

*Kallie O'Rourke – Irish girl (brother Sean).

James Ramsey – British ship surgeon who became clergyman, acquainted with Wilberforce.

William Wilberforce – member of British Parliament who fought to end slavery.

Sir Isaac Watts – hymn writer 1600s -1700s, British minister.

*Amazon Mary – mother of one of Anne and Elizabeth's students.

John Gilbert – white clerk; 31 years old when he married Anne in 1798.

*Rev. Smith – Methodist pastor.

John Wesley – founder of the Methodist Church.

Toussaint – led the revolution in Haiti 1700s.

Reverend Baxter – Methodist Pastor.

Bartholomew McDonald – Methodist missionary.

Charles Thwaites – white educator, married Elizabeth 1805.

# 1

# Father and Son

*Antigua, West Indies 1748*

The child sat at his father's large desk, waiting as patiently as an eight-year-old could. His eyes filled with wonder when his father opened a trunk, lifted out a beautiful mahogany box, and set it directly in front of the boy.

His anticipation fairly electrified the room. "Is this for me?" asked Barry.

John Hart leaned forward in his Windsor chair and focused his weathered yet still attractive face on his young son. "I ordered this paint box two months ago for your birthday, and it arrived from England on a ship this week."

Barry smiled in anticipation as he passed his slim brown fingers gently over the polished wood. The box appeared as a rare treasure to this creative child. He glanced at his father again before turning the shiny brass key and lifting the hinged lid. Barry gave an elated shout at the sight of the thin wooden sable hair paintbrushes and small porcelain water dish. The boy read aloud the label on the inside of the box.

"Colour Box—Thomas Reeves and Sons 113 Cheapside—London."

Barry's wonder grew when he slid open a small drawer disclosing an array of compressed, embossed blocks of paints in a myriad of colours, which gave a distinctive odor holding the promise of hours of pleasure to come.

The colour box prompted a flood of comments and questions from Barry. "Look, Father! So many colours are here! I can add colours to my drawings with these paints."

"Yes, if you don't see what you need, you can blend the paints creating limitless new colours of your own."

John responded with open pleasure to his child's continual inquisitiveness.

"Is my colour here, Father? Some people call me black, but I am not as black as charcoal! Am I? I think I am brown, but not dark brown. Am I?"

John's eyes flickered with amusement at Barry's observations.

"Barry, you are the most wonderful colour in the world to me. Perhaps there is no name for it."

"What colour are you, Father?"

A low Irish laugh emerged at the rapid-fire questions spilling forth from his son. "Most people would call me *white*," he said.

The child scrunched up his nose. "Milk is white, Father. You are not the colour of milk, and when you come in from the hot sun, you look red!" The boy paused as his father rumbled with laughter again.

Fiddling with one of the smaller paintbrushes, Barry spoke softly, "What colour is my mother? I know some people call her black. But she is not as black as our cook, Nelly, is she? I think my mama is the loveliest shade of brown. Maybe she is coffee with a little cream. Her colour must have less cream than mine, doesn't it, Father?"

Examining the colour box in front of them, John pondered the perplexing challenge.

Explaining to his son how the various shades of both brown and pale-skinned people came to be on this little island became complicated. John was not confident that he could put this in plain words himself, but he would go back to the beginning, telling his son of the events leading up to his birth.

Thinking back, John Hart recalled marveling at the stunning colours on his arrival in 1737. The Caribbean Sea, the flamboyant trees, the variety of vibrant toned fruits, and the striking array of fish were feasts for the eyes. Yet, he seldom noticed skin shades, not giving much thought to the slaves and their vast differences in appearance. Only after Barry's birth did John begin to see the slaves as individuals.

John began again to tell Barry about Ireland, though the story was somewhat painful to retell. Barry knew only a few lighter-skinned or white people. Yet, his father came from a country where black skin was not often seen.

"A long time ago, I lived far away in a country called Ireland. I had a business there until it no longer produced a profit. Hoping to try a new life, I bought this plantation in 1737 and brought my wife here."

Barry interrupted his father. "Did your wife want to come?"

"No, Barry, my wife loved Ireland, and it was a long and difficult two months on a ship to reach Antigua."

Barry climbed on his father's lap, and John Hart ran his fingers through the boy's soft curls as he continued the story of how he came to make this place his home.

"Why didn't she love it here?"

John frowned in remembrance. "Life here was so different for her and sadly those differences made her unhappy and clouded her eyes so she could see nothing but the memories of all she had left behind."

Barry asked his father, "What did she leave behind making her so sad?"

John paused, letting his mind drift back to occasions when he too had longed for his homeland, recalling the months of delay before he learned his parents had died in Ireland. But he had no regrets coming here. Staring down at his handsome son, he touched his cheek.

"We left all our family in Ireland, a lovely home in Cork, and lush, rolling green hills. My wife missed her friends. She longed for the shops with familiar things. The oppressive heat, the storms, and the troublesome mosquitoes on this tropical island overwhelmed her. The faces were so different here from those in Ireland, and this frightened her. There were few slaves in Ireland, and she grew increasingly upset by the differences in the lands."

"Why did you come to Antigua? I know I'm asking a lot of questions." The child bit his lower lip as he looked up at his father.

John Hart squeezed Barry's hand. "It's all right, son. Little boys are made to ask why. We chose Antigua because the British arrived here 100 years earlier, and sugar became a profitable business. My cousin lived here, and I suppose my feet itched for adventure."

"Did you love the island? Was it an adventure?"

"To be honest, the trip on the boat made me wish I never heard of Antigua. We were seasick for days, and when the storm hit our ship, it was more like a nightmare than an adventure. However, once we arrived and I began to adjust to the heat, I fell in love with the island and all it offered. The plantation house was pleasant, and though Ireland is a stunning country, nothing matched the beauty of our new home—the clear blue Caribbean Sea, the sweet pineapple, the beautiful wild orchids—it was all I could have hoped for."

"And when you came to this house, did you meet my mama?"

John reached for his clay pipe, taking his time to light it. How much should he tell an eight-year-old about what resulted in the birth of this beloved child? Pride and happiness washed over John as he stared at this son who had become a treasured and undeserved gift from God.

John rested his hand on Barry's shoulder. "I not only met your mother, I also met your grandmother, who was the housekeeper for the former owner for many years."

John wondered if Barry might someday realize the British owner before him was likely his grandfather, since Fanny Conyers, Barry's mother, had fairer skin and facial features hinting at a mixed racial background. She was more petite than others of her heritage, and her build belied a complicated lineage. John avoided any further details about his relationship with Barry's mother.

"Your grandmother was a wonderful cook for us. Your mother, Fanny, was about 20 years old when her mother died, and since your mother was the daughter of a house slave, it was natural she became our housekeeper."

"Did all of the slaves live in the plantation owner's house?" asked Barry.

"Oh, no," said John. "Most slaves lived in the shacks nearer the fields where they worked. But the owner wanted to keep Fanny's mother nearby, so Fanny grew up in the great house, along with the cook and others."

Barry returned to the subject of John's first wife. "Your wife never got to go home to Ireland?"

"No, shortly after your grandmother died, my wife also died. Yellow fever took their lives and became a memory I wish to forget."

The child barely paused for breath before he continued to overflow with questions. "Then you got another wife?"

Barry was probing where John did not want to go. Lifting the boy from his lap, he stood up and stretched. "Barry, could you go ask your mama to make us some lemonade, and see if she still has any of those currant buns left?"

Barry ran off happily and soon returned with his mother, the buns, and lemonade. Fanny curtsied. "Master, I can make you tea if you wish. Is Barry bothering you?"

"No. Thank you, Fanny. And Barry is never a bother. Well, perhaps occasionally," John said with a hint of amusement. He enfolded the boy in a tender hug, causing him to giggle—and giving contentment to John Hart.

With a flutter of envy over her master's love for her son, Fanny slipped from the room. Like his mother, Barry would grow up in the great house, but the similarities ended there. The man who fathered Fanny never cared for her. She also knew John Hart did not love her. With her mother gone, all she had was her son. Yet, Barry was enough for Fanny.

John pulled up a chair beside him. "Here, Barry, sit next to me while we enjoy our refreshments."

Swallowing the last bit of his bun, John watched the boy beam as he reached across to touch the brushes in the colour box. The extravagant gift was John's way of exhibiting a love that knew no bounds. Since John wanted no more questions, he suggested Barry take the paint box to show his mother.

Memories flooded John's mind and left him with mixed emotions. The path taken during the months following his wife's death resulted in Barry's birth. There had been little time for socializing, and trips to town occurred only occasionally. He had often read aloud to his wife to keep her from constantly enumerating the things she hated. After her passing, he spent many quiet evenings reading alone. One evening he spoke to Fanny. "I noticed when you dust my books you handle them with care. Would you sit and listen while I read out loud?"

Fanny sat on the floor not far from her master. To sit in a chair beside him would have been out of place.

John never intended to take advantage of his housekeeper, nor did he consider this time of reading to become anything more. However, following a long reading session, John had reached out to help the slight, fine-boned girl to her feet. He instinctively wrapped his arms around her and felt comforted by the sensation of holding a woman close.

His actions surprised them both, and he merely yielded to the strong desires of his flesh. Neither would have described what they shared as love, and the next morning he assured her it would never happen again.

John stopped reading to Fanny, going out of his way to avoid her except when necessary. He sensed her resignation to her expected role and the unexpected loss of friendship.

Some months later, John found the girl crying as she folded the clean sheets. "Fanny, what's wrong?"

She lowered her eyes, and a tear dripped from her chin. "I am with child, Master."

John felt mixed emotions. "And I am the father?"

"Yes, Master."

Because John's first wife had been unable to give him the children he longed for, he now felt anticipation mix with guilt when seeing his housekeeper's distress.

"I never meant to take advantage of you, and I am sorry for that. But I am not at all sorry I will be a father, and perhaps I will have a son after years of disappointment. He will be provided for as my child and will be granted freedom at birth."

Barry Conyers Hart arrived a few months later, and John Hart could not suppress his satisfaction. John proclaimed Barry the most handsome baby ever known. With hair soft and curly, eyes enormous pools of chocolate brown, and skin reminding John of the fields of winter wheat in Ireland, the child appeared perfect.

The boy brought much satisfaction, but soon John's heart filled with a longing for companionship beyond his infant son. Since his estate was located several miles from town, John only rarely mingled with those beyond his plantation, his life too solitary for anyone.

Not long after Barry's birth, John attended a dinner on a neighboring estate and met the widow Elizabeth Hillhouse Moore. This cheerful, attractive woman loved to read, and as they chatted about books, John felt hope. She was lonely and spoke of returning to her homeland in England. After calling on her several times, John asked Elizabeth to marry him.

Elizabeth did not question John about his evident fondness for his housekeeper's light-skinned son. Some questions were best left unasked.

A few months following their marriage, Elizabeth shared the news she was expecting their first child. She hoped for a son, and before long, they welcomed Gratianus Hart—a healthy baby boy—into their lives. John Hart had a legal heir.

Once Gratianus became a toddler, Barry took on the role of the shadow and protector. Elizabeth recognized the housekeeper's son acted with caution and care with her son. Regardless of Barry's background, the two boys were inseparable, and it seemed natural Barry sat in the evenings beside Gratianus as John read to them.

Unlike his first wife, Elizabeth enjoyed her life with John on the island. A natural equestrian, she often rode with John as he inspected the crops. But education for her son soon grew to be utmost in her thoughts. When their son turned six, John hired a tutor to educate him. Barry often sat beside Gratianus as the loquacious but boring instructor droned on about mathematics or history. Unimpressed with the available teachers on the island, Elizabeth was determined to return to England and enroll their son in a proper boarding school.

Both boys were upset when they learned Gratianus was leaving. Realizing her son was more upset at the thought of missing the slave's son than the idea of leaving his father bothered Elizabeth.

On a breezy winter day Gratianus and his mother set sail for England on a returning ship. John arrived home from the port to see Barry slumping on the veranda steps, weeping. John lowered himself to sit beside the boy, wrapping a strong arm around his small shoulder as

Barry rested his head on his father's chest. "'Tis a hard thing to miss someone you love. Gratianus has been a fine companion for you. I feel especially grateful you remain in my life. We will be fine together, with much to do about the plantation."

When the first letter arrived from England, disappointment overshadowed John. The arduous voyage had taken eight weeks. Gratianus and his mother became deathly ill from the rough seas. For weeks, Elizabeth feared for their lives and wrote she could not imagine ever wanting to experience a voyage like this again. The mere thought of a rocking ship left her feeling nauseated. Elizabeth would not return.

# 2

# Of Books and Bonds

Once more, John was alone, but the bond he had developed with Barry began to deepen. Gratianus remained the heir, but Barry captured John's heart. While the boy spent his days with his mother in the kitchen, evenings often found him in his father's study.

John took pride that the child had become fascinated with the books lining the walls from top to bottom in his father's library. The boy spent hours examining the books, delighting in the earthy smell and smooth feel of the leather-bound volumes. He especially enjoyed the illustrations. Often John declared the evening worthy of reading together on the veranda. Barry would sit curled up with his arms around his big shaggy dog, Oliver, while John read by lantern light in his lilting Irish brogue.

One day when the clouds were high and the air was clear after a fresh rain, Barry pointed in awe at the sunset. "Father, did you see?" Barry shouted. "The sun bowed in golden orange, then flashed a spectacular farewell in brilliant green before falling into the sea!"

John took pleasure in his son's exuberant spirit. "You described it well, Barry. Indeed, it was spectacular."

Barry rarely spoke the dialect so common among the field slaves. The child's vocabulary soon sounded like any British boy exposed to good literature at a young age. Eventually, John hired a different tutor to instruct Barry. Yet, the child had little idea he was privileged compared to other coloured boys on the island. He was too young to realize his life would always teeter between two social classes.

The dignified manner and bearing of his father became implanted in this child. He often entered the kitchen, speaking words emulating his father's inflections and mannerisms. At the same time, Fanny was content to have her son at her side while her master worked, and thus, Barry was also responsible for household chores. Barry helped his mother glean from the kitchen garden, toting a basket half his size. "Mama, the chickens used to frighten me. Now I know only the rooster is the one to watch out for. I like the feel of the eggs, still warm from the hens. When they see me coming, they know I will share kitchen scraps." Barry scattered the chicken feed, calling out childish chicken sounds.

Then he said, "Please, may I collect the guavas, since I have learned how to tell which ones are ripe. Their aroma is wonderful." He held a ripe one to his nose and gave a contented sigh. "I won't pick the green ones by mistake as I did when I was younger."

Fanny tousled his mop of curly hair, realizing it was time to cut it again. "After the guavas, please gather some of those ripe yellow passion fruit. We will make some jam later today."

"Will you sing to me, Mama, while we make the jam?" Barry asked. "Will you teach me a new song?"

During quieter days, Barry often sat for hours in the kitchen drawing and painting flowers, palm trees, fish, and lizards—wherever his imagination carried him. Barry seldom played with the slave children.

One Sunday afternoon he and his father walked along the beach at Runaway Bay. Barry took in the scene with renewed excitement. "Father, do you think I might paint the ocean waves? And look at the colours in the sky. They are like the colours in my box!"

Fanny adored her son and appreciated the world his father was introducing him to—the world of books and instruction in the King's English. The thoughtful child absorbed his disparate world—content to help his mother and listen to her sing softly as she worked—or listen to his father reading Shakespeare.

One afternoon John approached the kitchen, smelling the pungent scent of salt-fish, and hearing the nickel nut-seeds clacking when moved from each depression cup on the roughly carved wooden Warri board. He stopped for a moment outside the kitchen, hearing Barry's childish giggle as he told his mother, "I captured your nickels, Mama."

John contemplated for a moment playing Warri with Barry. Then it struck him that this game, handed down through generations from Africa, was something Barry's mother should share with her son. Many planters disliked the inclusion of anything formerly a part of the African heritage, but John appreciated the game. It stimulated learning about strategy and an awareness of the principle of cause and effect. He encouraged Barry to play. After Gratianus and Elizabeth left, John had begun teaching Barry how to play chess. By the time the child was ten, he could occasionally beat his father at their evening game.

At times, John felt a twinge of guilt spending almost all evenings with his son, excluding the boy's mother, but Fanny recognized the devotion bestowed on this child as rare. She determined to be content with the precious hours spent with her son during the day. Fanny had moved to the slave quarters when Elizabeth Hart left, and Barry had slept there when he was younger. Now John allowed him to spend most nights in the main house.

During the days, the child taught his mother how to play jacks and shared riddles John told him in their evenings together. Asking permission, Barry removed Shakespeare's *Romeo and Juliet* from the library, and read it aloud to his mother as she worked. Fanny cried when she heard the tragic end of the couple's fleeting romance.

The boy often retold the stories John had read to him the evening before. Requests such as "Father, please read me a fairytale tonight!" resulted from the child wanting to tell his mother stories she loved.

Both his father and his mother taught Barry the value of working hard to complete a task. The child was seldom assigned chores. He began to copy whoever he was with, striving to imitate them. Barry was only ten when given a horse of his own, sometimes riding out to the fields with his father to observe the management of the crops. Each passing year, John's hopes for Gratianus to return to the estate that was his rightful inheritance diminished.

When Barry turned twelve, he received a copy of *Poor Richard's Almanack* by Benjamin Franklin. John appreciated the author's maxims encouraging honesty, frugality, and industry. The following year, John ordered a copy of the next book by this American author and gave it as a birthday gift to his son. Soon Barry asked his father to buy him a copy of Franklin's book, *Experiments and Observations on Electricity.*

Barry often read from the local newspaper after John set it aside. As the boy's height and voice changed, John recognized he could no longer consider the boy a child. He suggested, "Son, you read so well I want you to write an article for the *Antigua Sun* newspaper. Work on it, and then we will edit it together."

The young man composed an article about the use of some local herbal remedies. After reading it, John removed his glasses and regarded his son. "This is good. Well done! We could submit the article under my name and see what kind of response you get."

After a trip into town a few days later, John told Barry, "Some folks congratulated me on a well-written article. My barrister, Blake, said it was the best I have ever written. I didn't confess you have surpassed me in your ability to write!"

Barry continued to write using his father's name as the author. Father and son found humor in the deception.

One day Barry laid the paper aside. "Father, this news in the papers coming on the ship yesterday gives accounts at least two months out of date. I am weary of such articles, knowing I must wait months to hear how a vote went in Parliament. I appreciate books more than useless newspapers. Thank you for having a grand library to share with me."

Were those tears Barry saw in his father's eyes?

"All thanks belong to God, for blessing me with the treasure of a son who loves words as I do," said John.

John's thoughts went to the son far away from whom he received news only every few months. The boys occasionally exchanged letters over the years. John still held out hope Gratianus would return to the island after his schooling.

During Barry's twentieth year, John became frail and spent more and more time sleeping each day. Finally, the doctor informed the household John's heart was failing. His barrister, Blake, visited the plantation to get Mr. Hart's affairs in order.

Barry sat watching as his beloved father slowly slipped away, agonizing as he drifted in and out of consciousness. When he was able to speak, John conveyed his disappointment that Elizabeth had taken Gratianus away to school and never returned. "Barry," John said in a weak whisper, "though by law Gratianus inherits the estate, he may never return to Antigua. I have written and told him how well you have been able to keep the plantation functioning over these last few months. Perhaps he will choose to deed everything to you." There was a lengthy pause as John moved his hand toward Barry who sat at his father's bedside. "You are the eldest, and everything I ever desired in a son." John struggled to get his breath. "You have been for me all the wonderful colours in the mahogany paint box I gave you when you were eight. You brought colour into my colourless life."

Several hours later, he was gone, leaving Barry alone with his grief.

Fanny comforted her son and listened while Barry explained how much his father had enriched his life. She knew John Hart could have ignored her son. Many owners did not acknowledge their outside children. She had accepted the hours when Barry belonged exclusively to his father. Barry grew up as the educated and thoughtful boy he was because his father had loved him and helped to build his character. Barry became conscientious and caring because his mother shared her own life-learned wisdom with her son.

John signed his last will days before his death, granting freedom to Fanny Conyers and several other slaves. The barrister spoke to Barry as they met in his father's office the day after John's death.

"John Hart legally granted you freedom even before you were born. The entire estate belongs to Gratianus as a legal heir, but John suggested you remain as the manager in his son's absence. He has provided a yearly allowance for you, and as soon as you turn twenty-one you will receive an additional gift of 200 pounds—*a most generous sum*."

Barry realized the barrister had only a faint understanding of the relationship he had shared with his father.

"What my father generously gave to me could never be written on paper or measured in money. I became rich years ago when he poured his love and life into me."

Reaching across his father's desk, Barry touched the colour box resting on a shelf. Memories of his father washed over his heart, a generous man with whom he had shared his life for too few years. He wondered what the future held.

# 3

# Changes and Chance Encounter

*1765*

After John Hart's death, learning to manage his father's sugar estate comprised Barry's whole world. Gratianus, who by law inherited the property, continued living abroad.

Producing sugar required intensive labor. Barry supervised the daily tasks with his overseer, at times working alongside the slaves. Harvesting of the mature cane began in the late fall. Prior to that they kept the fields free of weeds and the old leaves stripped from the cane. Spreading manure promoted the cane growth. After cutting the stalks with a machete, they transported them to the mills in ox-drawn wagons. At the wind-powered mill, hand-feeding the cane into large rollers to crush out the juice was a dangerous job. Then they collected and processed the cane juice through a series of boilers. Separating the molasses from the sugar crystals and packing both in barrels or "hogsheads" then taking them to the harbor for export completed the process. Following harvest, work began again to prepare the fields for the next year's crop.

Barry occupied evenings sitting on the wide veranda reading to his mother the stories she delighted in hearing, but he missed the lively discussions and companionship with his father.

Shutting the book, he announced one evening, "I fired Father's overseer today. His resentment that a person of colour could become the manager disturbed me. The bitterness and jealousy do not stop there—the slaves feel it too. I am trapped between worlds."

"Son, you is your own world. Some people not going to understand, so just let it be. You is wise to distance them that cannot see it."

Fanny's calm practical wisdom always reassured Barry. He knew the estate could not succeed without slaves, and he would never consider asking Gratianus about selling any of them. Somehow it would be worse than managing them with compassion. So, he toiled alongside his brother's slaves hoping to prove himself to them.

Exhausted by day's end, Barry welcomed sleep. Except for the hours he spent with his mother, he felt lonely and isolated. He had few acquaintances and even fewer friends. He felt no need of them while his father lived.

Letters sent to Gratianus detailed the progress on the estate. Barry's half-brother responded occasionally, but the gulf between their two worlds resulted in diminishing communication.

In the spring of his twenty-fifth year, Barry waited to read his mail until he and his mother had eaten their evening meal. As they sat drinking their tea, Barry opened a rare letter from Gratianus. Setting the papers aside, he said, "Mother, I want to read you a letter." He read,

> Dear Barry, it is with deep sorrow I report my mother has died after a brief illness. I have no plan to ever return to Antigua. You have managed the estate well, and I now wish to deed the land and my slaves to you. I have seen my lawyer, and you will receive a document with the recorded transaction.
>
> Fondly, Gratianus Hart

Barry shut his eyes, and the room grew quiet as Fanny waited for Barry to continue. He sat with his head lowered. After a few minutes, his voice quavered.

"I cringe at the thought of owning slaves, yet I have no funds to pay workers if I free all the enslaved working here. I am thankful for a generous brother yet trapped by his gift."

Fanny offered her advice—something she seldom did. "Gratianus be wise son to trust you with his inheritance. He knows you going to be a fair and understanding master. Your father prepared you for this. He knowed Gratianus never come back here. John Hart be a good man, and he had two sons would make him proud. You going do well, my son."

Barry gave his mother a half smile and squeezed her hand. She provided a wealth of encouragement and quiet confidence.

Months later Barry's life took a new turn by what some called a chance encounter. Barry journeyed to town for provisions. He enjoyed salt beef shipped from Ireland and rice and flour imported from North America. Before returning to the routine of home, he intended to swim at the beach near Fort James. Tired from laboring alongside his slaves for most of the morning, he hoped a sea bath would soothe his weary muscles.

He approached the white sand, and the sound of gently breaking waves calmed his lonely heart. The call of a lone seabird in flight broke his solitude. He inhaled deeply, treasuring the smell of the ocean. Shoes removed, Barry walked along the shore, enjoying the smooth, warm sand. The ever-changing blues and greens of the Caribbean Sea promised to lift his spirits. One moment the colours were a rich royal navy blue, and the next a beautiful translucent aqua topaz. The ocean provided a salve for his grieving heart. Gratianus entrusting him with the plantation appeared to be a final door closing their connection.

Suddenly Barry heard a girl singing! He slipped behind a coconut palm to discover who would sing with such enthusiasm about heaven. Creeping closer to the ocean's edge, he spied a girl intent on digging cockles from the wet sand, crooning to herself. Her radiance, not her singing ability, struck him. This girl had neither the appearance nor the voice of a slave. He surmised she must be a mulatto, her brown skin only a shade darker than his caramel complexion. Her perfect English sounded like a British subject.

Her face remained hidden as she bent over, collecting her shellfish. A mass of auburn-streaked hair surrounded her as a wild halo. While he refrained from laughing aloud at the sight of her hair, he observed an abandoned kerchief and straw hat lying beside her. Barry grew more curious by the moment. A swim would wait.

Not wanting to frighten the girl, he called out a friendly "hello" as she finished her song. The girl turned abruptly, spilling her basket of cockles into the damp sand.

Barry bowed. "Your song refreshed me, and I wish you had not stopped. May I offer to help you collect the cockles?"

The girl answered with an impish smile. "Sir, I do not know you, but your offer is most welcome *if* you might first introduce yourself."

Her teasing manner staggered him, and he found himself pausing to laugh before he answered. "Pardon me. I have not encountered a singing sea-maiden for some time, and my manners deserted me." Barry dipped again in a small bow. "I am your servant, Barry Hart of the Hart plantation."

"I am Anne Clearkley of Gambles." Her rich brown eyes sparkled with a hint of mischief. "Thank you, kind sir. I would welcome help collecting my sea feast for my sister's birthday."

Captivated by her generous smile, a curious pleasure warmed his heart. Some might not have called her beautiful, but her smile lit her countenance like a lantern's glow. Her splendid jumble of curly locks had now fallen into her eyes. Pushing it back, her sandy hand further added sparkle to this halo.

Fetching … delightful, Barry reflected, finding it difficult to respond. This girl was vastly different from the women he had known in his life—neither dark, timid slave nor white pretention, she resembled him, a blend of worlds.

Anne Clearkley appeared at no loss for words. "I never expected to meet anyone while gathering cockles for a birthday stew. I string the heart-shaped shells together after we remove the flesh. Where were you earlier when I collected some lovely tamarinds? They were way out of my reach I had to throw rocks to knock them down. Do you enjoy tamarind drink? I am making some for my sister's celebration." The girl flew between topics as a hummingbird flits from flower to flower.

Barry had never encountered a woman who spoke so freely. *Fascinating* came to mind as he found himself amused by her talking without a pause. Barry knew many of the free blacks on the island, but none of them spoke with the articulation he heard in her voice.

Knowing it would probably sound insensitive, he asked anyway. "Your speech, it has a rare and educated quality to it. Can you tell me why?" He stopped himself. "Oh my, how rude. I'm sorry. Please ignore me. I find I want to listen to you talk."

Again, her delicious laughter filled the air. She sat back down on the sand holding her sides. "Mr. Hart, it is rude, but my sisters tease me incessantly about my talking too much. No one ever gave me such a generous compliment about my voice before. You speak the King's English to perfection as well. So, we both are a bit unique."

Barry found himself amused again as he sat down beside her on the sand. Without a pause, the mesmerizing voice started up once more.

"To answer you, Mr. Hart, I suppose I do speak rather like the British girls with whom I attended school in London. My mother worked in the great house at Gambles estate. The master's son fell in love with her, and at my birth, my father declared I would attend school in England someday."

An incredulous Barry interrupted her. "You attended school in England?"

Pausing only to clear her throat, she continued. "Two years ago, my sister Margaret and I lived in London while we attended school. I suppose I attempted to fit in by speaking the King's English. Several of the students usually spoke rudely to me, creating a challenging time. I wondered if they resented my speaking with an educated voice or they disliked me."

"How could anyone ..." Barry stopped before he finished his thought aloud.

"How could anyone what? You sound like my sister, thinking I can read your mind."

"I hope you can't read my mind right now. I will confess I find myself wondering how anyone could dislike you."

Ignoring his compliment, Anne began to sift through the collected cockles to avoid gazing at Barry.

"My sister and I always squabble about my not taking better care of my hair or my manners. I do try to sound appropriate, but I cannot bother with looking proper. I am embarrassed you caught me while wearing a wet and sandy skirt. Do you consider yourself proper, Mr. Hart?"

Entranced by Anne Clearkley, Barry thought he had laughed more in the last hour than he had in an entire year. He could not answer fast enough before she began to speak again.

"My sister tries to dress me up and make me suitable. My mother is a free black who married Timothy Clearkley, a white gentleman who is a fine furniture craftsman. My white grandfather Clearkley remained an arrogant man. After my parents' marriage, he showed attention only to my father, while ignoring my mother, my sisters, and me."

Barry managed to slip in a word. "How could anyone ignore you?"

Unready to delve into the hurts resulting from her grandfather's choosing to ignore her, the girl added. "Now I have talked until I am dizzy with the details, leaving me curious about your story, Mr. Hart."

"My story appears to compare to yours. My father was a plantation owner whose first wife died. My mother was a house slave who had a child by the owner, John Hart. My father remarried … a widow, Elizabeth Moore. A year later, they had a son, Gratianus."

Anne prodded, "Having a brother must have been good."

"I delighted in having a half-brother to play with, until his mother decided to take him back to England for school. I was eight when they left. Missing both his wife and son, Father focused his attention on me."

"How long were they gone?" Anne probed.

"They never returned to Antigua. Two years ago, Father's wife died, and Gratianus recently deeded the Hart estate to me."

"Oh my. You own a plantation?" This girl was unafraid to pepper Barry with questions. He had always avoided disclosing the complicated details to others. This girl was different, and he wanted her to understand.

Barry continued, a slight regret in his smile. "My father's cousin, Thomas, recently deeded Royals estate to me, and it is next to the Hart Plantation. I am fortunate indeed to have had a generous brother and a cousin who provided for me. So, I inherited two estates, but my Antiguan family consists only of my mother and me."

The similarities of their backgrounds stretched down deep and left them both in a comfortable silence.

Anne spoke first. "We are the fortunate ones. I have learned to accept what I fail to understand. People will never consider us either black or white. Do you agree, Mr. Hart? Neither the slaves nor the owners accept us, but I thank God we both have freedom. So many people of colour are denied freedom."

Barry found no words to respond.

Jumping up, the sea-nymph declared, "My mother will think I took a book with me and got lost in reading while I should be digging cockles for our seafood stew. I am often guilty of delaying a chore at home. Reading is so much more delightful. Goodbye, Mr. Hart. If we meet here again someday, you can help me gather tamarinds."

Struck by the sudden loss of a girl he barely knew, still Barry experienced a baffling hope.

When Anne returned home, her mother gave her a gentle scolding for delaying their supper needs. "Instead of cockles, I thought you must have found a book buried in the sand," her mother teased.

Anne laughed, "I told him you would think so."

The stout but graceful Frances Clearkley stopped stirring the pot and put down her spoon. "Him? And who is this *him* you met who delayed you?"

Anne's eyes twinkled. "A rather charming young man who rescued me when I spilled my gathered cockles. He is Barry Hart, of the Hart and Royals plantations."

Alarmed to hear this news, Frances Clearkley's dark brown eyes sparked with displeasure. "I have heard of Barry Hart, and I'm not so sure you should consider developing a friendship with him."

Placing her hands on her hips, Anne replied with indignation. "Mother, I was collecting cockles with a kind and respectful young man. I thought him rather fascinating and quite handsome. We have some things in common, and it was a most delightful encounter."

Frances declared louder than she intended. "He owns slaves!"

Anne spoke defensively. "I have only met him once, and you talk as if we plan to marry! He inherited slaves. Much different than if he had bought them. And his mother was a former slave. Better a man of colour from a slave background to own people than selling them to some cruel owner."

While Anne removed the cockle flesh from the shells, Frances placed her hand on Anne's arm. "Thinking of one of our own being in possession of slaves is hard for me. I know of no other free black who owns people. Owning another person is not right."

"Mother, I don't even know if it's fair to call him 'one of our own.' He comes from two different backgrounds and different colours, as I do. I want to think of him as a very kind man."

Anne's mother reached for her hand. "Forgive me, if I sounded harsh. You are wise, dear Anne, and you have always been generous with people. You usually judge them on character alone. I am sorry. I only want what is best for you. I want you to marry a man of character, someone who will treat you as he should. Timothy has been such a wonderful husband and father. I only want the same for you."

Anne commenced separating the cockle meat from the shells. "Let's celebrate Lydia's birthday and not mention my mysterious helper. Now, if you will cook the cockles, I will make the tamarind drink and the ducana the girls love."

Frances noted Anne's reference to Barry Hart as "her" mysterious helper. "I already grated the sweet potato and coconut and set aside cinnamon and nutmeg to make the ducana," she told Anne. "Did you collect the banana leaves on your way?"

Anne raised her arms in exasperation and then wrapped them around her mother's soft waist. "No, Mother. I am sorry. My mind flitted as a bird on a blustery day. I will gather some from the garden before I make the tamarind drink. We can wrap the ducana together, once I gather the leaves."

As Anne danced her way out to the banana trees, Frances began to pray, "Please Lord, help me not to be judgmental. Show me when the time is right to let go of my child whom I love."

Anne's sisters considered the birthday dinner a success. The subject of a mysterious seaside visitor did not come up. The family devoured the fragrant ducana, and the love for her family warmed Anne's heart.

# 4

# Courtship Conversations

*1765*

The answer to Frances Clearkley's prayer came rather soon. The next evening Barry Hart called on her husband, Timothy.

The modest, wood-framed house impressed Barry as he approached. Anne had mentioned her father was a skilled carpenter. The delicate fretwork along the roofline undoubtedly displayed his skills. The picturesque house presented a wide veranda surrounding three sides, while blue shutters added to the home's character. Two girls sat on the veranda absorbed in the African game Warri. Barry called, "Hello. Is Mr. Clearkley at home?"

Before Anne's sisters could manage an answer, Mr. Clearkley appeared. "Good evening. May I help you, sir?"

Barry hesitated. He had never called on a girl before. "I am Barry Hart. I met your daughter Anne yesterday."

Towering over Barry, the man extended his strong, work-worn hand. "My wife told me you and Anne had quite a visit while gathering cockles at the beach. Did my small girl talk your ears right off you?" A smile formed and his blue eyes twinkled.

Relaxing slightly, Barry found his voice. "She fascinated me, Mr. Clearkley. I had failed to realize how quiet my life was until yesterday. Is Anne always so exuberant?"

Mr. Clearkley nodded. "Almost always cheerful, always talking unless she has her face in a book."

Barry blurted, "I have never courted a girl, Mr. Clearkley, and though I am 25, I am uncertain how to do this. Anne told me she is never too concerned with being proper, but I want to ask if I may court Anne properly. I know this is sudden, but I have never met anyone who compares to your daughter."

Timothy Clearkley appreciated Barry's forthright manner. He displayed both humility and confidence at the same time.

Barry held out a spray of crimson ginger lilies and fragrant plumeria. "These are for Mrs. Clearkley."

Overhearing the conversation from inside the home, Frances stepped onto the spacious veranda that her husband often referred to as the gallery. "Anne is correct. You are very charming, Mr. Hart." She thanked him for the flowers. "I will fetch Anne for you."

Anne lay sprawled across her bed, reading. She glanced up as her mother entered the room. "What does your look of amusement mean, Mother?"

"There is a gentleman downstairs, and perhaps he has beguiled me as he did you, my dear."

Jumping to her feet, Anne delighted to see the acceptance in her mother's eyes. "My hair is untidy, Mother, and my house dress wrinkled. What do I do?"

"Dear, precious Anne, if he is to appreciate you for yourself, he might as well become accustomed to your disregard for propriety. Tie a ribbon in your hair and join this young man on the gallery. If you keep him waiting too long, your sisters and father will begin to tell him tales you might rather he not hear."

Giggling filled the room. Tying a ribbon around her halo of hair, Anne raced downstairs. Trying in vain to compose herself, she opened the door leading to the generous gallery where her father and Barry Hart were in serious discussion.

Usually never at a loss for words, Anne could think of nothing to say except, "Good evening."

Her father rose. "Mr. Hart and I have appreciated our time together. Now I will excuse myself and be sure my younger daughters complete their day's lessons. Anne, try to let this gentleman get a word or two in before you talk his ear off." Mr. Clearkley turned to Barry and gave an understanding look. "You'll do fine, Mr. Hart."

Timothy Clearkley paused, viewing the couple with approval. Any gentleman who could leave Anne speechless, even for a short time, had accomplished a fantastic feat.

Barry cleared his throat. "Please sit, Miss Clearkley, and try to remember where you have hidden the angelic smile causing me to return tonight."

Anne's knees quivered as she lowered herself into the chair nearest Barry. Trying to breathe normally, a slow deep breath escaped through her lips. She managed a timid smile.

This silent version of the chatterbox he met yesterday brought Barry a nervous laugh. "I have not been very talkative myself in the years since my father died. I spend most evenings in the company of my books and my mother. All day I have anticipated listening to you chatter about whatever suits your fancy."

Abruptly Anne began to describe in detail her sisters' latest antics. She explained how they teased one another. Barry chuckled at her stories and felt his heart at peace. This girl just might eventually become his wife if he could ever slip in words to ask her.

Finally growing quiet, Anne asked, "When you were growing up, Mr. Hart, did you ever feel you were invisible to some people?"

Barry's smile turned to a thoughtful frown. "Was it the same for you, Miss Clearkley? I find it hard to imagine your being invisible to anyone. In answer to your question, my father never allowed people to ignore me. I was eight when his wife and my brother Gratianus left for England. Father's loneliness gave him the need to show me off."

"My own father always generously shared his love with my sisters and me. Yet, many white men are not like our fathers," said Anne.

"Once my father's second wife left, he never failed to introduce me as his son," said Barry. "Though I was an *outside child*, as people might refer to me, my father often said he thanked God for blessing him with me as his son. Despite my unplanned beginning, my mother respected him. He was a good man."

Anne said, "While at the university in London, I avoided some of the students. The glares and smirks hurt. Some white people talked as if I were deaf or incapable of understanding their cruel remarks—*as if I were invisible*. I felt as though they had used a scale and weighed the shade of my skin against theirs, deciding my shade was of no value."

Barry grew quiet, imagining this fetching brown-skinned girl outshining her privileged, white fellow students, who viewed her as upsetting the social structure that kept blacks in their place. Only the ever-present cacophony of the tree frogs disturbed the silence.

"I visited many places with my father and observed how some owners spoke to their slaves. Enslaved children cowered at the harsh voice of their master and must have wished they were invisible at times. Father and I often discussed the evils of the slave trade. He described it as a spider web, catching both the slaves and their masters in an inescapable trap. The harder they fought against the snare of evil, the more entrapped they became."

Looking into Barry Hart's soft brown eyes Anne asked the question troubling her. "So, do you agree it's acceptable for one person to enslave another?"

"NO! I inherited the trap ensnaring me. Gratianus had no desire to return to the island. Now I am trying to do my best to seek God's direction and guidance as I survive..."

Anne interrupted him. "And you need slaves to survive?"

Growing quiet Barry replied with conviction. "I pray someday we will see slavery destroyed, a time when every man, woman, and child become valued for their character, not the shade of their skin. My father never allowed anyone to ignore me, or frown on my mixed heritage. At the same time, I fear releasing those under my care might only bring them worse enslavement. There are no simple answers to ending this dilemma of slavery."

Reaching over, she touched the arm of Barry's chair. "An honest answer is what I hear from you, Mr. Hart. I loathe any child to ever feel invisible, yet I am not sure how change can happen. Ugly pride is a heart issue making some people think they are superior to others in God's creation. Some people will always be cruel. That is the problem with sin. Now tell me about your father and mother."

Grateful for a change in subject, Barry began, "Father had many interests, and he made me who I am today. My mother influenced me too, and she still does. Though she was his slave, she never spoke ill of my father. When I was a boy, I slipped into the realm of the kitchen and basked in her attention. I even learned to cook some."

Anne teased. "A plantation owner who cooks. I am impressed. What might you cook, Mr. Hart?"

"Be not skeptical. I make a rather tasty pepper pot and fried dumplings. Each of my parents spoiled me, I fear. At the close of his workday, especially after Gratianus left for England, Father's world became mine. We played chess, and he taught me to love books. Few children from a union such as my mother and father's are as fortunate as I."

Watching Anne twist the ribbons from her shirtwaist around her fingers, Barry recognized she must be nervous.

He knew the same feeling. "My father was Irish, and he taught me an Irish ditty about a lass named Annie. Someday I will sing it for you. Might I call you *Annie*?"

Anne nodded approval and turned strangely silent.

Barry patted the arm of her chair. "I have shared my hopes with you, but I am often too serious, too absorbed in my own thoughts. You can help me know and value the people around me. Your heart sees things I may have missed—Miss Annie Clearkley."

Anne stood up and began to pace the gallery. He imagined she must only be about twenty, but she possessed a confidence he found appealing.

Stopping in front of him, she spoke with determination. "Since I have given you permission to call me Annie, Mr. Barry Hart, I will step on your foot if I see you have treated anyone as invisible. Men sometimes do not see as clearly as women see. That is why God made us different. Oh my, am I chattering on and saying too much? I often do, you know." With this, she plopped back down in her chair and wrapped her arms across herself, to calm her excitement.

Barry delighted at Annie's fascinating fault and realized her ease in conversation might be a perfect match for his quiet manner.

Close to the equator, Antigua's twilight lasted only a few moments, disappearing by seven in the evening. As it grew dark Annie and Barry sat on the gallery—the moon adorning the sky with a sliver of light.

Annie called out to the man she could hear bringing the cattle near the house. "Old Joe, come meet my new friend, Mr. Hart." The man was dark as the night sky surrounding him, and only his sweet humming revealed he was there. His booming voice called out, "Evenin' chillun," as he walked on cheerfully singing to the livestock. "I love that man," Annie said.

"Would there be room in your generous heart to add another to those you care about, Annie?"

"Barry Hart, there might be room to add someone else to the folks I care about."

Barry cleared his throat again. "I want you to meet my mother. She tells me I am alone too much. When Gratianus left, I felt lost. When my father died, I felt a deep hole in my life. I despaired I would never find anyone who would be a companion on this journey called life." Annie's silence unsettled Barry.

"Love and security must have surrounded you as a child." Annie finally spoke. "My grandfather's rejection left a mark on my growing up years. Though your father did not marry your mother, he loved you. Someday I want to have a family of my own and provide children a haven of safety and love."

Over the next two months, Barry and Annie spent many evenings on the Clearkley gallery. Annie talked, Barry listened, and they eventually spoke of spending their lives together. After two months of hearing about this girl, Barry's mother finally met Annie. The evening Fanny prepared a dinner of pumpkin soup, red snapper, seasoned rice and johnny cakes for the couple was memorable. After dinner, Annie and Barry strolled through the flower garden, discussing his plans for the plantation. The fragrance of the night-blooming jasmine infused the air while the bands of pink-tinged sky descended into a dark night. Annie was oddly silent.

Finally, Barry asked her to sit with him on the gallery, and he prayed she would remain quiet long enough for him to speak. Picking a small cluster of the jasmine blooming beside the gallery, and reaching across to her chair, he tucked the fragrant blossoms into the halo of hair that first made him think of Annie as an angel girl. He began to sing with a hint of an Irish brogue.

*O, sweet Annie dear!*
*You are exceeding fair.*
*As lovely as the jasmine*
*That adorns your auburn hair.*
*With a smile like the sunshine,*
*You have captured my heart.*

*O, sweet Annie dear!*
*A halo of curls tumbles down*
*Around your glowing face.*
*Sparkling eyes of chestnut brown*
*Show love and gentle grace.*
*I pray we'll never part.*

"Annie, God has answered my prayers for a companion to share the blessings he has bestowed on me. Please agree to be my wife. Indeed, your gentle ways have won me, and without you, my life would be missing your happiness. I promise to protect and to cherish you always."

Her hesitation surprised Barry, although he knew Annie Clearkley could never remain quiet for long. A small lantern provided the only light on the gallery. As he eyed her closely, he saw tears. "What is it Annie dear; have I frightened you?"

Annie sniffled through laughter. "Have you never seen crying from joy, Barry Hart? Of course, I will marry you."

With a small smile she teased, "I have already begun to practice writing Annie Hart, and it is a beautiful name to me. Your song has charmed me. I will gladly be your Annie." She peeked at him coyly. "I might have said yes on the first evening you came to visit me."

She rose from her chair. "We should tell your sweet mother, and when you return me to my home, we will wake up my parents and tell them. Let's tell everyone we pass."

When she heard the news, Barry's mother was elated that he planned to marry Annie. Indeed, she erased his loneliness, and his happiness overflowed.

Soon Fanny made plans to move to the small but airy overseer's house. For the wedding feast Annie's parents donated a goat, and Fanny cooked a banquet for the family. Annie wore a simple muslin gown of white. Barry asked her to leave her hair the wild mass of curls he loved. The garland of ferns and Madagascar jasmine jeweled her hair like a crown.

Even the slaves benefitted after the family celebration, when at Annie's request, Fanny delivered the leftovers to the slave quarters.

Barry fancied he was the luckiest man on the island, if not in the world. The angelic sea nymph, Annie Clearkley Hart, was his.

# 5

# Family, Faith and the Fourth of July

*1768*

Barry spent long days working to keep the estate successful while Annie enjoyed Fanny's companionship. Annie relished life on the Hart plantation, and their love blossomed. They had been married two years when Barry's cup of joy overflowed with the birth of their first child.

Knocking at the bedroom door, Barry asked permission to see his wife. Frances Clearkley smiled as she ushered him into the room. Hovering over the cradle, he beamed as he viewed their newborn. His eyes lit up when he saw Annie. "We will call this child Anne, after you. I promise our Anne and all our children to follow will have my devotion."

Annie smiled weakly. She loved this tranquil and charming man.

Frances cradled her newborn granddaughter. "Your blessings are many, precious baby, many indeed," she whispered. Frances noticed the baby's stunning eyes. "Good gracious, Annie, your daughter possesses light blue eyes! They remind me of the shallows in our Caribbean Sea. I think her caramel skin is lovely, though it will probably darken in time. The child is perfect, and her healthy cry is exactly what a mama wants to hear."

Barry began to draw circles on Annie's delicate hand. "I intend for our children to become the best educated on our island. I want them to have the same love of learning my father bestowed on me. I have already informed Mr. Fairway, the newspaper editor, we will be wanting a tutor soon."

Pausing, he proclaimed, "You will always be my Annie, but the baby's name will be Anne. I pray she will resemble you in many ways."

Though exhausted from childbirth, Annie replied, "How thoughtful of you, Barry, to be considering an education for this child when she has barely even nursed from my breast! You are prepared to fill her with the words you love so much. Naming her Anne pleases me. I am praying our Anne becomes a person of knowledge, like her father."

Barry placed his fingers on Annie's lips. "You, my dear, had an education in England. I merely had a father who loved knowledge and shared his library with me."

Kissing his fingertips, Annie nodded. "I need to rest. But first … glimpse at dainty Anne's startling eyes. They are as you described your father's eyes. Her skin is fairer than mine and resembles yours." Reaching up, Annie gently touched Barry's cheek. "I hope she will also inherit your freckles."

Another baby was born a year later, but he survived only a few days—bringing grief to the Harts at the loss of their first son. Barry reassured his wife that God would give them strength to endure this overwhelming loss. Though heartbroken, Annie understood their need to trust in God. Her faith comforted her, and she trusted their future to God's design. Baby Anne's antics helped to relieve the dark days. As their little girl took her first steps and began to repeat words, Annie prayed more children would someday fill their home.

God answered their prayers with the birth of a second daughter, Elizabeth, two years later, a serene baby who brought them much pleasure. The Harts delighted in their two little girls, and in 1774 baby Jacob joined them, bringing Barry the satisfaction that he now had a son who would someday inherit the plantation.

Annie never wanted her children to be jealous of a new baby. When Gratianus—named for Barry's half-brother—began to kick in her womb in 1776, she held each child's hand close to her belly and declared, "The baby is saying, 'Hello, family. I want to join you.'"

Annie encouraged and admonished each of the children as they matured. Both Barry and she spoke to them often about having faith in

Jesus Christ as being of the utmost importance. "I pray often God will use you," Annie told their firstborn. "Never forget how blessed you are. Ask God what He would have you do with these privileges. Do not keep them just for yourself, but share your blessings."

Sitting at her mother's feet, Anne questioned, "How will God use me, and why does He care about me?"

Annie rubbed her daughter's back. "Pay attention to the opportunities God gives you. I only know He can use you if you are alert to His direction, listen for His voice, obey His word. God has given you a keen mind and strength to follow, even if it might be difficult. Trust Him always, follow Him always, and He will direct your steps. This is His promise."

*1776*

Young Anne often thrilled with delight as she watched her parents. One day at the end of August 1776, the eight-year-old girl gazed out the window into the garden and saw her father twirling her mother round and round—her mother's skirt now in full circle. Her parents were affectionate, but not often did Anne see them in such a playful mood. The scene reminded Anne of a whirling dervish, like the drawings of Turkish men in one of her father's beautiful books. Knowing how devoted they were to each other made her feel secure. Even at her age, she sensed it was a private moment, but curiosity overruled her caution. Anne flung open the door and burst outside to greet them.

Spontaneous as always, Anne blurted out, "Why are you excited, Father?"

His eyes revealed a cautious pleasure. "I am not sure I can explain my elation in words. I do not know if a faraway event will touch our lives, but changes in distant lands fill me with hope for transformations here in Antigua."

Pulling on her father's arm, Anne pled, "Please try to tell me, Father. I want to feel excited too."

Barry began, "I heard the news today about an event occurring on July 4. The British colonies in the Americas wrote a declaration of independence from England."

The child looked perplexed. "Why does this make you so happy, Father?"

Barry kneeled beside her. "I think you can understand this. White owners here consider their unfortunate slaves as property, not as people. Free people of mixed blood do not have the same privileges white-skinned people have. The men in power deem me unequal due to my colour, meaning I cannot vote, nor can I serve as a juror in a court of law."

Leaning down, Annie squeezed her daughter's hand. "This faraway news gives us hope that someday changes may come here, bringing equality for all."

"Will it matter to our little island, what countries so far off decide?" Anne asked.

"The founding fathers of the new country wrote all men are created equal. All men," her father said. She squealed with delight as he picked her up and whirled her around the way he had whirled her mother earlier.

Anne struggled to understand. "Will Antigua declare all men equal too?"

Annie embraced both her husband and daughter, as Barry explained. "Not yet, my treasured child, but this news fills our hearts with optimism for the future. I trust you will see changes in the way those in power choose to value people unlike themselves in your lifetime, ending a predicament I inherited years ago. Yet, it will change our livelihood when it happens."

Placing an affectionate kiss on the top of her head, Barry wondered what the future held for his children. The future always brought surprises, some heavy with distress. There had been the thrill of expectation and the anticipation of a wedding for Margaret, Annie's sister. During the time Annie and her sister attended school in London, they had met a pleasant young white man. Shy, bookish Stephen Matthews became interested in a friendship with Margaret. His parents did not approve, and they insisted he complete his law degree. Defying his parents' wishes, he corresponded with Margaret Clearkley for six years. Their letters sealed the conviction they should marry, and Stephen finalized plans to move to Antigua.

As Margaret completed her wardrobe, her heart anticipated years of married life. Her younger sister, Lydia, shared in her gladness and helped with the wedding plans. For eight weeks, Margaret awaited his ship, expecting her wedding to take place shortly after his arrival. Then the staggering news reached them. The ill-fated vessel on its voyage to Antigua had sunk, and Stephen had drowned. With Margaret's dream of marriage shattered, and 17-year-old Lydia taking the tragedy almost as hard as her older sister, the Clearkley home felt overwhelmed with gloom as they grieved along with Margaret. Though Lydia had never met Stephen Matthews, she had shared in the excitement when her sister had read aloud some of his letters.

Annie began to consider how to help Lydia. She needed to think about happier things than the death of their sister's fiancé and the dashed plans for a wedding. Since Lydia was intent on someday becoming a teacher, her mother, Frances, encouraged her to serve as Anne's tutor. The noise of Annie Hart's lively family would help dispel the sadness, giving Lydia a mission to turn away her thoughts from the sorrow enveloping the Clearkley home.

Lydia was not the only one who found comfort in the Hart children's education. Not many weeks after she began to tutor the children, Barry sat outside observing them. The children were taught outdoors under the shade of the large mango tree near the front veranda. Barry turned to Annie. "Though she is three years younger, watch how Elizabeth absorbs much while sitting beside her during Anne's lessons."

Annie nodded. "Anne and Elizabeth are inseparable and appear to appreciate having my sister as their tutor. Our daughters will have opportunities open to them because they are well educated. Thank you, Barry, for providing a larger world for them than most children have—most especially than most *girls* are given. Only God knows what they might achieve."

Holding hands, Barry and Annie rocked in their wicker chairs. Barry thought of his own upbringing. "Education is the key to unlocking future doors for our children, doors usually shut tight to children of colour."

The Harts grew to a family of seven with the addition of Charles in 1779. Charles was full of spunk, and the six Harts attempted to keep him out of mischief once he began to walk.

Jacob, Gratianus and Charles thrived on sunshine and fresh air and rarely lingered inside except for their required studies. Anne and Elizabeth flourished as they acquired knowledge, and were rarely without a book in their hands. The girls loved to quote the witty sayings found in their father's childhood book, *Poor Richard's Almanack*. As they prepared for bed each night, Annie would begin, "Early to bed and early to rise ...," and her children would chime in with "makes a child healthy, wealthy, and wise."

Most evenings, the family relished time reading together. The girls often played the pianoforte Barry had had shipped from England. Peace, faith, love, and children filled their comfortable home.

While Gratianus and Charles napped, 13-year-old Anne attempted to instruct seven-year-old Jacob in the courses Lydia had taught her and Elizabeth that morning.

On her own, Anne spent hours engrossed with her favorite books in her father's library. She sat rocking baby Charles while she recited Milton, and he cooed as if he understood. Elizabeth sat nearby sketching. She had heard about the colour box of paints given to her father when he was about her age and hoped that someday he would share the colour box with her. Oh, what a treasure that would be! To think of all the colours and possibilities!

The children often studied in the afternoons beneath the canopy of the mango tree near the outdoor cooking shed. The smells of seasoned goat meat or the sweet aroma of ducana wafting from the coal pot distracted Jacob, making it difficult to pay attention.

One afternoon as they sat under the mango tree, Anne became exasperated with Jacob. "How can you be bored by all I am trying to share with you? I know you appreciate having stories read to you, but you avoid doing sums. Please, Jacob, don't waste what learning you are given."

Struggling to teach Jacob, Anne noticed the slave boy, Joe, peeking from behind the cooking shed. Following the boy around the corner, she discovered he had been scratching in the dirt the words she had spelled out for Jacob. "What are you doing, Joe? Do you know your alphabet?"

The youngster hung his head. Anne quizzed him further, "How do you know the letters?"

Joe raised his head, and his dark eyes pooled with tears, since he feared to tell her more.

"You are not in trouble," said Anne. "How did you learn your letters?"

Joe managed to whisper, "Jacob, he tell me 'bout dem and de words when we play together."

Now Anne laughed. "At last, I know Jacob is listening when I try to teach him. You are not old enough to work in the fields, Joe. What do you do all day?"

"Me help Cook gather coal for to cook de meals." Joe became less frightened. "Me wash de vegetables and Cook lets me stir de pot."

"And you listen while I struggle to teach my brother." Anne shook her head at this surprising news.

Again, Joe lowered his eyes and nodded.

"I am pleased, Joe. I am not angry with you. You write your letters well." Anne could not help but think how wrong so many were who proclaimed that slaves were incapable of learning to read. Cook called to the boy, and Anne watched him dart to the kitchen garden. She listened as Cook instructed Joe to gather vegetables for the slaves' supper.

After supper, the younger children went to bed early. The day had been hot and humid. Anne and Elizabeth sat with their parents on the veranda cooled by the evening breeze.

Anne blurted out the question plaguing her all afternoon. "Why can't slaves learn to read?"

Barry blinked in surprise. "Whoever told you that? Of course, the slaves can learn anything we teach them, but they work from first light until the bell rings for their evening meal. After the evening meal, many of them work in their own gardens, so they have provisions to sell at the Sunday market."

Their mother began to fidget with her handkerchief. "I suppose most could learn, but they are worn out and weary by day's end. I imagine they see no reason to learn."

Anne viewed her father's countenance etched with regret, much like the expression she sometimes saw on her brother's face when caught disobeying. Shaking her head, Anne announced, "This is so unfair. I spend hours trying to help Jacob learn, and he demonstrates trivial interest. Yet, today I discovered Joe, who assists Cook, possesses a keen wish to learn. Why should we deny Joe the learning Jacob cares so little about?"

Her father's concern mixed with pride at Anne's insight. "Life is often unfair. I experienced the privilege of a father who granted my freedom before I was even born. If it weren't for my father, I might be like Joe. Yes, each member in our family needs to remember that opportunity comes with responsibility."

Wrapping her arms around her daughter, Annie intuitively told her, "What a gift you have for compassion, Anne. You try to teach Jacob even when he appears uninterested. Barry, do you think we could allow Joe a few hours each day to sit under this inspiring teacher-to-be?"

Barry touched Annie's hand. "How could I turn down the request of two such lovely girls? Of course, Joe may join you. I will explain to Cook, and he must help her before and after his lessons."

Anne rose and perched herself on the arm of her father's rocker. "I am eager to see if Joe can inspire Jacob to pay more attention while I teach. To find Jacob teaching Joe himself was amazing! Thank you, Father."

Elizabeth sat quietly sketching while her parents discussed education. The ten-year-old had surpassed what many adults could do with charcoal and paper.

Annie held up the lantern to see Elizabeth's sketch. "What is your newest drawing?" asked Annie.

Elizabeth held out a drawing of a boy scratching out words in the dirt.

Annie said, "I will see to it Joe has a proper slate and a bit of chalk to write with before tomorrow! How pleased I am with my talented and caring daughters. I am anticipating how God will direct your future."

Beginning the very next day, Joe joined Jacob most afternoons and copied words onto his slate. Jacob's competitive spirit helped him pay better attention to his studies.

At the end of the year, when Lydia completed her time as the children's tutor, she returned home. Barry hired a tutor for the children. Life on the Hart estate was serene, with both crops and children flourishing.

# 6

# Upheavals

*1782*

Anne and Elizabeth gathered enough guavas so Cook could make jam—if they could only keep their brothers from devouring the not-yet-ripe fruit before the women had enough to make the treat. The plentiful rains produced fruitful trees. One guava was large enough to fill Anne's hand.

The sisters left silly little notes in their efforts to stop their brothers' antics. One day they copied down a poem. "*Jam is sweet, a lovely treat. So away, away if you wish jam to eat.*" They hung it on a branch to remind their brothers not to touch the guavas. Now, Anne's apron held enough guavas to make a batch of jam. She wanted to show her parents the fruit of her successful poem.

She had not intended to listen in on her parents' conversation, but their voices drifted past the half-closed door. The tension in the room filled every corner, and the distress in her mother's soft words startled Anne. "Barry, please assure me we will be safe here in Antigua."

Slipping inside, this 14-year-old could not help but ask, "Safe from what, Father? Has something happened?"

Both parents turned abruptly to stare at their oldest. Her father stepped toward her as he shut the door. "I do not want to frighten the others. If I tell you, then you must keep it to yourself."

Alarmed by their tense expressions, Anne nodded her agreement. Her parents kept little to themselves, often sharing with their children the severe effects of drought or the dangers of illness on the island. Her father motioned to her to sit down beside him.

"St. Kitts, Nevis, and Montserrat suffered an attack from the French, and the French Admiral Comte de Grasse has captured all three islands surrounding us. You remember seeing these islands in the distance on our visits to the Caribbean side." Her father stopped. "The French now control Guadeloupe to the south, Montserrat to the southeast, and St. Kitts and Nevis not much further away to the west. The enemy now surrounds Antigua."

Immediately Anne understood their concern. Antigua was in great danger from the aggressive French. "I am thankful we do not live on those other islands, but they are so close to us. Will we be safe here?" Her eyes searched her parents for reassurance.

Her father's pursed lips replaced his usual smile, "Because of the Naval Dockyard and its warships, Antigua remains secure. Besides, we are well protected by forts around the island. They say the new fort at Goat Hill is impregnable, and Governor Shirley has begun work on the fortifications on the heights above the Dockyard." Her father continued, "Since the defeat of the British fleet in the American colonies last year, France shifted her military activities to the islands here. Spain and the Netherlands entered on the side of the revolutionaries. These countries covet islands to grow sugar, tobacco and indigo. So now, with the French base on Nevis and St. Kitts, they are within sight of us."

Anne appeared confused. "But didn't you tell me we sympathize with those North American colonies?"

Barry almost grimaced. "Even so, we are a British possession, and France would love to capture this island. We have heard stories of how brutal the French can be against captured territories. Our forces experience severe opposition. De Grasse boasts of 6,000 troops and 50 men-of-war ships. Since the French and the British have fought over the possession of St. Kitts for over 100 years, a battle is inevitable. Sadly, war involves our neighbors on St. Kitts once again."

Now Annie spoke as she rubbed her daughter's back—her habit when comforting her children. "The Almighty keeps us secure in His hand. These are battles between the Navies, and we can only pray for peace. There is nothing else we can do. We rest there."

Gathering his daughter into his arms, Barry began to pray for those at war, on the seas, and on his neighboring islands. As he finished his prayer, he asked, "What is the lovely aroma I detect coming from your apron? Have you added some weight recently? I suspect you have devised a way to keep your brothers out of the guava trees."

Relieved to turn to a more humorous topic, Barry snatched a guava from Anne's apron and devoured it.

"Father, I'm beginning to wonder if it was really the *boys* snatching those guavas before they had ripened. If you are patient, we will turn these guavas into a jam we can *all* enjoy."

Two months later, Anne's father called her into his office. He shut the door, while her mother watched. With a mixture of relief and excitement he spoke. "I must tell you the news I heard in town today. Word came down that Admiral Rodney won a sea battle near Guadeloupe and captured Admiral de Grasse! The British fleet sank many of the French warships. The talk of the town buzzes with the news of breaking France's sea power."

Anne thanked her father for trusting her with this news, but Barry cautioned both his wife and daughter. "The French are still a danger. However, Governor Shirley is going forward strengthening our defenses surrounding English Harbour, and he is building barracks for more soldiers, with several men-of-war that will now be based in the English Harbour Naval Dockyard. Those ships include thousands of soldiers and sailors, and we should be secure from invasion."

Anne embraced her parents. "Thank you, Father. This morning I read Psalms where it tells us, 'Some trust in chariots, and some in horses, but we will remember the name of the Lord our God.' I have been attempting to trust only in God."

## *1784*

In 1784 a severe tropical storm ravaged Antigua interrupting the Hart family's normally peaceful life. This storm, the most significant storm in Barry Hart's memory, devastated his plantation and ripped at his heart. The violent storm raged over the small island for the better part of two days. Across the island, crops lay shredded. Inside the house, an even more devastating storm threatened to dismantle his family.

As the violent storm diminished, Annie gave birth to another son. Barry wanted to think Annie and their son were all right, but something felt wrong. While Frances Clearkley asked Barry to give her a few minutes to ready Annie so the girls could see her, their father slipped out of the house, checking to be sure his slaves had survived in their shelter under the main house. He quickly instructed the field hands to recover whatever they could salvage.

Barry returned as Frances Clearkley stepped out of his wife's room and rested the tiny bundle she held into Elizabeth's arms. As Elizabeth took the newborn, she struggled to calm the uneasiness within her.

Sixteen-year-old Anne glanced at her little brother, noticing his labored breathing. Her grandmother appeared cloaked with a clashing mask of both agony and relief. "Though the house is hot and stuffy, I feel a cold chill within me. Something is dreadfully amiss," Anne said.

Embracing Anne, Grandmother Clearkley briefly rocked her back and forth, then indicated for her to go into her mother's room. As Barry started to follow, she held her hand up indicating he should wait. He sank into a chair, lowered his head, hugging his arms around his body protectively.

Wrapped in fear and dread, Anne entered the bedroom, terrified at what her grandmother's dramatic embrace foretold. Anne knew from the beginning the birth of this baby was different. Labor started nearly an hour before the storm arrived. Although shuttered from the howling wind and crashing of debris, for more than a day, her mother's agony and screams had echoed throughout the house.

When Charles had arrived five years before, Anne and Elizabeth had taken their other brothers outside and they had overheard little. This time they heard the unmistakable sounds of anguish as their mother labored.

Anne's anxiety deepened when she saw the pile of bloody sheets on the floor. With Charlie's birth, her mother had bled some, but nothing like this. *No, not this much.* Kneeling beside the bed, she rubbed the delicate hand. "Mother, tell me what to do."

The answer heightened Anne's fears. "Listen to me. I must tell you something before I go."

The lump in Anne's throat made answering difficult. "None of us can go anywhere. The storm has flooded the roads. The large mahogany trees felled by the winds during the night block anyone coming or going. I want you to rest now. Do not tire yourself with talk."

Annie Hart slowly stretched her arm toward her daughter. Her tangled and damp auburn hair surrounded her pale forehead. "There is a note for you in my Bible. I wrote it before the pains grew too strong. Read it later. I love you dearest ..."

Her mother's words grew fainter, as Anne fought to hear, to comprehend what her mother struggled to say. "Mother, please, I want to understand."

Tears covered Anne's cheeks. Was her mother giving her a blessing because she was about to die? No! Her heart refused to think of her mother leaving them. "Mother." She covered her mouth with her hand.

Barely audible now, her mother repeated, "Always remember my love. Bring Elizabeth and your father. Be strong, dearest."

Rising on trembling legs, Anne kissed her mother. Uprooted and broken, much as the giant mahogany trees in the roadway, Anne whispered, "Yes, I promise to heed your words." *I promise.* Her heart broke as she quietly went to get Elizabeth and her father.

Seeing Anne's anguish, Elizabeth tenderly handed the oddly still bundle to her grandmother. Struggling with grief, Elizabeth and Father entered Annie's room to say goodbye to this delicate, bronze-skinned beauty who had brought so much happiness to this home.

Falling on the bed beside her mother, Elizabeth caressed the tangled damp web of auburn hair. Elizabeth often thought of her mother as an angel. Her radiant smile communicated joyfulness and serenity. Now, her face mixed pain with peace.

"Mother, I love you more than I can tell you. Everyone is so solemn. I am afraid, and I don't understand. Say you will recover. Please tell me you will."

"Yes, Elizabeth, I will heal in the arms of Jesus." Annie spoke in a hushed tone, "A part of me will always be with you ..." Elizabeth feared this was goodbye as Annie laid her hand on Elizabeth almost as if she were imparting a blessing.

"Now, please let me speak to your father."

Choked by tears, Elizabeth slipped out of the room. She knew Father needed time alone with his wife.

Kneeling beside Annie's bed, Barry pled silently with God before he rose and embraced her. He choked back the tears. Annie had always possessed the ability to fill their life with assurances. She knew how to express wisdom and encouragement. Since the first day they met this proved true. He could compose written words, but he found speaking more challenging. Annie gave him a faint smile, and he swiped at his cheeks.

"Barry, I know you will hold the family together with love, but try to talk to them daily." Annie struggled to catch her breath. "Speak of God's creation and His love. He blessed me with a man who loved me well."

Only God could keep her there with them, and it appeared the Creator desired her to brighten heaven instead. "Annie, from the moment I heard you singing on the beach, my heart has been one with yours. You gave me laughter, helping me discover how much God loved me." Barry struggled to tell Annie one more time of his love for her. At that moment an indescribable wave of peace washed over Barry, as he knew he must say goodbye to his beloved. "You know how much I love you and our children. You read my mind and my heart when I could not find the words, always knowing what to say to each one of us. God gave you to me. I will not blame God if now you are His alone."

Within moments, Barry's Annie went to be with God.

Grandmother Clearkley sat outside the room cradling the tiny bundle. His death followed soon after Annie's, and he was now safe in the arms of Jesus too.

Barry consoled Anne and Elizabeth, crying as they clutched some papers. The family Bible lay open beside Anne. She handed her father the tear-stained note.

Dearest Anne,

Follow your dreams as if I were there to help you. Listen to God. He will direct you. You are privileged, and now you must share those privileges with others. Share your God-given dreams. Share your gift for words, and help others see with your vision what they may otherwise ignore. Be a voice for those who appear to be silent. Care for your sister and the boys. Love your father. Someday you will do much more—way beyond helping your family. Love, Mother

Barry glanced at Elizabeth and she handed him the note her mother had written for her.

Dearest Elizabeth,

You are my gentle, thoughtful darling. I love that you write poetry and draw. In your drawings you capture the heart of a person. Will you do me a favor? Someday sketch all of you children surrounding me and give it to your father. I love watching your heart overflowing with compassion. May the Lord himself direct your compassion and guide you. Help your sister and always love your brothers and obey your father. Love, Mother

The girls realized their mother somehow knew she would not recover from this childbirth, but they wondered how they could move forward without her guidance.

The financial blow dealt by the storm compounded the devastation of Annie's death. Mourning his loss, Barry plunged into the task of replanting. As Barry sought to restore the estate, his daughters immersed themselves with caring for three active brothers.

Knowing their mother's deep faith, Elizabeth and Anne sought solace in the Methodist chapel. Dr. Thomas Coke, the newly appointed Methodist bishop, visited Antigua on his trip to the West Indies a few months before Annie's death and baptized both sisters. Though he stood only a little over five feet tall, both Elizabeth and Anne viewed Dr. Coke as a giant of a man. One evening during a meal at the Hart home, Dr. Coke revealed his bold ideology and views on slavery.

Dr. Coke told the Hart family of his meeting with George Washington. "Washington asked me to speak before the United States Congress. I doubted they would allow me to profess my views on slavery, so I declined." He folded his arms across his broad chest.

"You said 'No' to the President of the United States?" Elizabeth blurted.

Dr. Coke pursed his lips, "When you are not allowed to speak the truth, it is better to be silent."

Both sisters agreed they did not want to be silent about their faith or bury their longing to teach others. They resumed their studies as best they could.

Barry implored his daughters, "I want you both to continue your education. Many girls in your position would think of their future as tied to this plantation, linked to your brothers. I do not know how many more years I can keep working as I do. We still only make enough to survive, though I often work as hard as my people do. You girls should have expectations beyond the estate, visions of eventual marriage and homes of your own."

"Father," Elizabeth protested, "I want this always to be my home. I want nothing more than to care for all my family."

Barry shook his head. "Both of you fill my heart to overflowing with pride in your abilities. To see how much you're both like your caring mother gives me peace. Your minds are sharper than hers and mine combined, and you both have hearts reflecting your mother," he said proudly. "Your ability to teach your brothers exceeds my aspirations, and the boys tell me they learn more from the two of you than from our overweight, overpaid tutor I had hired. You both possess a wealth of wisdom. I may not be able to leave you much as an inheritance, but I pray I gave you a love of learning and a quest for wisdom."

Anne held her sister's hand as Elizabeth clung to their father. "You have given us a love of truth and taught us to stand for what is right," said Elizabeth. "There is no greater inheritance, Father. Because of you, we will always be wealthy."

Reaching an arm around both of his daughters, Barry Hart did not attempt to hide his pride in his two girls. He loved his sons, but his daughters made life full.

# 7

# An Answer Named Esther

*1785*

Responsibility could have been Anne's middle name. After her mother's death, 16-year-old Anne took on many of her mother's tasks. Her ability to organize the household pleased Barry's grieving heart. Yet Anne knew she needed more help than 13-year-old Elizabeth could give. A surprising answer about the needed help came from the local newspaper.

Few Jews lived on the small Caribbean island of Antigua. Anonymity for any non-coloured remained rare on this 10- by 12-mile island inhabited by 30,000 slaves, with a white population a mere 2,000. To be Jewish in Antigua meant nearly as many hardships as the free coloured experienced.

Anne rushed into their bedroom, clutching the newspaper. "Elizabeth, have you read the latest news?"

Elizabeth remained in her comfortable position, curled up on her bed with a book capturing all her attention, with little interest in the newspaper. Without taking her eyes from the page, her reply was simply an uninterested, "No."

Sitting down on the bed, Anne dropped the newspaper in front of her sister and persisted. "Elizabeth, listen. This might be God's answer."

Elizabeth shut her book in exasperation and stared at her sister. "What are you talking about?"

Pointing to the article, Anne began excitedly, "I just read about the recently imprisoned Jewish man. I know he has a daughter my age. I saw her in the small Jewish store in town. We have never spoken, but I noticed her stocking the shelves. 'Esther,' her father called her, and as she turned, her sad expression caught my attention."

Dismissing the urgency in her sister's voice, a frustrated Elizabeth picked up her book. "The rest of her family will take care of her," Elizabeth mumbled.

More exasperated than ever, Anne insisted. "No, I never noticed a mother or any siblings, so she must be alone. We need her here."

Elizabeth put her book aside and smiled at her sister. "And you have a plan to help both the girl and us. Am I right?"

Finally, Anne had captured Elizabeth's full attention. "If Father reaches a point when he cannot manage the estate, how would our family survive?"

Understanding her sister's plan before she voiced it, Elizabeth said, "We must pray Father remains healthy, and if we can help this girl, perhaps she can help us with Charles."

Anne sighed with exasperation. "At last, you are listening to me. Yes. Please pray while I go speak to Father."

After their mother's death, the family managed because their widowed Grandmother Clearkley had moved into their household. But life turned more complicated when Grandmother passed away only a month ago. Though the loss for the Hart family proved great, their sorrow was tempered by their hope of heaven. Still, the many duties remaining for Barry and his girls occupied their lives.

The challenge for the girls to continue their studies while they assisted their father was overwhelming. Grandmother had cared for Charles while the older children attended to their studies each day, helping the girls manage all the tasks necessary to maintain the home as a place of refuge and retreat.

Charles often disrupted the studies of his older brothers as he was too immature to join them. Father discharged the tutor after the financial losses caused by the storm. Thus, all summer, Charles trailed behind his mischievous brothers. The question remained. Who would care for Charles while Anne helped her other brothers and Elizabeth with their lessons? Charles needed supervision, as he thrived on trouble.

Barry insisted the girls must return to their own private studies. He spent most of his days, except Sundays, working alongside 22 of his 32 slaves. Six of the slaves he owned were children who were too small to work. The two elderly slaves cared for the slave children because they were too old to work the fields. Barry contemplated allowing his son Charles to join the slave children while the older children attended to their studies.

The Africans, forced to learn English when brought to this British West Indian island developed their own sing-song dialect. If Charles played all day with the slave children, his English would match that of his playmates. Barry remained adamant his son would grow up speaking the King's English. Annie would want this.

Anne approached her father as he sought the evening breeze outside. He smoked his clay pipe and relaxed on the veranda.

"Father, I believe God has given us an answer."

Barry turned to gaze at his oldest. "Which perplexing question did you present to God, my thoughtful daughter?"

"What we will do with Charles once we begin lessons again. I think we should consider asking Esther to live with us as our housekeeper."

Barry raised his eyebrows, taken aback. Anne continued, "You know. Esther, the Jewish girl. They have arrested her father. Surely, the law classifies her as *white*. The new law requires we must hire one white for every thirty slaves. If they count Old Molly, deaf Zacharias, and the children, we need to hire a token white to be compliant with the new law."

Humor blended with caution in her father's countenance. Barry was both pleased and sad as he realized again how Anne sounded like his Annie. "How old might this Esther be?"

"I don't know, Father. She and I have never spoken. She seems to be close to my age, maybe sixteen."

Her father cleared his throat and proceeded with a skeptical smile rising to the surface. "So, you know nothing about this girl other than she is white, young, and Jewish."

Hands resting on her hips, Anne responded. "I know she needs us, Father. And God placed her on my heart because we need her to care for Charles. You know he disrupts the studies of the other children. Please allow me to ask her."

Barry relit his pipe and leaned back in his chair. "You are both kind and wise, Daughter. I trust you to manage this need. The added loss of Grandmother affects both our hearts and our requirements."

Never one to hesitate once her mind grabbed onto an idea, Anne decided to seek out Esther the next morning. She asked Elizabeth to watch the boys, gathered her parasol, and headed to the Jewish shop in town.

A padlock secured the heavy wooden shop door. Knowing the family probably lived above Rosenthal's Grocery, Anne stood in the street and called out. "Esther! Esther, I wish to speak with you."

Anne imagined the girl alone and frightened. Hearing no answer, she called again, "Esther, I have come to help you. Please speak to me."

The window above the small shop opened. A tear-streaked, red-faced girl with disheveled hair stuck her head out.

"Who are you, and why do you want to bother me? Go away."

Anne smiled and exclaimed, "God has sent me to help you, Esther. Please come down, and I will tell you."

Now the girl sounded skeptical and angry. "Whose God told you to come? My God or your God? What do you want from me?"

With confidence, Anne declared, "I think the God of Abraham would want me to bring you home, Esther. Our mother died, and my sister and I are attempting to care for our three brothers. We need house help, and I imagine you might need us. You will find our home a safe place."

No answer came from above, but Esther forcefully shut the window, and Anne sat down to wait and see if this meant the girl might be answering "yes."

Praying as she waited, Anne considered what would be the result of this spontaneous plan. Thinking about her home, she realized even family could be a challenge to live with, and Esther's personality might prove difficult. Charles needed a firm hand, but he also needed love and a watchful eye. Both sisters showered Charles and his two brothers with love. Their mother had always been a fount of joy and serenity. Struggling with exasperation over the behavior of her brothers, composure turned into a distant goal for Anne. The tremendous feeling of being scattered in too many directions enveloped her, reminding Anne of her own shortcomings.

Elizabeth, calm Elizabeth, served as Anne's strong right arm. Her sister often provided the tenderness Anne feared she lacked when overcome by the task of raising three brothers. Contemplating all this, she asked the Lord to help Esther be His provision, not her own impetuous idea. Then the window opened, and Esther called down.

"Pssst, girl. Go around back to the mango tree."

Anne hurried through the alley to the large mango tree below what must be Esther's bedroom. The aroma of sweet mangoes saturated the air and she realized she was hungry.

"Stand back," the girl instructed as she lowered a rope with a large bundle attached. Hitting the ground with a thud a strange clank filled the air.

Anne watched, startled at the size of the bundle, as Esther lowered herself by the rope. She climbed the rest of the way down by way of the tree.

"Go ahead and gather mangoes if you want any. They have locked the shop below, and I cannot take the food supplies remaining inside, but the neighborhood children will glean this fruit if we do not."

Esther appeared to be the one giving instructions. This was usually Anne's role, and it seemed strange. Soon mangoes bulged from her apron pockets. Her brothers thought you could never have too many of them. Curious, but trying not to pry, Anne asked, "Is it all clothes in the bag you lowered?" She could now see Esther used a sheet to lower the oversized bundle.

"I only have a few clothes. But I am bringing a heavy pan I use to prepare chocolate, along with a supply of cocoa I kept in my bedroom."

Cook? The thought jolted Anne. Could Esther cook? Anne had not even considered what Esther's job might involve besides keeping a keen eye on Charles. Yet, she remained assured the Lord would have her entreat this girl to come to live with them.

Cultural differences surrounded the free blacks' lives already. Whites looked down on them merely because they were free coloured. Some slaves also resented their freedom. Envy came from one side, while snobbery emerged from the other. Jews in Antigua suffered almost as much animosity from the white plantation owner class as the free blacks. Anne chose to include a Jewish girl who appeared both bitter and grieving. Walking toward Esther, Anne held out her arms, hoping the girl would not hesitate to embrace a coloured girl.

Esther stopped, glanced away, and then broke into a sob rising from her depths as she fell into Anne's outstretched arms. They stood that way for a long time, until Anne reassured her. "It will be all right."

Unexpectedly, Esther moved away, turning crimson as her angry words flew. "My father, my innocent father, remains in jail! How dare you say it will be all right? I don't know what will become of him. I don't know what will become of *me*, and you tell me, *it will be all right*?"

Anne hung her head in shame. "You are right, Esther. I can't tell you all will be well. Please forgive me and allow me to try to make what may never be all right at least a little better." Anne pled with the upset girl. "I told you before, we need you, and I believe you need us. Please, can we try together to make things as good as they can be for now?"

Attempting to lift Esther's large bundle, Anne discovered it was both heavy and awkward. "Esther, can we divide this and carry it to my home?"

The sullen girl gave no answer but untied and redistributed the items into two bundles. Supposing it best to keep her foot out of her mouth, Anne said not a word. She lifted one of the packets and turned to begin the journey home. Esther blew her nose on a handkerchief and followed.

Anne reflected as she walked home, that Elizabeth might discern better how to comfort this girl. Forced out of her home, Esther now anticipated living with this girl's family instead of her own. The humiliated Esther had likely considered this mixed-race girl beneath her before that day. Now she would undertake the care of this girl's three rambunctious brothers.

As they arrived at the plantation, Esther finally spoke. "I am afraid I must appear ungrateful and rude. My life has always been Father and me alone. What will I do? Who am I now?"

Before Anne could think of an answer, Elizabeth joined the two girls. "Welcome home, Esther. Anne told me your name. I am Elizabeth, Anne's sister. We will show you to your room, and you can rest."

Astonishment overflowed from Esther as she whispered, "My room?"

"Actually, I should have said your bed. Anne and I will share a bed, and you will have mine. We three girls will share a room. The boys have a room and Father his own room, besides his office."

A touch of astonishment appeared in Esther's eyes as she questioned, "You would give up a bed for me?"

"Of course. We rejoice we have something we can share. Goodness, whatever makes your bundles so heavy?"

Esther answered defensively. "I brought my chocolate pans with me, as well as my supply of cocoa, stored in my room, and my recipes. Father gave me the responsibility of preparing chocolate to sell in the store. My mother taught me how to make chocolate from cacao when we lived in Curaçao."

Now Anne spoke with resolve. "Please be patient with us, as we will try to be with you. We know nothing about cooking chocolate, but I tasted it once, and found it delightful. We understand how it feels to be excluded. Now, come to see our room." The girls took her hands and walked her up the broad steps of the plantation house that would now be her home.

# 8

# Harsh Realities

*1786*

Anne sat savoring the breeze on the veranda and watching her father secure the wagon to the hitching post after returning from a trip to town. As he made his way up the steps, she noticed his slumped shoulders. He never completely succeeded at disguising his emotions.

Surprises did not sit well with Anne. She wondered what could be wrong. Her insistence on maintaining an unchanging routine gave her direction and consolation. On the contrary, her brothers thought she was too regimented and often saluted behind her back when she barked out instructions.

"Father, was everything good on your trip to St. John's?"

"May I have a moment with you in my office, Anne?" Her father lacked his usual smile. The privilege of being the oldest and the task of managing her siblings also meant she remained in her father's confidence for more significant matters.

Anne stood in front of his desk, while Barry sank into his chair. He ran his hand over the colour box sitting on a shelf beside the desk. He longed to draw from his own father's memory and wisdom, as he tried to find the right words to tell Anne what confronted them.

"Father?" Anne brought him back to reality.

"Please sit." Barry motioned. Distress etched his face. "I was summoned to see a lawyer this morning, to be present at the reading of the will for Judge Blizard. You might remember his children live off-island, and his wife died some years ago."

The Hart plantation shared a border with the Blizard estate. The families did not socialize as such, but the Judge had always been neighborly.

"Did the Judge bequeath something to you?"

Barry stared at a paper in his hand. Gazing up he reached across the desk to touch Anne's arm. Her mother would have understood how to break the news to this beloved daughter. Words to soften the blow he must share with her eluded him. He gripped her hand. "No, actually he left something to you, Anne." Barry hesitated, as shock widened Anne's eyes and concern etched his own. He asked, "Is there something you haven't told me regarding Judge Blizard?"

"He left something to me?" Anne blurted louder than she expected. "Why would he do so? What could he have left me?"

Somewhat relieved, Barry understood her genuine confusion. He contemplated why the Judge left something to her. "The Judge was known both for his fairness and his sense of humor. You will not find humor in his gift. I have no idea how to prepare you for what it is." Her father shut his eyes momentarily, and upon opening them he studied his daughter. "The fact is, he has given you two of his slaves."

Anne jumped from her chair and placed both hands firmly on her father's desk. "NO! Tell me this is not so. I hate the very idea of slavery." She sank back down into the chair and shook her head as if to remove her father's words. "This can't be."

"I knew this would upset you. I thought about it during the ride home, and I want you to trust me to help you with this."

"Of course, I trust you, Father, but this is an unfair burden for a girl. This is not right."

Barry squeezed Anne's hand. "Would it be better if these two slaves were given to a harsh owner? Sometimes we are forced to choose between the lesser of two evils."

Taking a deep, resigned breath, Anne began to tell her father a story offering a possible explanation for the Judge to include her in his will.

"Some months ago, Aunt Margaret and I were out riding near the edge of our property, next to the Blizards' land. The Judge was out riding too, and he invited us to join him for tea at his estate. Aunt Margaret said yes, as the man appeared so eager for company. During tea, he questioned me regarding my views on slavery—as a free black. I boldly told him slavery is a blight on any country allowing one person to enslave another. He laughed at me, but said I presented a good case. To cover for my brash reaction, Aunt Margaret began to gush over his beautiful tea set and his fine furniture."

Barry raised his hands in understanding. "Your story explains the other mystery. He also left your aunt all his furnishings," he paused, "including the tea set." Barry leaned back. "You must have impressed him, and your aunt amused him. Perhaps he remembered that her fiancé died on the voyage from England to Antigua, and he may have sensed some kinship with her in his own loss."

Pacing always calmed Anne. She stood up and began walking back and forth. She turned. "What can we do?"

Barry rose and took Anne's hands, bringing her to a standstill. "We will trust God that meeting Judge Blizard and your afternoon tea were providential. Please understand I would never buy two new slaves, but I certainly could keep two additional men working."

"Men?" Anne raised her voice. "I was given two men?"

Her father gently touched one finger to her lips, and she quieted, laying her head against his shoulder. "This is too much. I can't bear to think I own another person, let alone two men!"

"We will think about this and talk again tomorrow. Next week is when the two are scheduled to come."

The following day when Anne entered Barry's office, he rose and closed the door. "I trust you have not yet disclosed Judge Blizard's bequest to your sister?"

"I am wise enough to not burden her with this dilemma."

"Good. For now, I believe it best to allow people to think I inherited these slaves. Of course, if I ever must sell them, God forbid, I would give you the money."

"Oh no, Father! Giving me money would feel like the 30 pieces of silver Judas received for betraying the Lord. If I could wash my hands ceremonially, I would. I realize it is better if they are with a sympathetic master. Yet I can't bear the thought of playing a part in two people torn from the life they once knew."

Barry nodded, shutting his eyes in hopes of erasing the subject. "We can't set them free, unless they have a way to survive, and a means to make a living supplying their own needs. Slavery is a blight, but we do not have an answer. The law compels owners to supply clothing, food, lodging, and all medical care. I know it does not compel them to be compassionate, only caretakers. I regret you are caught in this trap I have experienced since I was 25."

Anne could not answer her father. She did not want anyone to question why she was upset. To avoid revealing her emotions to Elizabeth, she left the office to walk to the cook shack. Visions of slaves bound to a system of life she abhorred seemed to march alongside her.

Glancing towards heaven, she pled, "Please God help me bear this heavy burden. Help me share it with you alone. I trust you know I am now trapped as my father found himself trapped into this vile ownership of enslaved people."

After Anne celebrated her seventeenth birthday, she asked her father to allow her to teach more than the few slave children on the plantation. The adults also longed to learn, so several evenings each week Anne walked to the tobacco drying shed to instruct any adult slaves who wanted to learn. Elizabeth always accompanied her and often helped with teaching the alphabet. Several months after learning Judge Blizard had bequeathed two slaves to her, she noticed a new man in the small group gathered for instruction.

She bit her lip as she walked over and stuck out her hand. "Hello, I am Anne. Welcome to our class."

The tall young man, a handsome blue-black, timidly took her hand, "Dey does call me James, but me want to be called Quano."

Not hesitating, Anne asked, "How old are you Quano?"

"Seventeen, Miss. Me tinks. Many years past, my mother done sold. Not even me Massa remember what day me born."

"Can you read?" asked Anne. "Are you familiar with the alphabet?"

The boy told her, "Me learn de names of letters from de others, but me can't write."

"Well then, Elizabeth will help you catch up to the others." Anne motioned for him to sit.

Later Elizabeth said, "Recognizing how Father feels about slaves, I don't understand why he took two from the Blizard plantation. As tragic as the Judge's death was, I can't comprehend Father's reasoning."

Anne was reading a book and held it up so Elizabeth could not see her trembling lips. "Yes, it is sad."

A month later she observed another new man, an older slave maybe a few years younger than her father, helping unload the wagon. He glared at Anne, and she turned and bolted into the house. His scowl was a dagger to her heart. Shame washed over her, remorse for a circumstance in which she had no choice.

That evening she talked to her Father in his office. "Is the man aware I own him? Why did he give me such an evil glare?"

Barry attempted to calm her fears. "The slave knows you are my daughter. He is angry and rightfully so, but the others will try to help him feel safe. For some people resentment can turn the heart to stone. His back is scarred from years of whippings, and I imagine his heart is filled with anger and bitterness," said Barry. "When I told him about the reading class, he spit out a word I have never heard, but I understood it fully. He will not be joining your class. He frightens even me."

Anne asked, "Was Judge Blizard a harsh master?"

Barry shook his head. "They say he was a just judge. Perhaps his overseer was cruel. Avoid this angry slave. If he knew he was given to a girl, it would only make his fury worse."

"I'll fix you some tea, Father. Thank you for warning me."

Elizabeth particularly delighted in teaching the 12-year-old-slave, Ophelia, to read. The large-eyed, ebony-skinned girl showed promise. She was becoming one of the brightest students the sisters taught. While striving not to show favoritism among her father's slaves, Elizabeth found Ophelia had worked her way into her heart. Unafraid, the striking girl asked her master's daughter all the questions swirling in her mind. Elizabeth had no answers for some of those probing queries.

"Why, Miss, me born a slave and you born free? Does God love you more? Will me ever be free as you, Miss?"

The rapidly fired questions left Elizabeth shaking her head and answering louder than she meant to. "No!"

Ophelia peppered her teacher with more thoughts. "No, God not love me as much you? No, me never be free?"

An infrequently exasperated Elizabeth responded with a quavering "Yes, God loves you, Ophelia. Yes. I pray you will be free. *No*, I do not know why you are a slave and why my father and myself are not chained to this evil system created by man."

Plaintively Ophelia said, "My papa, he say me must not ask questions. My questions dem be bad, Miss?"

"No, to ask questions is not wrong. But if your papa tells you not to ask, it is because he does not want your mind troubled when there are no answers. *At least not yet*. We can pray for answers, and we can wait, but to struggle against things we can't change only serves to make us angry."

Several days after this discussion Barry asked his daughters if they wanted to go with him to St. John's. He had an article to take to Mr. Farquhar at the newspaper, and the girls could help him select provisions in town. The girls appreciated the rare privilege of spending time with their father, just the three of them. Esther told them she would keep the boys from getting in trouble. This young Jewish girl had made herself indispensable to the family. The cool December morning and the gentle sea breeze that signaled Christmas was near saved them from the exhausting heat.

When they arrived in town, Barry gave his daughters a list of necessary purchases, requesting they also buy a bag of sweets for the evening. Anne had packed a lunch to eat before the ride home. Barry suggested after they bought their supplies, they could walk down High Street towards the water. He would join them for lunch after he finished at the newspaper. The girls ordered the necessary items from the grocer, leaving the clerk to package them. They carried the bag of sweets and the lunch basket with them as they walked down to the ocean.

After engaging in a rather lengthy discussion with Mr. Farquhar, Barry imagined his daughters were becoming impatient.

Bidding him goodbye, Mr. Farquhar said, "If I were you, I'd avoid High Street this morning. They are holding a slave auction down by the boats."

Barry did not wait to answer the newspaper man. Turning, he ran towards the place where he hoped to find his daughters. As he approached the harbor, he saw people jammed together, waiting for the spectacle of an auction. Where were Elizabeth and Anne?

The girls had never seen slaves sold. Such things were not ever a subject he discussed! He did not want them plagued by the raw evil displayed when people bought and sold others as if they were mere animals. He found his girls huddled together in an alley between two buildings, the lunch basket knocked over in their haste to escape what they must have heard, and what he feared they must have seen. The noise of the crowd prevented Barry from calling out to Anne. When Barry touched her arm, Anne screamed, unaware of his presence. Clinging to Elizabeth, Anne was trying to shield her sister from the auctioneer's cruel words.

As he gathered his daughters in his arms, Barry could hear the auctioneer shouting, "See the fine figure of this girl. She will bear many pickaninnies to work your estate."

Men began hooting as Barry heard cloth ripping to expose the girl's nakedness. He cringed as the auctioneer called out, "Look at her healthy teeth. Who will bid 200 pounds?"

Barry guided his girls away from the disturbing sights and sounds and the wretched odors of the auction. The ever-practical Anne turned back to collect the basket, leaving their discarded lunch to stray dogs. Horror had replaced hunger. Barry could see Anne held back her tears to be brave for Elizabeth. Once they were away from the throng, Anne began to weep and clung fast to her father's arm. They hurriedly walked back to the shop.

"Forgive me," pled their father. "I am grieved you should witness such a revolting spectacle. I had no idea they were holding an auction today. I am distressed that I could not spare you from such a sight."

After he settled the girls in the wagon, Barry quickly collected the provisions from the store. On the ride home, Barry told them again how wretched it was they had observed such a tragedy. Elizabeth lay with her head in Anne's lap, holding tightly to her sister's waist. Silent.

Finally, Anne spoke. "Father, I feel such fury, yet I do not blame you. I saw a girl who was about Ophelia's age, they ripped her covering, and I heard them laughing. The girl spoke in a foreign language. She sounded as if she cursed them, then I saw the man knock her hard across her cheek. There was the rank smell of the meat market, reminding me of the hucksters calling out for people to buy. God must weep when he sees what man has become. I am ashamed my own father owns slaves. I am sorry, but it grieves me."

Barry hung his head. "Of course, it hurts you. I have avoided viewing the slave market, and I try to treat the people God entrusted to me with care and respect. We do not have an overseer because so many of them are cruel, using brutality to control. Sin causes unspeakable things. If only I could keep you from knowing the depth to which so many have fallen."

But Barry knew he could not.

# 9

# Easing Sorrows

*1786*

Hearing her father laugh, Anne tried to remember how long it had been since she experienced the delightful sound. The heavy sorrow of losing his wife nine months earlier had begun to lift. Now, as they walked together, and the dog playfully ran circles around them, she sensed the approach of a serious discussion. His pace slowed, and he grew silent. Several times, his mouth began to move, and it seemed he wanted to say something. He cleared his throat and began speaking rapidly as though the words would disappear if he did not say them quickly.

"Anne, you are bearing your load of the work with love and resolve, but I fear it is becoming too heavy for you. Though Esther has indeed been a Godsend, I want your sister to begin sharing more of the responsibilities. Jacob and Gratianus still need to continue with their education, and you do an excellent job."

"We will be fine now, Father. Don't worry about Elizabeth and me."

"Soon it will be time for Charles to take up his studies. Do you think it wise of you to spend the precious little time you have to yourself teaching our slaves in the evening hours? I know Elizabeth assists you with the annual sewing distribution for our people. Though Esther purchases the necessary provisions from town, I think you will exhaust yourself." A stiff frown marred his handsome face, making this appear as a mandate, not a request. Barry rarely spoke with such insistence.

Though hesitant to admit it, Anne experienced exhaustion at the end of each task-filled day. Fitting in many of the responsibilities her mother and then grandmother had provided for the large family required many hours of tiring labor. The law required an annual provision of clothing for each slave. A few of the items they purchased. Both sisters spent hours each day sewing and knitting many of the necessary clothing items. But if she must give up doing something, she certainly could not stop instructing her father's slaves. Her father had asked her if it was *wise*, but it was as necessary for Anne as food or sleep or shelter. She abhorred the thought of owning people, as though they were sheep or cattle. Sharing knowledge lessened the dilemma, the guilt, the regret that she—not only her father—but she, secretly owned two slaves. Teaching made her feel she was creating a breach in the web that might someday allow the slaves to survive. Her words turned into a plea.

"Father, I must educate the slaves. You and Mother agreed. I need this." Sensing her mother's affirming presence as she taught, remembering how she had always encouraged that endeavor, Anne experienced agony at the thought of not instructing the slaves.

Having more he needed to convey, her father took her hand, since he needed to finish this talk before others were around to hear. Tipping back the oversized hat protecting her from the scorching sun, he stared into her eyes.

"I never realized how much your mother did until she died. She cared for the slaves' physical ailments, sewed their clothes, and bought the necessary food for Old Molly to cook for them. I am grateful Old Molly remains able to cook and care for the pickaninnies. Sometimes, she watches over Jacob, Gratianus, and Charles as well. Gratianus would rather play cricket with the slave boy than study."

At her father's calling him a "slave boy," a frown soured Anne's expression, and she dropped his hand while planting her hands on her hips.

"Please, Father, can't you call him Aaron? He proves himself a bright lad and more eager to learn than Gratianus. True, our slaves do refer to their little ones as pickaninnies, but they are babies, beautiful babies. Aaron could do well for himself if given the opportunity. I pray in my lifetime we will see freedom for all the slaves. When freedom comes, they will need education and skills beyond fieldwork more than ever."

"Anne, perhaps I do not yearn for freedom for those enslaved as much as you do. You are young and idealistic. When I inherited the plantation and the slaves, I experienced feelings to match yours. I began to see there was more to it than erasing an injustice. Freedom will bring justice to the slaves but alter our lives as well. Workers for my small estate are a necessity, though I have considered how I could run the estate if forced to hire laborers. Frankly, I don't think we would succeed."

"Except for God's grace, Father, it could be you and me toiling long days in this unrelenting sun, although I know few masters are as thoughtful and generous as you. While I understand you cannot grant your slaves freedom, at least we can grant them the opportunity to learn."

"You would make a persuasive lawyer. I am grateful God granted my freedom. As I look in the mirror each morning, God reminds me of His grace bestowed on me. Though my skin is rather light, I remain a black man. To another point, I brought you on this walk today to ask you to extend grace about another pressing matter."

Again, he struggled to find the words. "No woman can ever replace my angel, Annie. No one. However, I need you to realize eventually I will remarry."

Barry's daughter was unprepared for this. She had surely heard wrong or misunderstood. Had her brother accidentally thumped her head hard with a cricket bat, making her ears ring?

"Why do you need to marry? I will continue to care for the boys, since my studies are almost completed, and I can keep up with the needs of the slaves."

She kept blinking, feeling she had slipped into a dream and would wake to find he had not said he planned to marry.

"Anne, there will be a time when you think of yourself, when you marry and have a home of your own. I do not want to hold you back."

"Hold me back? You have done everything to enable me to be so much more than any other free coloured I know. You provided a superior education, one far beyond what even most white children on this island experience. Mother showed me how to have compassion for the slaves, filling my heart with understanding and love."

Touching her hair reminded him of his Annie. Barry was without words. Dreading the awkward topic, he plunged forward. “I recognize no woman will take your mother’s place. None could be a match for her wisdom and care. But at the close of the day, as I rest my weary head on my pillow, then I miss her the most. I always shared with Annie the challenges of my day. She soothed me as a mother who satisfies a hungry baby with milk, becoming my anchor, my light in the darkness of life’s trials. Now, I only ask the Lord to provide someone to listen to me as nightfall approaches. You are a rock, Anne, but I need a wife, whereas you are almost ready for a husband.”

Feeling as though she might choke, she tried to imagine what her father could be saying. Both the thought of her father remarrying and the possibility he believed she should marry came as a blow.

“Father, who would want to marry me? I am blessed, but too well educated, too opinionated to be desirable. Many think I am too compassionate to the slaves. No, I will never marry, yet I can try to recognize your needs. I will pray you find a companion, but I do not expect to marry.”

Pacing as she did when contemplating a problem, Anne halted before continuing. “Free black men often learn a trade or a skill early, yet never experience the luxury of education, such as you and I were given. I absorbed every book I could, so I make these men feel inadequate. A few men at church have spoken to me, but all too soon they realize I have a mind. Most free black men want a woman to be only a wife and mother. I would embrace that, but I want more. I want—I need—to share the blessings God gave me. Most men are shocked and immediately become uninterested when they learn I envision a school for slave children.”

Anne’s insight often overwhelmed Barry.

Removing her hat, Anne began to crush the edges as she twisted it around. “I only aspire to share the privilege you provided to me with as many people as possible. I am happy, having purpose, and contentment. Thus, in generations to come, I hope to have a part in educating slaves to be all they can be.”

He empathized with her observations, yet he needed for her to grasp his own situation.

Barry smiled weakly and attempted to change the subject. "I have good news. The Methodists paid me another thirty pounds as payment for the property I bought two years ago from Mr. Nanton, with a Methodist chapel in mind. Next year the church will pay me the final payment, while work on a new chapel will soon begin on the large lot on the corner of Tanner and Temple Streets."

More words were unnecessary. Anne spoke the truth about free black men, yet it pained him to think she might never marry. They walked back to the house in silence, with each unable to provide an answer to the issues they had unlocked.

Not long after this discussion, Barry's yearning for a wife became a reality. Elizabeth Sharp, a free black, worked as a seamstress. She had failed to find a man to suit her taste until she met Barry when he came to the tailoring shop where she worked in town. Miss Sharp was 29. Barry, though 17 years her senior, remained a charming man. And he owned two plantations, and that alone made any free black man attractive.

The young seamstress presented a sharp contrast to Barry's muscular frame and caramel colour. Her figure had more substance than the lean, almost petite, fair-skinned African women in his own family. Her curves and softness were without the muscular tones brought on by physical labor. The daring hats and stylish clothing Miss Sharp created complimented her figure and colouring. Perhaps Barry wanted someone who did not remind him of his Annie. Elizabeth Sharp did not.

Over several meetings and walks in the evenings, they had agreed to marry, but Miss Sharp did not meet Barry's family. Both imagined such a meeting might bring an end to the easy relationship that had become both comfortable and desirable for the two of them. Barry feared the prospect of joining herself to a family of five children might dissuade the young woman, so he avoided bringing her home. Barry warned her of his three boisterous sons, while explaining his two older daughters shared in the upbringing of his boys. He began to speak to his daughters about the woman he chose. He knew he was acting in haste. No one needed to tell him, but the craving for a wife clouded his judgment. Though

Barry forewarned his family, the girls were astonished when their father announced he had already asked Elizabeth Sharp to be his wife.

Miss Sharp was nervous about meeting Barry's family. At least he recognized the thought of five children was somewhat overwhelming for her. This would, in fact, be quite a change for all. However, marriage to a man who owned a plantation was already beyond her imaginings.

Barry Hart and his future wife arranged a private wedding at the courthouse. The girls knew he would bring Elizabeth Sharp Hart home for the first time directly following the ceremony. But when the woman walked in beside their father, the children merely stood and stared.

"I want you to welcome my wife to our family," said Barry. "Because we already have one charming Elizabeth, I decided to call my new wife, Liza." He took her hand. "Liza, may I introduce my family: Anne, Elizabeth, Jacob, Gratianus, and Charles."

"Children, please welcome Liza into our home as she is now officially a Hart along with the rest of us."

Charles gave a small bow and his brothers quietly offered, "Nice to meet you," saying it almost in unison.

Not sure what to say, Elizabeth said, "Welcome home." Anne managed to gaze past Liza and announced, "We have prepared a meal. Are you hungry?"

Trying in vain to disguise their amazement, both sisters glanced at each other. This woman appeared years younger than their father and dressed in a manner their mother would not have considered proper. Liza removed her elaborate hat, embellished with feathers. As her hat pin fell to the floor, the family realized they had become so quiet they heard the pin drop. Even the boys were shocked into silence.

Father had made his choice. There would be no discussion with him about this, and the girls knew Liza deserved for them to accept her. Anne wrapped her arms around herself and knew her smile and greeting were less than authentic. Elizabeth, always quick to make peace and extend grace, now smiled at her father's wife, even if her heart did not feel it. Barry's sons chimed in with questions. Liza's small dog bridged the boys' inability to know what to say.

"What's his name? May we play with him? Will he chase a ball?"

"I call him Oscar, and he loves to chase balls. Though it might take a while for him to feel comfortable with you. He is not used to children."

Accustomed to life on her own, Liza imagined it indeed might take some time for herself to feel comfortable with this large, boisterous family.

Barry's daughters asked if they could now serve the special meal they prepared—yams, eddoes, chicken in savory rice, and a coconut cake. The girls also arranged red hibiscus and variegated green, red, and yellow crotons to decorate the large table.

Once all seven gathered at the table, Barry's new wife was overcome. Not yet thirty, she was now the mother of two almost grown girls. Her well-crafted dress of silk made her feel uncomfortable as she noticed the children all dressed in plain cotton. Liza wished Barry had talked more about his family situation, and she began a mental list of all the changes she wanted to make to the estate house. Liza trusted she could charm her husband into agreeing to new curtains and cushions for the chairs. Accustomed to having only herself to consider, a sudden awareness her life was about to change dramatically struck her, but she determined to adjust to the existing family and prize her newfound life on the plantation.

Both Hart sisters struggled to fathom why their father chose to marry Elizabeth Sharp. Stylish and young were possibly part of the appeal. The loss of his beloved wife of eighteen years had aged him, and perhaps he would never again display the light-hearted, quiet charm that drew so many people to him. However, many still considered Barry Hart, at age 46, youthful.

Annie Clearkley Hart had always demonstrated a disregard for external adornment, charming Barry with her modest, unpretentious, and sincere inner qualities. Liza Sharp Hart appeared to have high regard for outward appearances. The girls tried not to compare their father's chosen bride with their beloved mother, yet the glaring contrast astonished them.

Weeks after Barry married her, Liza invited a friend from town for tea. Cook brought in fresh mango buns, then returned to her outdoor kitchen. Liza bragged as she poured the pungent ginger tea, "I am fortunate indeed Mr. Hart will spoil me. Some of those haughty white women think a woman of colour has no sense of creativity. I know my husband will support my taste for fashion. Of course, I have also accepted a family of five spoiled children, including those three noisy boys. Their sisters will fill the role of nanny for the boys, so I will have time to sew and take my ease in this home that is now mine."

Overhearing this self-centered conversation when they slipped into the house for water, the girls quietly moved back outside. Elizabeth recovered her composure first.

"We need to pray for Father. We can't question why he married this woman. The boys are still our responsibility, and together we will give them all the attention they need."

"Elizabeth, I need to guard my heart because right now my feelings for Father's wife are not those of love or respect. I will willingly—no, I will readily—care for Jacob, Gratianus, and Charles, but how can we show respect for her? How can we do this?"

Elizabeth peered out across the field to where their father worked alongside the slaves.

"We will do this because Mother would expect it," Elizabeth paused, "because Father needs us to accept his new wife. We will do this because God extended grace to us, and because God loves her, and Father chose her. Remember the story Father told us about how he impetuously chose Mother? Maybe this time, Father chose rashly based on his loneliness. We will choose to love her. God being with us, we must."

"Elizabeth, you are so much wiser than I am. We need to go find those boys."

# 10

# Becoming Proper Methodists

*1786*

Barry's daughters were relieved to see some of their father's light-heartedness return as he balanced time between his new wife and the children he adored.

While supporting the girls' choices whenever conflicts arose, Barry explained to his wife that she must treat the girls as adults. At first, problems occurred over the girls' involvement with the Hart slaves, since as a free black, Liza had experienced little interaction with enslaved people. Minor grumbles arose until Barry's wife accepted that she must not challenge Barry's loyalty to his family.

Not long after the Methodist Church began in Antigua, the Hart family began to attend. At the supper table one evening, Liza contended the Methodist Church lacked the proper respect their family should receive as landowners. Since the Methodists attracted 3,000 slaves and a handful of less than 30 whites, Liza questioned if they might attend a more proper church. The girls never considered their father to have a temper. Now, they observed otherwise as his voice deepened with irritation.

"Proper? Proper, you say? There is nothing proper in the manner the established Church of England treats the slaves or free blacks," Barry set his jaw. "The girls are free to worship God in the church of their choice. *In fact,* I choose to worship God alongside my fellow men and with my daughters and sons. Worship is about truly honoring the indwelling Christ. Church is not a place to display a new dress," he asserted. "I have never cared about being proper. I learned that years ago, and I taught my family the same. No, it was Annie who taught my girls true worship has nothing to do with being proper."

Rising from the table, Barry walked outside. Casting a bewildered glance at Barry's family, Liza followed him.

"Barry, I am sorry, and I will not interfere with how you raise your children. I'm struggling to understand the girls' involvement with your people. Yet, I do know how you love your daughters. Perhaps I have some jealousy of your love for them, but I trust you will allow me to choose how I intend to raise our child?"

Barry spun, and his anger turned to confusion. "Are you telling me God is going to bless us with a child?"

"Yes, Barry, but this will be *our* child—a child we can pour love upon."

Barry tempered his smile with disappointment.

"Liza dear, I wish for you to love all my children, ours and those here before you joined this family. I need you to love them, and I long for them to give you pleasure as well. If they sensed you needed their affection, it could make a difference, since the girls especially are generous in their love for all those in need."

Barry trusted there would be no further discussion about his daughters' choices, while hoping his family would continue to extend grace to all—even when it was not given in return.

Liza's pregnancy soon after they married added another element to the adjustment period. Barry took his daughters aside, asking them to try to be understanding. Remembering how tired their mother had been when pregnant helped the girls be sympathetic. In the days following, Anne and Elizabeth worked at having an agreeable arrangement with their father's wife. Barry hoped if he gave it enough time, his wife's mood might adjust and clear, much as the ever-changing weather in Antigua.

Barry struggled with a longing that the care of the boys not become a burden for his daughters. He desired for them to experience much more. Elizabeth's poetry thrilled him. Her skill to both articulate and write surpassed his. His girls were copies of their mother, Annie, caring little about pursuing what others considered proper pursuits for free-black girls. Liza, on the other hand, wanted Barry's daughters to care more about their appearance. His days were full, and by the time he ate his supper, he was ready to rest. On one such evening as the sun was setting and the evening promised a full moon, Liza requested a walk for the two of them.

"Barry, are you aware of how the church controls your daughters?" Liza began. "I offered to sew for them, yet they wish for simplicity rather than the more recent styles. The girls are attractive, but the way they dress reflects poorly on you."

Barry's expression told her she had already said too much. Sadness clouding his features, she tried again. "Having my ideas rejected hurts me. If they could at least try some of the modest trimmings I have offered them. Even the slave women care more about their Sunday dress than your daughters. At least the girls care enough about their complexions to wear their bergère hats when they go out. But I could make those hats the envy of many women, if your girls would allow me to add feathers and silk ribbons." Liza continued, but she did not miss the set of Barry's jaw growing tighter. "I am not interfering, but I am trying to improve them. I thought if *you* told them this is important, then they would change their minds."

Barry stopped and drew in a deep breath. "No, I will not speak to them. This is what *you* want, not what I wish to see. I thought I had already made it quite clear you must treat them as adults. Both Anne and Elizabeth know their own minds," Barry declared. "I know my people. When they earn a little money selling produce, they spend it on fripperies. However, this goes contrary to my daughters' nature. They find pleasure in dressing simply." Barry turned and began a fast-paced walk back to the house. He was afraid if he said more, it would be in anger.

The impact of Anne's decision to simplify her life grew more evident one evening when Liza requested her stepdaughter entertain the family by playing the piano. She declined, announcing a recent decision that her talent for piano playing filled her with pride, and she had resolved to forgo this pleasure.

Liza exclaimed, "Honestly, Barry, the girl acts obsessed with these Methodist ideologies. You must control her better."

Barry had taken great pleasure in hearing Anne play the piano. He thought her decision rash and unnecessary too. His boisterous sons hushed as Anne watched for her father's reaction.

"Anne, I delight to hear you play," said her father. "Piano playing can be to God's glory. Still, I will not compel you to follow any rule-book to satisfy others. You must come to conclusions of your own and have courage to follow the convictions God gives to you. If you strive to please God, I see that as best," he was speaking to all of them while addressing Anne. "The Almighty is more concerned we trust in Christ than with the externals we display to the world. Take care your decision to avoid things others take pleasure in does not create a false pride in denying yourself."

His daughter hesitated before replying, "I will consider this, Father. Now I want to be excused to walk in the cooling night air before I go to my bed."

While everyone knew Anne and Elizabeth did much to keep the Hart ship afloat, they also understood Barry was the captain of the ship. The family waited for him to indicate how he expected them to react.

"We live in a country bursting with people who treat others with disrespect," Barry proclaimed. "In this house, we will always honor each other, including respecting Anne's choices. God bestowed on her incredible compassion for others. She will think through her decisions, but never let me hear any of you mock her for having convictions."

A mere nine months after their father remarried, Barry's children welcomed their new half-sister, Sarah. Elizabeth and Anne knew all too well childbirth and its complications could be life threatening. They waited patiently for Liza to regain her strength, recognizing she seemed baffled by the demands of a newborn. Often when baby Sarah began to cry, Liza would summon one of her stepdaughters to take the infant.

Welcoming the opportunity to cuddle her baby half-sister, Elizabeth declared, "We need to give Liza time. I see a vacant gaze in her eyes and wonder if she is afraid."

Anne was less generous. "Afraid she might lose her figure for fashionable clothes."

Elizabeth frowned. "Won't you consider how our noisy brothers often disturb her when she tries to rest. Not only that, but the baby keeps her awake much of the night, so don't be ungracious and judgmental."

Anne began to pace as she listened to her sister's reprimand. "Of course," she stood still and spoke thoughtfully, "You are right. Stop me next time I complain."

Holding Anne's hands, her sister squeezed her fingers. "I will nudge you when I see exasperation spoiling your attitude. You have been creasing your brow so much lately, I am afraid it will stay that way."

Anne hung her head. "Is it actually so often, and so obvious?"

"I noticed Father appeared hurt the last time Liza asked you to take the child. You never say no, but I could see you were vexed."

Anne touched Elizabeth's cheek. "I need a walk. Sorry for my poor example, and I thank you for your correction. I have been judgmental and given little thought to how hard all this has been for both Father and Liza."

Baby George followed a year after Sarah's birth. Liza struggled through weeks then months of emotional anguish. The mental fog surrounding her was reminiscent of the fog occasionally seen in the creek bottoms. The girls took turns caring for the toddler, Sarah, and baby George, as well as their own brothers. Increasingly, Liza distanced herself from not only her own babies but also from everyone else.

*1788*

Adding Liza and the two babies complicated the Hart household. Esther, though no older than Anne, took on the role of mother-hen. She watched over Anne and Elizabeth as well as Charles. Daily she ordered the sisters outside to spend an hour after lunch as a brief rest from their many duties.

The sisters retreated to a blanket under a large mango tree. Elizabeth often detected moods Anne tried to keep to herself. Hearing her familiar sigh, Elizabeth tapped Anne's hand. "All right, what troubles you? And don't try to deceive me by saying *nothing*. You have been staring at the same page for much too long, and you have sighed three times in the last few minutes. The weight of the world should not rest on your shoulders alone. Tell me."

"I can't hide anything from you. You understand me better than I understand myself most days. I detest whining, and if I talk about this matter, it will become exactly that."

"Go ahead," teased Elizabeth. "Whine a bit. Then I can help whatever is bothering you. Besides, holding troubles inside is never good, and at least I'll know how to pray for you."

A slight smile surfaced on Anne's troubled face. "I treasure this daily hour when we escape outside, while Esther watches over the children, and I regain my sanity. Today I am thinking of Mother, remembering the times when she was expecting our brothers. I don't know if you remember, but she often sat rocking while singing to the baby swelling her belly," said Anne. "She'd call me over, place me up on her rapidly disappearing lap, and place my hand to feel the baby move. Elated to be expecting, she adored each child before it was born. I don't see Liza doing this."

Anne waited for this to sink in. "Mother called us her treasures, and she delighted in caring for Father and each of us children. I see how Liza struggles more with each pregnancy, and I imagine losing her figure does little for her pleasure of dressing stylishly."

Elizabeth nodded with understanding. "And you are troubled by Liza's inability to have pleasure in her two precious babies she and Father added to our family? Yes. I understand. I ache for her and whatever is missing in her life. Yet, there will soon be a third child in as many years."

Admiration for her sister reflected in Anne's pale blue eyes. "You always attempt to understand a person who does nothing but irritate me. I am ashamed, Elizabeth." Anne admitted, "I struggle with a small voice inside me saying, 'My doing all the mothering she should be doing is unfair.' I want to help Liza, but I also try to imagine what she would do if we were not here to take care of her babies, as well as our brothers."

"Yes, unfair, but necessary," Elizabeth clenched her hands tightly. "I'm not sure she could do it if we were not here, and I fear something is broken inside Liza."

Anne rolled her eyes. “I got rather upset when she asked me to walk Oscar this morning. Caring for the children is one thing. Walking her dog was the last straw.”

Elizabeth shut her sister’s book. “Father is not blind. He knows how hard it must be for us, and it is equally wearisome for him. He chose her, and all the children are his responsibility too. We must tell Father we understand his struggle and are praying for both him and Liza. We’ll talk to him about this after we have our noon meal.”

Each day the slaves listened for the noon time blowing of the conch shell. Noontime meant a break from the sweltering heat for everyone. Sitting in whatever shade they could find, eating food prepared for them by the elderly slave, Old Molly, everyone rested until the conch shell was blown again at half past one.

The Hart family ate together at the long dining table in the house. Father often retreated to his office after finishing his meal. After a lunch of salt fish and pumpkin, Anne knocked on her father’s study door, knowing he would return to supervise the slaves soon.

“Father, I want a visit with Old Molly. May I walk out to the fields with you?”

Barry picked up his hat, his smile brightening. “You know I delight in a walk with a lovely girl by my side.” Barry suspected his daughter had a plan to present to him. They had only walked a short way, when she took his arm and stopped.

Swallowing hard, the words she had been rehearsing tumbled out. “Elizabeth and I want you to know we understand how your wife struggles to cope with the changes taking place. We do all we can to make things easier. I understand this situation must trouble you, and we want to know if there is more that we can do to help.”

Barry grew quiet. When he finally spoke, his voice choked, and his distress pained her. “I wish I knew what to do myself. I have always been impetuous, choosing your mother practically the first time I met her. I imagined I could choose just as well the second time.” He rubbed at his chin. “I fail to understand why Liza is unable to adjust to having children. I thought she would love all of us.” Barry focused down. “I realize she can't connect even with our own babies. I grieve when I see you and Elizabeth caring for them. If I could afford a nurse, I would hire one."

He tried to clear the sadness these thoughts stirred up. "My wife came into this large, busy family as an outsider. Esther provides invaluable aid, and because both she and Liza experience the sting of feeling like an interloper, Liza responds best to Esther's support. You are now twenty, and Elizabeth almost seventeen. You should be enjoying your last years at home. I am sorry for this burden."

"Father, I have upset you. We thought it might help to tell you we understand."

Her father's evident regret lay heavy on Anne's heart, and she wrapped her arm around him, rocking him as if soothing one of his babies. "We will get through this, Father. Elizabeth and I have no plans to leave. You could never have foreseen Liza's response to having children, and we realize she needs our understanding, not our judgment. Do not fret for Elizabeth and me."

"You are a match for your mother in more than a name. Annie always extended grace upon grace to cover all my mistakes."

# 11

# Blessed to Be Free Blacks

*1789*

Counting on her memory of her father often granting favors in honor of special occasions, Elizabeth found her father on the veranda where he had retreated with pipe and lantern to relish a rare moment alone. "May I speak with you, please?" she asked hesitantly.

Barry patted the seat next to him. "I detect a plaintive plea approaching my heart. Yes, my dear, ask."

She cleared her throat. "Father, we received a letter today from Uncle David. He asked us to bring him some of our Barbados cherry bark for his gout, because he remembers Mother taught us how to concoct a suitable remedy."

Her mother's sister Aunt Grace and her husband, David, lived around the south side of the island in Old Road Village. After her mother's death and her father's remarriage, the family saw Grace and David Cable infrequently. From St. John's to Old Road and home again required two days of travel by wagon, a lengthy trip.

"Father, next week I become eighteen. I would consider it a gift to go to Old Road to deliver the medicine and spend time with Aunt Grace. May I be the one to go to them?"

"I blink my eyes, and here you are a lovely, grown woman. For you to travel alone would not be safe or proper. If Jacob agrees to go, it would be an adventure for both you and your brother. Though Jacob is only fifteen, he is quite mature, and will look after you." His eyes twinkled, grateful to be able to repay Elizabeth for the sacrifices she made daily.

Kissing her father's forehead, she started off in search of Jacob. Turning back, she gave her father one of her radiant smiles. "Bless you and thank you."

Elizabeth reminded Barry so much of Annie he experienced a prick of pain. When she was out of sight, he wiped away a tear. Though now married to Liza, he still missed Annie Clearkley Hart.

Elizabeth planned what she and Jacob would need for the trip. They would travel almost twelve miles on rough dirt roads. They must take enough water and food to sustain them if any unforeseen problems arose with the wagon.

Finding Anne in their room, Elizabeth blurted out her news. "I am taking a birthday outing to Old Road to see Aunt Grace and take medicine to Uncle David. Jacob will go with me. I will pack a blanket in anticipation of a picnic lunch along the seaside. Oh, I do so love the sounds of the sea."

A flash of envy struck Anne, but it left as quickly as it came. Anne kissed her sister's cheek. Elizabeth spent almost all her time tutoring and caring for her siblings and now half-siblings. Her sister deserved this getaway. "I can't imagine a better present than a trip around the south side and a quiet lunch, just you and Jacob."

Elizabeth plopped on the bed with a contented expression. "I love all our family, but solitude is seldom our companion. Jacob and I might not even talk, with the sound of the wheels on the road becoming all I want to hear. No crying, no whining, no questions" she paused. "Yes, it sounds delightful— a perfect day."

Rolling over, Elizabeth said, "I want to take the remedies to Uncle David, but I also long for the adventure of seeing the south side of the island." She shut her eyes as if daydreaming. "I would love to sketch the view across the ocean to Montserrat, with the changing blues of the sea. We will go past Darkwood and Urlings before reaching Old Road."

Anne's eyes twinkled. "My mouth waters at the thought of the pineapple fields below Boggy Peak." She took a deep breath. "I can smell them now."

Elizabeth flopped her arms out across the bed. "Desiring to take only Jacob and not the rest of you is a mite selfish. Yet I will barely sleep tonight anticipating tomorrow."

Jacob loaded everything early in the morning. Antigua's proximity to the equator meant almost no twilight and an early sunrise. Elizabeth packed her parasol to protect her from the worst of the sun's penetrating heat, sure to be noticeable even before eight in the morning.

As they drew near Darkwood Beach, she turned to Jacob. "Let's stop here long enough to go down and cool our feet in the water. I delight in the tang of the sea grapes growing along the shore as well as the beautiful view of Montserrat from here."

While Jacob walked down to the water, his sister stepped into the bush to relieve herself before they continued the rut filled road. As she tidied her skirts back down, she heard a sniffling sound, followed by a plaintive plea. "Please, Miss, please help me."

Elizabeth resisted an urge to scream. The female voice sounded desolate. Turning, she could see matted, flaming red hair, and the much-sunburned face of a white girl clearly in great distress. The girl's faded brown homespun dress, what remained of it, appeared shredded. She wore no shoes, no hat, and her hands were raw. Clearly the girl had suffered from an ordeal leaving her battered and frightened.

Elizabeth questioned the pathetic creature. "Who are you?" she asked gently. "What are you doing here in the bushes, and where is your family?"

At the last question, the girl started to sob. "They're all gone now. Sean died, and I am alone."

Pushing the bushes back further to better see the girl, Elizabeth asked, "Who are you, and who was Sean?"

The girl's bloodshot eyes shone with tears. "Can I trust you?" she quivered. "Please do not turn me in. I cannot go back. My only brother Sean died to protect me. Please … Miss … I am Kallie O'Rourke."

Elizabeth peered back to where her brother Jacob skipped stones into the sea, while his bare feet splashed in the waves. "My brother is waiting for me. Let's sit with him, and you can tell me how we can help."

Kallie's words overflowed with fear. "No, please. I cannot meet a man. I cannot. I will tell you how Sean died, and you can tell me what I should do, but please don't make me go back."

Elizabeth called to her brother, "Jacob, I will be a few minutes more. Go ahead and start picking the sea grapes, please."

A surprised Jacob walked further away from where Elizabeth remained concealed with this sad girl.

Shutting her eyes, as if trying to erase the memory, the girl softly confessed. "I killed him, my only brother Sean. I should have remained in Montserrat."

Hearing the girl came from the island of Montserrat, 26 miles across the rough sea, left Elizabeth stunned. "Montserrat! You sailed from Montserrat? Why do you say you killed your brother?"

Elizabeth removed the dainty handkerchief tucked in her bodice and handed it to the girl, who quietly sobbed.

Kallie's words poured out. "I escaped, and Sean helped me when he stole a boat. We failed to plan what we would do once we reached Antigua. Sean was afraid if someone saw the boat, the authorities would know where to come search for us. He thought if it appeared the boat sank on the reef, they would believe we perished. My brother took the boat out where the water was deep enough to sink it as I watched from here."

Her words choked, "Then I saw the mast strike Sean in the head. I watched as he sank along with the boat. I thought he would surface, but he disappeared. Sean could swim, yet I cannot. Now I am all alone, and I don't know what to do." Kallie covered her mouth, attempting to stifle her sobs, her red face etched with anguish and guilt.

Never one for dramatic reactions, Elizabeth bowed her head, pleading with God for wisdom, then continued questioning the girl. "Kallie O'Rourke, I hear the ring of an Irish name. I am trying to understand why you were fleeing Montserrat." Elizabeth was amazed by this girl's story. "I am sorry about your brother, but you did not kill him. From whom were you fleeing? Explain before Jacob imagines something is wrong and comes searching for me."

Kallie poured out more of her story. "Indeed, my brother and I took transport from Ireland to Montserrat four years ago. In Ireland, we lived as a poor but happy family before our mother and father both died of a sudden fever," said Kallie. "I was 12 and Sean 14 when the Overseer of the Poor placed us in a workhouse for orphans."

Elizabeth nodded at the girl to go on. Kallie reflected between her tears, "I worked in the fields day after day. Sean spoke to me one Sunday, telling me a man offered to take him to an island called Montserrat. He told us many Irish lived there, and Sean would be an indentured servant. The man said he would pay my brother's passage and bed and board for four years. After four years, a small plot on Montserrat would be Sean's own land. The thought of such an island sounded as if an answer from heaven," she paused, "not knowing it would resemble hell. Though a beautiful island, yet deceptively so, it seemed as a place designed to kill us."

The sunburned girl's expression clouded with grief. "Sean should have gone without me, and he would have been fine. Yet, he insisted he would go to the island only if the man took me as well. Imagining the island was close to Ireland, I was excited."

The girl clutched Elizabeth's hand. "Oh, Miss, the journey took two months on a stinking boat, crowded with Irish men, women and some children, all signed to become indentured servants," she whimpered. "On arrival, they sent Sean and me to work in the cane fields alongside the Africans. Those were horrible, brutal years of working all day in the torturous sun. I only saw Sean on Sundays. We finished our four years as indentured folk two weeks ago."

"Why did you flee?" questioned Elizabeth. "Help me understand what has caused you to fear."

Kallie hesitated. "They told me because I am only a girl, I must work an extra year in the man's house as a house servant. At first, I had relief I would not be working in the sun. I became horrified when the girl I shared a room with explained to me the master's true expectations of me."

Words poured out, "Miss, I am a good girl, and I could not remain there. I could never endure a life of disgrace! When I told Sean what she had said, he decided we must steal a boat and flee to Antigua. We could see your island from ours, and we didn't think it was impossible," she gasped. "Oh, Miss, 26 miles is so very far by sea. Sean observed some men sailing on his Sundays off, and he asked some questions, but he had never sailed. He knew where they docked the boats. Sean only wanted to protect me. What do I do now?"

Telling her to remain hidden, Elizabeth walked to the wagon and brought bread and cheese, as well as a bottle of ginger drink to the girl. Kallie whimpered as she took the food and drink.

"I will help you, Kallie, but you must understand this puts me at risk. If the authorities of Montserrat cast blame on you for the theft and destruction of the boat, they will consider you a criminal." Elizabeth scrutinized her. "They could also hold me accountable for what Sean did if people learn I helped you. First, I do not want my brother involved in this. I detest lying. I will not lie to my brother, but I will tell him he must not question me."

Elizabeth continued, "We are traveling to my uncle's place not far from here, but first we will go by way of Claremont Plantation. I have heard the woman who owns it recently experienced the death of her husband. I have never met her, but I understand she is a Quaker. I know the Quakers see slavery as a terrible iniquity, and it sounds to me you were as a slave in Montserrat.'

Kallie wiped at her tears. Elizabeth told her, "I heard this woman hires freedmen, working for wages. I trust she will hire you. I doubt authorities will go there to search for you." Elizabeth paused, "I will not tell you to lie, but you could alter your name. If the authorities question the mistress of Claremont, she can say in all honesty she never met Kallie O'Rourke. In remembrance of your mother, you could use her maiden name."

"Oh, Miss, God sent you with a plan. I will do as you say."

Elizabeth touched the injury on the girl's raw, sunburnt hand. "Before my brother returns, you must climb into the back of the wagon and cover yourself with our blanket. I will ask Jacob to go first below the Claremont estate so I can pick some herbs before we reach my aunt and uncle. I will uncover you, and you must follow me into the bushes, from there you will see the plantation on the hillside. Do not tell the mistress your entire story. Give her whatever name you choose. Tell her you need help and need to work. I believe she will take care of you. Do not tell her or anyone of my part in this."

Kallie squeezed her rescuer's hand. "Oh Miss, you are an angel sent from God. I will do as you suggest."

Giving the foul-smelling, disheveled girl a hug, Elizabeth motioned for her to hide under the blanket while she called to Jacob.

Jacob noticed her tears. "What's the matter?" he asked.

"Please don't question me, Jacob. I need you to trust me." Her brother nodded, confused by her distress and failure to answer. Aware the wagon seemed heavier as they left the beach, he considered the possibilities. Elizabeth requested they ride up near Claremont Estate to gather more herbs before they arrived at their aunt's home.

Jacob spoke with irritation. "I saw what you brought from home. What do they have growing here you don't have already?"

His sister gave him a warning stare, and Jacob knew he must do as she requested. Before long, Jacob pulled the horses to a stop below Claremont, and Elizabeth climbed down.

Elizabeth gathered her basket from the back of the wagon, Jacob turned, and Elizabeth called out, "No, Jacob, please turn back around. I will be right back, and we will go to Aunt Grace's."

Jacob muttered as he turned around. Elizabeth motioned to Kallie to get down and pointed towards the brush behind her. The girl quickly darted towards cover. In a few minutes, Elizabeth returned and told her brother. "I'm extremely weary and ready to be at Aunt Grace's home and treat Uncle's gout."

The horses followed the dirt road and took them slowly to their destination. Aunt Grace stood, hoeing and tending her garden. She rushed to embrace her niece and nephew as she called out. "Just look at you two! Welcome and thank you for coming," she said. "Now let's get you inside for a nice drink of passion fruit juice."

After the refreshment and a short chat, Elizabeth brewed the concoctions she brought for Uncle David. He told them he had done some work while on a ladder and later experienced a flare-up of his gout.

The next morning Jacob and Elizabeth said their goodbyes and left early to return to St. John's and their family. After a long silence, Jacob stated, "You are too quiet."

Imploring Jacob with her eyes as much as her voice, she pleaded, "Please, Jacob, you must trust me. We cannot say anything about what took place— excuse me, about what did *not* take place back there at the beach! I am protecting you. The fewer who know, the better."

"Father supposed I would be protecting you on this excursion, but I'm inquisitive and vexed you don't trust me."

"Yes, Jacob, and curiosity can get many people in trouble, so we will say no more about this. I want you to realize how blessed you are, fortunate to have a family who loves you. And Jacob, thank you for having faith in me."

Elizabeth's mind turned to her last view of the poor, heartbroken, girl standing alone. She prayed for the Quaker widow to show love and mercy, asking the Lord to comfort Kallie. When tears came without warning, Jacob knew he'd have to let the subject remain a mystery.

Arriving home, Elizabeth greeted the children and her sister, thankful her father worked in the far-off fields of the plantation. "Anne, after so many hours riding, I feel the need for a walk. Want to join me?"

The Hart sisters kept almost nothing from each other. As they left the house, Anne stared at her sister, "Is something troubling you? Is Uncle worse?"

Elizabeth tried in vain to hold back the tears, thankful her large straw hat kept others from seeing her suffering. "I need your wisdom, but if I tell you what occurred, you must promise not to tell Father. I am afraid I did a dangerous thing, but I would do the same again." She admitted. "Do you realize how fortunate we are? When I view the white women of our island, at times I feel jealousy rising. But I met a white girl who left me with gratefulness we are free blacks, not poor whites."

"You met a white girl from Old Road on your journey?"

"No, I rescued a poor Irish girl from Montserrat, and she appeared more red than white. I wish I had thought to tell her to peel an aloe plant and rub it on her blistered skin. I never saw anything so tragic. She and her brother stole a boat to escape the island where they served as indentured servants, but what she told me saturated me with both sorrow and anger." Elizabeth stopped and shut her eyes trying to erase the memory of the poor girl's burned skin. "No matter what they name them, for their indentured years, the Irish receive no better treatment than the slaves do."

Anne encouraged her to continue. "The girl told me there are thousands of Irish on Montserrat working as slaves. Her brother died—drowned—trying to rescue his sister from a dangerous situation."

"God placed you where you were for His purpose. How reassuring to know you rescued someone, and I'm a little jealous. God has told us whatever we do for one of the least of these brothers and sisters of His, we do for Him. This girl sounds like one of those *least fortunate,* and you did for her as unto the Lord."

Anne stopped and turned to study her sister. "Elizabeth, your birthday outing came at the time God placed the girl on your very path. Tell me no more, and I will forget this conversation. You are right. This would distress Father, and he must not know. I will pray for the girl, but I don't suppose you can reveal her name to me, can you? I am praying God gives you peace about whatever you did." Anne smiled. "We needed this in order to remind us to count our own blessings."

The sisters walked home arm in arm. Relief washed over Elizabeth. Talking to this beloved sister always made things better. "There are others in need of help. I know we can make a difference in the lives of those who have heavy burdens. Could it be possible God can use two females blessed to be free blacks?"

Anne watched her sister expectantly. Elizabeth blurted, "Blistered red skin is as unsightly as anything you can imagine. Thank you for helping me to see the good in this. I pray next time I will know to trust an all-loving God who places on my path those who need my help. I am fine now. Indeed, you and I are fearfully and wonderfully made and blessed beyond measure."

Gently rubbing circles on Elizabeth's back, just as their mother had lovingly used her tender touch to soften times of hurt, Anne now ministered to her sister.

# 12

# Tales of Men of Character

*1791*

The Hart home seldom qualified for any definition of quiet, and the recent birth of Ruth increased the number of babies for Liza and Barry to five, thus raising the clamor as well. In the mornings, both sisters instructed their brothers, and now Sarah and George were old enough to join the classes. In the evenings the girls slipped away from the noisy house to hold night classes with their father's people. Both sisters hoped to share the privilege of the education they had experienced while growing up as free coloureds. Teaching those men and women hinged on their view of everyone deserving respect, dignity, and a chance to learn.

When a girl, Anne heard her father read the *Declaration of Independence* of the United States, and she grasped at an early age the principle of "All men are created equal." All men. The United States declared the bold statement in 1776, but in her view, they failed to act on the declaration.

Envisioning a day when slavery in the West Indies would only exist as a bitter memory on her small island, she longed to prepare those enslaved for life for freedom once it came. Literacy provided a level of independence they could not gain otherwise.

The tobacco drying sheds held some benches, and a lantern provided enough light so the students could see a sizeable board Barry had painted black. The girls wrote using a chunk of limestone marl or sometimes chalk, and the students memorized letters and words written on the board. Lacking individual books, the teachers and students relied on rote memory for learning. Many made their way to the drying shed night after night, however weary they were from a day spent in the fields. Though exhausted in body, learning fed their minds and encouraged their hearts. Holding a school in the barn was not without risk. Many owners were set against educating slaves. The rewards made the endeavor worthwhile.

Resembling the breeze or a storm blowing, news spread rapidly across the island. Though the girls did not seek to teach others not belonging to their father, it did happen occasionally. Students concealed their new-found knowledge due to their gratefulness for the sisters' teaching. If caught sneaking back to another estate, they would not admit they had been at the Harts'. The dread of a slave revolt caused the island whites to be suspicious. Thus, those held in bondage often created false excuses for being out after dark.

Even though Barry encouraged his daughters in their endeavors, he had cause to be concerned for their welfare. Occasional work at the newspaper brought Barry into contact with travelers from England. Most visitors wondered about the circumstances surrounding a mulatto man who owned other blacks. At times, Barry heard from a visitor nuggets of information the editors of the local Antigua newspaper concealed from their readers. Knowing his daughters possessed deep compassion for the oppressed, one day he recognized a news item of great interest for them.

On the pretext of seeing the progress completed in the tobacco and cornfields, Barry asked his daughters to walk out in the fields with him after the noon meal. A gentle breeze softened the heat of the scorching day. As they neared the bench beneath the mango tree, Barry motioned for them to sit. The shade offered a welcome relief even though the girls had taken their parasols, and he wore an oversized straw hat.

"Girls, I heard some news I want to keep between us for now." Barry placed his hands on his knees and rubbed them back and forth. "But before I tell you today's news, I need to tell you of a man I met twenty years ago, a meeting that had much influence on me. The man was James Ramsey, a British ship's surgeon who lived on St. Kitts."

Anne could scarcely wait to ask her father more about Ramsey. But Barry held up his hand to stop the girls from interrupting him. "While visiting Antigua, Ramsey inquired if any free-black men owned slaves, and he requested a visit with me," Barry continued. "During his visit he asked me some questions, yet it was apparent he wished to bare his soul."

Elizabeth interrupted. "Father, why would a ship's surgeon want to do such a thing?"

He smiled wryly at his impatient listeners. "Because on his first voyage to St. Kitts, he boarded a slave ship requesting his medical help. What he saw on the ship deeply scarred his mind, giving him nightmares. Doctor Ramsey told me of the conditions on board, but don't ask me to repeat his description of the horror." Barry continued, "You have heard some stories. I have no wish to speak of the details he revealed."

Constrained by their father's words, both girls waited for him to keep going.

"Not long after we met," said Barry, "Ramsey resigned as a ship's surgeon, traveling back to England and studying to become an Anglican clergyman."

Anne interrupted. "You mean he left the practice of medicine to become a clergyman?"

Barry shook his head to clarify his memory of the inspiring man. "He wanted to do something more to give hope. Returning to St. Kitts, he not only served as a clergyman, but also treated indigent patients, both black and white, for spiritual and physical help."

An excited Elizabeth held her hand up as if she wanted to break into her father's speech. "Wait, Father. I remember reading a pamphlet by a Doctor Ramsey, *Essay on the Treatment and Conversion of African Slaves in the British Sugar Colonies*. I thought it shocking."

Barry patted Elizabeth on her hair as if to calm her down. "Yes, he wrote that essay about five years ago, and it caused an explosive uproar among the British owners."

Again, an excited Elizabeth interrupted her father. "I have respect and admiration for his courage. He lived out his faith, not talking or merely writing about it, but living it."

Barry turned sorrowful, "News arrived of his death a few months ago, and I thought about his legacy, knowing I needed to share his encouraging story with you both."

This news saddened both girls. Elizabeth pressed her hands together as if in prayer, resting them on her chin. "Thank you, Father. I wish we'd met him."

Barry swallowed a lump in his throat as he continued. "There is more current news. Lately I learned of a man, William Wilberforce, who recently gave a speech in the British House of Commons. I brought a copy for you girls to read." He handed the paper to his daughters.

Clutching it, Elizabeth read aloud.

> Let us not despair, it is a blessed cause, and success, ere long, will crown our exertions. Already we have gained one victory, we have obtained, for these poor creatures, the recognition of their human nature, which, for a while, was most shamefully denied. This is the first fruits of our efforts, let us persevere, and our triumph will be complete. Never, never will we desist till we have wiped away this scandal from the Christian name, released ourselves from the load of guilt, under which we at present labour, and extinguished every trace of this bloody traffic, of which our posterity, looking back to the history of these enlightened times, will scarce believe that it has been suffered to exist so long a disgrace and dishonour to this country.
>
> —William Wilberforce, speech before the House of Commons, 18 April 1791.

Overcome with emotion, Elizabeth composed herself. "Who is this man, Wilberforce, Father?"

"Wilberforce became a Member of Parliament only five years ago," said Barry. "He is a young man of great vision, and a close friend of another young man, William Pitt, who rose to Prime Minister in 1783."

The girls struggled to take in all this information without shouting, but they motioned for their father to continue. "Wilberforce met Mr. Ramsey, becoming influenced by his stories of the horrors on the slave ships, while he also became a staunch supporter of the Methodist pastor George Whitefield."

An excited Anne jumped up. "I have heard of George Whitefield. But what I want to know is did Wilberforce put his trust in Christ? I have heard it is rare for British politicians to also be believers."

Barry held up his hands, wanting them to stop interrupting him. "Wilberforce did come to know Christ, and as you imagined he encountered many protests when he experienced conversion." Their father lowered his voice as if the mango tree shading them was listening. "My daughters, God supplied a young man of conviction and courage to help even us as free-blacks. Sadly, many in England see his firm belief in God's principles as a social transgression."

All three knelt and praised God for William Wilberforce and Ramsey, understanding how God created these men for such a time as this. They rose to their feet, dusting the earth from their attire, feeling clothed in anticipation.

Barry took both girls by their hands. Slowly, they began to walk towards the far field where workers toiled quite a distance from their discussion. He walked between them, with an arm loosely linked through each of theirs.

Though there was no one around to overhear, he lowered his voice again. "Girls, I brought you out here to implore you to use even more caution. The same events giving us such expectations also mean the opposition will become more antagonistic. Resentment deepens toward anyone who dares support the radical idea of abolition, and those caring about the slave situation are beginning to suffer persecution." He paused, needing them to heed his words. "I am proud of you and support you, yet I also fear for you." He stopped and studied his beloved girls, hoping they understood the need to display more restraint.

Elizabeth, though often the quieter sister, placed her hands on her hips. "I don't see it as a radical idea, Father. And I refuse to let fear guide me. I will be cautious, but God will be my guide, *not fear!*" Clearly this discussion deepened her resolve to be a part of the change.

Barry swallowed his fear and began walking. "Many whites express concern about the chapels and church producing discontent and making the oppressed restless. On other islands, the Baptists, as well as Moravians and Methodists, attract scores of slaves to their services." Pausing again, he watched their faces as he hoped his words took root. "Recently some brutal attacks on the missionaries by the planter class took place."

His voice grew more intense. "The severity of these retaliations will only grow due to Wilberforce and others supporting abolition."

Anne remembered what she heard in town. "A token is being produced, marked with the emblem of a kneeling slave in chains. The token reads, *Am I not a man and a brother?*"

Although understanding his anxiety, Anne had already determined that her actions, the same as Elizabeth's, would not hinge on fear. She studied his reaction. "Father, helping others learn to read gives purpose to my life. If I were not here to teach my brothers and now my youngest sister, you might hire a tutor for them. But if I do not teach these people ..." She hesitated and spread her arm out towards the workers in the far-off field. "They will remain ignorant. Then what jobs can they secure when slavery does end?" Anne could not hide her frustration. "I pray it will end, and when it does, they need to be ready to do more than cut cane, sweep floors, or wash laundry! Elizabeth and I know the danger of teaching them, but teach we must, and teach we will!"

Anne's words rang bright with steadfast determination. Barry understood his girls' resolve to prepare people for a future beyond slavery. Feeling both pride and heavy concern swirling for control in his heart, he turned quiet, his lovable smile changing to a frown. He took their hands as they headed for the far field.

"I hear *fire* when you speak, Anne. I admire your passion, but please do use prudence and tread carefully. Hope delayed can make the heart grow sick, and freedom will come, but slavery will not end anytime soon." Barry playfully touched the tip of Anne's nose to ease the tension. "You must not encourage these folks to expect the end yet. Educate them and allow the timing to rest in God's hands."

The girls linked arms together with their father. Keeping this overwhelming fountain of excitement from bubbling over would be hard. While the girls' personalities balanced each other out, Anne appeared ready to take a sword and go to battle like Joan of Arc. On the other hand, Elizabeth's gentle heart soared with her father's news. Now this spirited but brave daughter danced about, circling her father and sister while singing.

Come, we that love the Lord,
and let our joys be known,
join in a song with sweet accord
and thus, surround the throne.
We're marching to Zion ....

As Elizabeth circled them singing, Barry advised her again, "I'm sorry we cannot do as Sir Isaac Watts' great hymn says and let our joys be known. I trust you girls will not give a word of this latest news to your brothers, or Liza, or anyone." He moved his index finger back and forth. "Soon the grapevine will be buzzing with rumors of things happening in England, though I have never figured out how news can travel so fast. This battle to end slavery will be long and it is a battle only God can end without bloodshed. The owners become aggressive when they fear for their financial endeavors."

"Do you think we could have bloodshed here in Antigua, Father?" Anne asked.

A sudden breeze gave some relief from the heat, but the air turned heavy with tension. Barry had pondered for a couple of days before deciding his daughters needed to hear even more tragic news from him. As they stood there, he weighed his words carefully. "I dread telling you more news. Though not yet common knowledge, I overheard something at the newspaper office about the events on Saint Domingue."

Again, Barry lowered his voice, though the wind would not carry his words beyond his audience of his two daughters. "Saint Domingue's government agreed to allow mulattos, born of free parents, to vote for colonial assemblies. The mulattos had already begun demanding what they believed was their right, but while the whites focused on the rumblings from the mulattos, the government did not learn of a planned revolt. The people rallied together by drumbeats in the night, set fire to cane fields, burned plantation homes, and murdered whites. The mulattos there were afraid of the enslaved since jealousy survives with a treacherous result."

Both girls appeared shaken by the seriousness of this last revelation.

Anne dug her toe through the dirt. "What took place, even more evil?"

Barry could not bear to observe his daughters as he told them. Scuffing his shoe in the dust, he gazed down. "Yes, I am sorry to report they murdered over 2,000 whites and destroyed nearly 200 sugar estates, with over 10,000 of the enslaved also perishing. After the explosion of hatred and evil, they also destroyed coffee and indigo settlements."

Elizabeth asked, "How could all this death happen so easily?"

Letting out a slight moan, Barry told them, "The authorities executed some, while others died in the fighting, and some starved to death." Barry wanted to finish. "I imagine when owners here learn of this, they will become even more apprehensive of permitting meetings. I heard the whites and mulattos in Saint Domingue are now at war with each other." Slowly Barry glanced up staring at both of his girls. "Change is coming, but at what price? We must pray for our brothers in the islands, recognizing them as brothers, be they black, white, free, slave, destitute, or even plantation owners."

The gravity of Barry's words disturbed them, as if a heavy wind had struck them instead of the faint breeze on this day. The three formed a triangle as they stopped under a tree. The flowering cassia gave them shade. The spines could inflict pain lingering for days if one were to step on a cassia thorn, reminding them of the dangers all around them.

"The owners will never see all men as equal," Anne's face was etched with heavy sorrow.

Barry pled. "This is why I advocate for patience and prayer about eventual freedom for all. Freedom must happen decently and with order." He repeated it slowly, "Decently. With order."

Elizabeth clung to her father's arm. "This news is from an island far away. How will it change life for us in Antigua?"

Barry patted his daughter's hand. "The whites will now imagine the threat is greater and will be even more opposed to what you girls want to do. So now you should realize how all these events happening in England, Saint Domingue, and other islands will affect our lives. Your lives."

Elizabeth shook her head in dismay. "Divisions of black against mulatto, poor against the wealthy, and even the Africans against the Creoles must grieve the heart of God."

Barry enfolded the girls in his strong arms, conveying deep love mingled with concern. The girls recognized how much their slave-owning father craved the ending of this practice while knowing it would change his own life dramatically. Their admiration for their father grew with the knowledge of his association with the British surgeon and clergyman, Ramsey.

Barry told them he needed to do some work in his office. Elizabeth said she wanted to consult with Esther. Each of them was deeply thankful Antigua did not suffer from the intensity raging on other islands.

Anne walked by herself to the cook shack. She knew Cook would have gone back to her dwelling by this time. Anne longed for a few minutes alone to form thoughts into a plan. Her first thought was how much she wished she could share this news with Esther. Though rarely vocal about her feelings, she understood how Esther identified with those despised or rejected by others. Esther was extra supportive of Liza after the birth of her latest baby.

Thinking back to those first months after Esther joined them, Anne remembered how Esther's jaw had tightened when the family spoke and sang about Jesus. Then Esther's Jewish father died in prison, leaving her hopeless for a return to life as she had known it. Over the years Esther became more accustomed to hearing talk about Christ. Both sisters reminded Esther how they considered her a gift from God, and her response softened over time. She even smiled more often lately. Anne knew when Esther heard this news via the grapevine, she would appreciate the glimmer of hope for the oppressed, a ray of hope for all who suffered persecution and injustices.

For now, Anne knew all she could do was pray and trust God to work. There could be no plan except to obey her father about using caution.

# 13

# Spider Web of Slavery

*1792*

Barry's oldest daughters Anne and Elizabeth filled their days with providing education for their brothers and eventually for their father's second family. The sisters wondered how they could have managed without Esther's assistance. Time to themselves proved meager.

Barry Hart was a capable man but often felt overwhelmed with the duties of operating the plantation without an overseer. As Barry's sons matured, they helped more with chores. In order to lift some of his burden, Anne and Elizabeth also took on many of their father's tasks.

Twice a year the sisters sewed replacement garments to clothe the people working the estate, but the family also had needs. Liza began helping a few months after she gave birth to her sixth child, baby Thomas. Before her marriage, Liza had devoted herself to making the newest fashions. Now function, not fashion, dictated the clothes she made. Since neither Anne nor Elizabeth enjoyed sewing, they agreed to purchase the cloth and cut out the garments, and with Esther serving as nanny, Liza could happily sit for hours making clothes for the Harts' growing needs.

Unlike thriving larger estates, small ones such as the Harts' depended on a commitment from all family members to carry their load. Most of Barry's people grew much of their ground provisions: yams, okra, bananas, and eggplant. Old Molly did most of the cooking for the workers. The girls delivered to her the weekly allotment of salt fish, beans, rice, and cornmeal.

While Elizabeth and Anne sensed sincere appreciation from most of the slaves for teaching them to read, they saw envy in the eyes of a few. The resentment and jealousy toward a free-black family owning other people was openly evident with one of the men, and his attitude troubled the girls.

Both girls craved respite, and sometimes on their visits to the quarters, they stopped to help Old Molly shell peas or grate coconut. She had a sweet voice, even in her later years, and she often sang as the girls sat working alongside of her. To go from the large, noisy, child-filled house to the small cooking shack was a soothing balm—a place of refreshment—the sweet slave singing as she toiled.

Barry allowed the men time to build sleeping quarters—small stone rooms they roofed with crushed sugarcane stalks. Some owners only provided what others commonly referred to as wattle and daub huts. When the rains came, the mostly mud huts became a prescription for illness and disease. Those on Hart's land had more consideration than many of Antigua's enslaved. Still, the girls could not reconcile this practice of owning others as an unavoidable part of life. The evening classes salved the girls' consciences.

One evening as they walked to the workers' quarters, Elizabeth probed, "Anne, does it bother you to be a part of this—sewing the clothes, providing the food, even helping with medical needs for Father's people?"

Anne responded, "I love Father, I respect Father, and I know he did not buy these people, but it grieves me to be a part of this in any manner. How will God ever clear up this man-made mess? Teaching these people to read is right. I pray someday they will be fully responsible for their own needs."

Elizabeth joined her arm to her sister's as they walked. Elizabeth broke the silence. "Such responsibility will only happen if they learn to make choices for themselves. Many people think Africans can't reason, treating them as children. Teaching them to read is vital, but we must also teach them to reason and become responsible for their own choices."

"Father once spoke of finding himself trapped in the spider web of slavery. Though the untangling of this web of evil is overwhelming and without answers, God placed us in a position of giving assistance to both Father and the folks living here."

Anne turned to her sister. "*Yes!* We must attempt to convey not only learning, but wisdom from above—God's wisdom. Freedom will come. Perhaps we are like Moses, tired and afraid but leading these people through the wilderness. Moses had grumblers, and we do too. Moses encountered obstacles, and we have mountains of those. Nevertheless, God gave us a task, a quest for freedom and equality for all. We can pray God covers the mistakes we make."

They strolled toward the cooking shack. "I question sometimes how it would be to live a life away from here, and to be married, having children of my own. For now, God has entrusted us with Liza, and this second growing family, and we need to trust God one day at a time."

The two provided strength to each other. Anne, always the leader, took her sister's hand and pulled her forward. "Now, let's hurry this delivery to Old Molly. I want to teach her the Isaac Watts hymn we heard in church last Sunday. Her memory far surpasses my own. She will memorize the words in no time."

Old Molly might never learn how to read, but she proved full of wisdom as she admonished Barry's daughters. The woman had belonged to the Hart family even before their father's birth. No one knew her exact age. They had always called her "Old Molly," but they knew she had the wisdom of many years stored up beneath her graying hair.

After a visit with the beloved slave, the girls headed for the drying sheds where they taught in the evenings. They knew the way well and did not mind the bats swooping past them, nor the minute tree frogs serenading them with their familiar night chirping. They often carried a small lantern as they walked the well-beaten path. The light helped the sisters watch for the tarantulas and centipedes.

On this evening, the girls walked without a lantern, the full moon illuminating their path. They approached the sheds later than usual because they had taken the time to visit the cook shack. The girls walked silently, absorbing the beauty of the island's night sounds. Both wore modest cotton shifts, covered by aprons. Their sturdy leather brogans protected their feet from the hefty, furry horse spiders that came out after dark.

Without saying a word, Anne held out her arm to stop Elizabeth. As they approached the schoolroom shed, four men sat outside with their backs turned, not noticing their presence.

The girls listened to one of their students talking. At first, they assumed the men were entertaining themselves with Anaci stories, the African folklore tales the girls grew up hearing. Both the Africans and the Creoles, those born in Antigua, took pride in telling the oral stories passed from one generation to another. Soon they realized the storyteller was sharing a personal story.

"Mary she be a long-legged gal. De white folk took to calling she Amazon Mary. Proud she be of she size. She not mind de name. She be a handsome woman, skin as black as de darkest night, full lips as a juicy mango, hair short as de shortest cut cane. She spirit as big as she size. She be good with de sick, all who know she love she."

The girls listened as the men encouraged the storyteller. "One night, Amazon Mary she be caught leaving she plantation, going out in de night under a full moon to see she man. Praise be she master found she—not de overseer, cruel as a jumbee—always we be in fright of he. She master he always be firm—not mean. De whites dem still be afraid after de revolt."

The girls knew the story of the revolt well. Only a few years before, the enslaved in Antigua had planned revenge on the whites. The attempted attack resulted with those who planned the revolt burned to death, or with broken backs on the wheel. White men still feared the gathering of blacks together. The girls continued listening.

"So, Amazon Mary, she know de whip she going get. She tears fall. Proud and tall she stood. She done told de master it be love, not hate dat sent she sneak off in de night." Several of the men grunted in agreement.

"She say, 'I love me man, and me cook plantains me grew to take for he.' She shove de ting of boiled food, wrap in banana leaves, to de master. 'If dis be a weapon me carry, it be a weapon of love.' She be one brave wo-man. Dat night a group of men from de field slowly come round Mary. Dey call out 'Even'n Master.' The master he be fraid as he see de people all bout him. De men soon round Amazon Mary. She stand taller above dem all."

The storyteller continued, "One man in de group call out, 'Please, Master, our Mary she love she man, and she go out some nights. She come back before daylight. Mary work hard, and she do you good day pon day. Same how you love you wife, Master. Me tink some nights you want de comfort of a warm body beside you.' Den de master he laughs. De workers say, 'Dis be true Master. We begs you let Mary go to she man.' Dey good peoples."

The girls listened while the speaker finished his tale. "Den de strangest ting did happen. De old master he tell Amazon Mary climb up behind on he horse. She no gets beating. De master give she ride go see her man. Master let she off near de edge of de quarters on de next place. Master he say 'you must tell others of good and generous master who believes in true love.' When she get on de ground, Mary kissed de boot of she master, den she offered him she cooked plantains, but he tell she dem belonged to de man she love."

Elizabeth clung to Anne's hand as she heard the man tell the remainder of the story. "Some whites dem tink we got no love and family. Amazon Mary, she be my mama, and she teach me love and respect, no finer woman. She old now and she man gone to heaven. She still sells in de Sunday market, be gray-headed—not so tall, but she be a fine mama."

The story seemed complete. Anne started singing as they approached the men, not wanting to embarrass them by letting them know they had overheard the tender story.

The following Sunday Elizabeth went searching for an unusually tall, gray-headed woman selling her wares in the market. She asked another vendor, "Is that Amazon Mary over there?"

Elizabeth approached the weathered, but still stately, old woman. "Hello, what do you have for sale?" After purchasing some guineps and tamarinds, those tart gooey fruits the boys loved, she handed the woman a small packet containing a new apron. Elizabeth knew she must offer some explanation. "I have met your son, and you should be proud of him. This apron is a gift because … well, just because. Have a beautiful Sabbath, and God bless you."

She thought she saw tears in the old woman's eyes. If the woman had questions, Elizabeth realized she had no answers. She would never tell her student she met his mother. Elizabeth felt slightly guilty for overhearing the story told by a proud son, but richer for having heard the love story and for meeting Amazon Mary.

Barry insisted his oldest girls each have a day apart from the children. As the years passed, contrition often washed over him regarding his two selfless daughters. Liza needed almost constant assistance with her children. Occasionally, Barry wondered what Elizabeth and Anne might have chosen to do with their lives if he had not remarried and created a need for them to remain at home.

Anne, now nearly 25, frequently chose to spend her solitary time beneath the towering mahogany trees in the graveyard. There with only the silent company of headstones, she found peace. She often read a book or merely absorbed the silence and serenity she found among those who made no requests or voiced complaints.

Elizabeth liked people-watching in the bustling market when it was her day free from the chaos of a house full of children. So, a few weeks after she met Amazon Mary, she returned to the Sunday market in St. John's after church services accompanied by Amy, one of her father's people.

The pleasure of going as an observer with nothing required of her at the market pleased Elizabeth. Hucksters, with their brightly coloured head ties, sat beneath the trees spreading their wares around them. The aroma of ripe pineapple mixed with the pungent smell of salted fish, limes, and mangoes, blended with the scent of the harbor. She enjoyed the pleasant hum of the many hucksters bidding all to come and see their wares, and took pleasure in listening to the haggling between the sellers and purchasers. Unlike the children's squabbles at home, here there was no need to intervene. Amy had walked away to see if she could find a soursop to purchase. They would soon begin the trip back home, but first, Elizabeth wanted to buy a lobster for a special soup to celebrate her father's birthday.

Busy relishing all the sights, she started to cross the small roadway dividing the sellers of seafood from the vegetable hucksters. She failed to notice a wagon loaded with pineapples traveling down the narrow road at a fast clip. When a strong arm grabbed her, she screamed. The horse pulling the pineapples shied, and some pineapples fell along the dirt roadway. An angry man jumped from the cart of tumbled fruit and began cursing her. As her rescuer held fast to her arm, Elizabeth stared at the well-dressed white man. She did not recall ever having seen him before. Though dressed simply, the man appeared to be a gentleman.

"You are not hurt, are you?" he asked calmly. Not waiting for an answer, he stepped in front of Elizabeth as the pineapple seller approached with fire blazing from his eyes.

"She damage me goods," the man contended, pointing at Elizabeth.

A young woman slipped up beside Elizabeth and whispered, "James will protect you and deal with him, no need to feel afraid."

Elizabeth turned to question her. "Do I know you?" Noticing wisps of bright red hair escaping from beneath a lovely, but unadorned bonnet, she peered closely at the attractive woman and gasped, "You are, you are …"

The girl smiled impishly. "Yes, I am from Old Road Village, and my name is Catherine. This is my husband, James, from Claremont plantation. And you are?"

Elizabeth clutched the girl's hand tightly. "I am Elizabeth Hart, and I am remembering meeting a girl some three or four years ago, near Old Road Village. You remind me of her."

The woman lowered her voice. "Yes, and I trust my appearance is a wee bit better now." She straightened her Quaker style bonnet and glowed with a lovely smile.

As Elizabeth fell into Catherine's arms, laughter mixed with tears overcame both women.

With confusion, James turned and asked, "Catherine, is the girl all right?"

Catherine beamed. "Thank you, James, she will be fine. Might we purchase the bruised pineapples and quiet this irate man? Elizabeth is an old friend of mine, and I have not seen her for years."

The two women stepped from the street as James purchased the few pineapples and a large burlap bag to transport them. Elizabeth could not keep her eyes from the lovely transformation of the young woman standing beside her.

When James rejoined the two women, Catherine implored him to finish his errands while she visited with Elizabeth. James questioned, "Exactly what do I do with these pineapples, dear wife?"

"Oh, please leave them as a gift for Elizabeth." He bowed and walked away.

As James left to shop in the market, Elizabeth thanked Catherine for the pineapples. "I am so grateful I did not need to deal with that enraged man. We are unable to grow pineapples on our side of the island. How generous of your husband to purchase them."

Placing her arm around Elizabeth, Catherine declared. "No, it is I who am deeply thankful I could return a favor for my guardian angel. I have thanked God over the years for your appearance on such a fearful day at Darkwood Beach."

Elizabeth blinked as if clearing the memory. "I prayed for you. I wanted to return to Claremont and ask about you, but I knew I could not. I never dreamed I would see you again. I never imagined I rescued such a beautiful girl."

Catherine explained her story from the point where Elizabeth left her below Claremont. "The Mistress took one glance at me and started weeping. She never asked why I had shown up or how I came to know of her. Healing my wounded body and soothing my frightened heart, she was as a mother to me. Her son, James, had been away in Barbados attending school. He returned, and I discovered God planned for me not only a mother, but also the provision of a godly husband. We married a year ago. Thank God you directed me to Claremont, where I found all I needed and more. I have never forgotten my guardian angel." Catherine clasped Elizabeth's hand. "God placed James and me here at the market where we might become reacquainted. I want to know about you, Elizabeth. Are you married?"

"I doubt I shall ever marry, but I am content teaching school to my father's second family and his people," Elizabeth answered.

Catherine did not conceal her astonishment. "I assumed you were a free black, but I didn't know free blacks ever own slaves."

Elizabeth seldom needed to explain her background, but now it became necessary. "My father inherited a plantation and the slaves there after his white father died. My father is a compassionate man and a reasonable master. I know the word compassionate is rarely linked to the word 'master,' but for him, they go together."

"Elizabeth, I suppose you knew when you directed me to Claremont, since it is one of the only estates where they hire laborers and treat them fairly, that I would be safe there. For me to be there was not by chance. My husband opposes slavery, and I am pleased to hear you are teaching your people. If only slaves receiving an education could become commonplace."

Elizabeth touched the scar on Catherine's hand. "Your beautiful face did not scar from your terrible sunburns of years ago. I never imagined I would know the end of your story. I will watch for you again when I come to the market after church," Elizabeth said. "Thank James for rescuing me. Now I must find Amy. God be with you, Catherine, as I know He will guide each step of your life."

# 14

# Shop Girls Don't Read Milton

*1795*

The Hart home was almost as bustling and noisy as the market. The swelling household continued to increase, with newborn Mary following Thomas, bringing Liza and Barry's children to seven. Amid everything, Barry's wife turned more bewildered, more withdrawn. At times the toddlers clung to either of the sisters, avoiding the woman who birthed them. Many days Barry's wife was wrapped in a daze. When the cloud did lift, she smiled and told the children she loved them, but she seldom interacted with them on an individual basis. Esther had an ability to comfort her, and the girls often discussed how God provided this girl for such a time as they were experiencing.

The ever-present heat weighed heavily on the struggling, overwhelmed Liza. The climate of Antigua affected more than merely human comfort. Some years provided an abundance of rain, and others brought severe drought. When the rain came, it came in torrents, dumping as much as fifteen to twenty inches in a day. Prolonged rain proved destructive to crops as everything began to decompose, and the rotting stench pervaded the land. In contrast, drought sometimes lasted six to seven months and devastated the crops. Sugarcane, cotton, indigo, and tobacco thrived on the repetitive, gentle showers. Anything affecting the crops affected humans and animals as well.

The rains stopped in 1794. Simply stopped. Crops died. Cattle and goats perished. Water brought in casks from Montserrat came with a price higher than a barrel of rum.

One evening, Anne waited until the busy household quieted before she approached her father as he sat on the veranda. She slid into a chair next to his. "Father, I know this drought is hurting us. I could seek a position as a clerk in one of the shops in town while Elizabeth continues teaching the children. Please let me help in some way."

Searching Anne's blue eyes, Barry returned a slight smile. "You are always thinking ahead. Don't add a burden that I pray will not be necessary," he said. "God knows how we need rain. I manage to cart water from the pond to the plot of vegetables for our table. I believe we will butcher another cow soon and sell the meat because we haven't water for all of them to survive."

Her father grew quiet. He pulled up a long-ago memory and smiled. "Do you remember when you were a child, your mother read the Bible story of Joseph and how he prepared for the years of famine? I have set aside money each year, anticipating an eventual crop loss. Thank you, for your offer. Any shop would be fortunate to have you."

Now her father winked. "Since you are much more educated than the shopkeepers in St. John's, I fear your knowledge and efficiency might intimidate them. If I were a shopkeeper, I would not hire an assistant as intelligent as you."

Anne pled, "I want to help. I want to feel of value to you and the family."

Beaming at his beloved eldest, Barry took one of her hands. "You are of more value to me than you can know. I pray someday a wise man, strong enough, sure enough of himself, will recognize what a treasure you are. Sadly, many men are neither wise, strong, nor intelligent enough to know true gold when they see it."

Barry quietly said, "However, until the day a wise, strong man does appear, I count our family fortunate to have a resident educator. I know my exhausted wife fails to thank you. Both you and Elizabeth are a part of the harvest set aside for the lean years. You girls feed us in a way I never imagined, and no, our pockets are not so low that you or Elizabeth need to be shop girls."

"Oh, Father, stop, or I will become proud. How I long for enough water for a proper bath, as well as water to indulge my love of flowering plants, and enough to drink until I am satisfied."

Barry frowned. "You must always drink enough, regardless of the drought."

Anne leaned back in the chair, cupping the back of her head in her hands. "Father, I have been reading John Milton, and he speaks of the vulnerable earth. I realize with this drought how fragile the earth is and how tempted I am to doubt God can solve this problem without me. I struggle not to be so impetuous. I know I need to wait on God."

Barry gave his daughter a momentary frown. "Shop girls never read Milton! No, you could never be a shop girl. Since the birth of baby Mary, Liza has become less patient with lack of water to bathe and other irritations of the drought. I will not excuse her whining, or her short temper. I can't begin to tell you how much your attitude and Elizabeth's sweet spirit help me through these rough times."

Remembering the experiences of the past year, Barry said, "I never want to take advantage of your gracious care of this family. Perhaps this week, you and Elizabeth could take the children for a late afternoon sea bath, which might be refreshing and help the attitudes of the boys as well as the younger children. A quiet afternoon to herself might help Liza rest and improve her outlook as well."

The sea bath proved to be a boost to all their spirits. The boys ran in and out of the lapping waves. They all sat on the sand, finding delight in the colours of the setting sun before they walked home.

With ten siblings to care for, most evenings Elizabeth and Anne retreated to their bedroom following their hour of tutoring the slaves. Often Elizabeth read or wrote a hymn in the evening, but after their sea bath that day she began composing a letter.

Elizabeth's pen glided across the page with the ideas and images flowing from her heart to the paper. Recently, she read a letter revealing another writer's thoughts on slavery. Letters like the one she was writing circulated among those advocating abolition. Her mission was to send a message of her own to those fighting for freedom.

She laid her pen aside. The ink nearly dried, and the words burned into her mind. Looking at her sister, without saying a word she passed her the letter. These two remained as tightly knit as twins. With Anne's questioning gaze, Elizabeth nodded. "Please read what I have written and tell me if it is clearly stated. I am reluctant to show this to anyone but you."

Expressing her thoughts on paper regarding this evil made Elizabeth apprehensive. She had read the reports about the persecution of those brave inhabitants on other islands who dared to speak out against the evil trade. For the owners, the issue had little to do with right and wrong. Abolition threatened the eradication of a privileged way of life.

After reading it Anne paused, often cautious with her advice to her sister. "Thank you, Elizabeth. Your letter reveals such insight and expresses the truth about the situation so clearly. I especially appreciate your words. *I cannot lower the standard of right or bend a straight rule to favor a crooked practice.* Such a vibrant statement, filled with nuggets of gold."

Elizabeth took the letter. "Do you think I write too boldly? I know there are some compassionate white men who write about this, yet they still seem ignorant of the severe trials and injustices inflicted on slaves in the West Indies. I didn't tell you, but I have written to this society once before, hence they wrote back seeking my opinion again. Many in this organization are concerned, yet they only receive second-hand observations of cruelty. Since I belong to neither the white nor the slave community, they want to know what I have seen."

"I think it fitting you have described what you have observed." Anne's face glowed. "You would make a convincing and articulate barrister-at-law in a courtroom."

"I only aspire to convey to those who fail to see this practice as morally wrong— an opportunity to view Africans as humans and not cruelly treated animals. I wish they could understand how a mother's heart breaks when her owner sells her child to another plantation. I want them to feel the mother's heartbeat as if it were their own."

Anne squeezed her sister's hand. "Yes, I approve how you described the owners as *unenlightened mercenary mortals*. You made it personal by explaining what grieves you most. You showed how some masters dash the wishes of any who try for decency and virtue, exposing how they often crush modesty and morality. As you said so clearly, slavery in the West Indies renders every part of these beautiful islands equally iniquitous."

Elizabeth reflected. "I am unable to describe in this letter the worst situations that I know exist in this part of the world. I see in my mind an endless list of complicated ills brought about by this unjust practice, knowing many of the enslaved fear to complain. The years of servitude have bruised and broken their spirits. Few of these poor folks can explain their disadvantages, though they may feel them keenly. For many, this is the only life they have ever known."

Anne's eyes revealed her concern. "Elizabeth, your letter demonstrates how the actions of many masters become the work of corrupt, fallen men who displease God. These owners inflict such abominations, deceiving themselves into believing their actions are acceptable to God."

"I want those who live in England to understand what is happening here on our islands. In some other countries, you will not find the same amount of idleness and excess we see here among white men," said Elizabeth. "I read of Europeans who lack independent fortunes who often labor with their hands."

Anne's eyes filled with amusement as she chuckled. "Father always made sure each of us learned to work with our hands. Though at times it was hard, I am thankful Father raised us not to be spoiled, pampered women, incapable of hard work." Then she turned serious. "I question if there are other masters as kind and considerate as Father has always been. I know he understands our feelings, but you should not share this letter with him."

The sisters guarded what they expressed to their father, striving not to burden him further. Elizabeth agreed. "Father could never be considered a typical master—far from it. Remember when he told us he made himself sleep in one of their huts so he could experience how they lived? I also chose to describe in my letter how some treat poor white people almost as badly as they treat their slaves. I will never forget the terrified Irish girl I met at Darkwood Beach four years ago. The whites, indentured and debarred from their civil and religious rights, also suffer. I am grateful I saw Catherine in the market, and I know she is fine now."

Anne tapped her finger on the paper. "I do question a part of your letter. You mentioned the person who wrote to you asked if any solicitude by them could make a change in the matter. You told them we have reason to believe a brighter scene is approaching. Do you think so? Some days it feels nothing will ever change. You sound more hopeful than I am," Anne said. "How brave you are to write and discuss this matter with strangers. I am in awe of your courage." Anne now noticed the silent tears running down her sister's sweet face.

Elizabeth replied, "Please, don't! Your understanding touches my heart."

Her tears ceased as Anne told her, "I am proud of you. So many remain apathetic about the plight of our black brethren. Your poem included in the letter gives glory to our Lord and Savior, and it thrilled me." Anne read her sister's poem aloud.

> 'Love as He loved, a love so unconfined
> With arms extended will embrace mankind,
> Self-love will cease, or be defeated, when
> We each behold as many selfs as men,
> All of One family in blood allied,
> His precious blood, who for our ransom died.'

"Well written, Elizabeth. Lovely. Christ died to redeem us, and we fall so short of showing His love to others. Your poem is rich with insight."

Thanking her sister, Elizabeth added, "My heart shudders at the cruelties we read about in Mr. Boucher's pamphlet and Mr. Cowper's latest writing. Communicating with others who struggle to understand the evils of this blight helped me. What I read confirmed that I cannot ignore the plight of those on our islands less fortunate than our family. We inherited being born free, and we possess what others cannot. Thank you for understanding my attempt to reveal my heart to others."

Expressing the burdens of their hearts in individual ways, these sisters remained united in focus. Clasping the letter to her chest, Elizabeth smiled with gratitude at Anne.

# 15

# An Unlikely Setting for Love

*1798*

Perpetually bursting with clamor and laughter of so many people, the Hart home lacked privacy. For years, Barry encouraged Anne to take Sunday afternoons as her *alone time.* The graveyard provided the solitude she craved, as well as an escape from the loneliness she experienced at times, despite her large, loving household.

She often took a book to read and a piece of bread and cheese. Sometimes she shared her lunch with the friendly bananaquits darting past, their yellow feathered breasts and prominent white eye stripes so distinctive. The antics of the marauding goats climbing over the tombstones offered another pleasant change. At home, the responsibility to keep all the children obedient occupied her mind, but here she could laugh at the capers of the lively goats.

After the service, Anne sat under one of the generous mahogany trees watching as the seeds spiraled through the air, while her thoughts, like the airborne seeds, gently swirled. She was thirty, unmarried, and restless. What did God intend for her to do now with her life? Her brothers, dependent on her and Elizabeth for so many years, were all grown up. Father kept talking about the possibility of moving to Trinidad or Barbados, islands further south in the Caribbean.

Startled, she heard someone behind her clear his throat, she tried to rise too fast from her seat on the ground, and lost her balance. A strong hand gripped her elbow and saved her from falling. "Hello, Miss Hart." John Gilbert immediately apologized for not announcing his presence, asking if he might join her. Surprised he had called her by name, she was at a loss for words.

Of course, Anne had noticed John in the sizeable Methodist congregation. How could she fail to see one of less than a dozen white men who attended? The church served about 3,000 coloured worshippers who came when they could, whereas the non-coloured in the congregation numbered fewer than thirty. Finally, Anne managed a few words. "How do you know my name?" He revealed a shy smile. "Several times, I have heard you teaching before the service, and I've admired your gift for applying truth clearly when you teach children."

"I come early to pray with Reverend Baxter. I asked him who it was I heard instructing the children and knew I wished to meet you." He cleared his throat. "I know of your father, and when the service ended, wanting to meet you, I came to find you. Please say you don't mind."

"Why?" she choked out.

"Why would you mind, or why did I hope to meet you? Frankly, your voice drew me to find you." John was tall, slim, and sandy-haired, and his warm, genuine smile lit up his rather ordinary face.

"Mr. Gilbert, it is unwise for anyone to see you alone with me. Surely you understand."

"I understand I am lonely, and when I heard your voice, my heart seemed lighter than it has been since I lost my wife. Your voice reminded me of hers."

Turning away from the pull of John Gilbert's magnetic smile, Anne raised her eyebrows. "Mr. Gilbert, you are not deaf, but you must be blind! I am coloured. You will discourage eligible white women if anyone notices you here with me."

"Miss Hart, are you sure you are not the one who is blind? How many godly white women did you see in the service today? Several must be old enough to be my mother, several married, and some indeed too young to consider a man of 31 years. Please hear me out." He paused waiting for her to indicate she would listen.

Seeing his expectant expression, Anne nodded and then lowered her eyes. She leaned on the giant mahogany tree for support.

"As a boy of sixteen, gravely ill with yellow fever, the wife of the Wesleyan preacher nursed me back to health—explaining how I could also be spiritually healthy. I became a follower of Christ. When only 22, I married and joined the Methodists. Though it surprises me still, I even began to preach in some distant places. My wife died of an infection two years ago."

Anne cleared her throat. "I am sorry for your loss and thankful to hear you came to know Christ at an early age. I also came to Christ when a girl. But I must go home now because it is ill-advised for us to be alone."

"Miss Hart, we are hardly alone. Do you see all these saints surrounding us?"

"Dead saints who can tell no tales, Mr. Gilbert!" She began to laugh, a nervous laugh at first, then changing to genuine amusement at her own words. John Gilbert joined her in laughing at her intended pun. His gentle wave of laughter covered her, and unexpectedly this was the right place to speak to this lonely man.

As she composed herself, Anne realized her heart seemed lighter too. She studied this man. Though not particularly handsome, his eyes displayed kindness, and his voice resonated sincerity.

These thoughts made her nervous, and she began to move towards the path leading out of the graveyard. Peering around, she said, "Sir, forgive me if I misunderstand you, but you must know we can surely not be friends. We come from separate worlds. We are foolish to continue this conversation."

"I will be praying for you, Miss Hart."

She felt trapped. Their discourse made her uncomfortable, so she turned away from this unusual encounter. "Goodbye, Mr. Gilbert."

After she arrived home, she kept the encounter with Mr. Gilbert to herself. Since she shared almost all her feelings with Elizabeth, it left her thinking about why she avoided discussing this unexpected meeting. All week, thoughts of Mr. Gilbert began building a nest of confusion in her mind.

The following Sunday, Anne found herself searching for the bold Mr. Gilbert. Picking his sandy-coloured head out of the crowd of slaves and free coloureds was easy.

Most people left for a noon meal. Waiting until the church was almost empty, he approached Anne, causing her heart to flutter at the idea of what he might be after. He smiled. "Might I interest you in a walk among your silent companions of the graveyard? On such a lovely day I would appreciate some company."

Seeing no one around to hear his request, Anne hurried out the door. Now, where should she go? To the graveyard as Mr. Gilbert had suggested or a brisk walk home without glancing back? Mr. Gilbert's hopeful smile caused her to return to the place where she often rested beneath the mahogany tree, surrounded by a colourful hibiscus hedge. She stood sheltered under the tree and imagined he would find her.

He had followed her, and Anne's sudden deliberate breath caused Mr. Gilbert to laugh. Knowing she should laugh at herself as well, she smiled. This kind, lonely man merely fancied a talk, so she turned to him. "So how are you this lovely Sabbath, Mr. Gilbert?"

He waited a moment. "I am better now because you have not avoided me. I believed you might run away at the very sight of me, Miss Hart."

"Mr. Gilbert, if we are wise, we will not start something that cannot end well."

"Excuse me, Miss Hart, but I am an honorable man. Please do not think my intentions are impure in any way. I found myself drawn to your voice and inquired about you. Everyone tells me how you unselfishly serve both your father's large family and the Methodists."

In defense of the direction she believed he might be going, Anne held up her hand to halt him before he said too much. "Mr. Gilbert, I do serve those I love and my church, and I plan to carry on. My life is full, and my heart satisfied. I am content." Anne realized she had uttered this forcefully, almost rudely, and she was seldom rude.

John Gilbert summoned the courage to speak. "I, on the other hand, am *not* satisfied, and God has placed within my heart a desire to marry again. But I am searching for a woman who is not focused on herself. I have been asking God for a woman who focuses first on Christ and will include me on her journey."

At his declaration, she took a deep breath and spun her back to Mr. Gilbert. "You do not know me, Mr. Gilbert. You cannot mean you are considering me. I am coloured. I am unsuitable for you. Surely you realize this fact."

He touched her arm, and as she turned, he said, "I am considering you may be the answer to my petition to God to remove this ache in my heart. How could it matter if your gentle soul resides in a body adorned by a skin shade only slightly darker than my own? I work in the sun much of the day and my skin is almost browner than yours."

John took her hand and held it next to his own. "See, Miss Hart. In many ways, we are not so different."

She stared at him as if he had offered her poison to drink. Her rapid breathing and elevated pulse restricted her voice. Pulling her hand back, she turned and walked away from this strange meeting—her mind racing to consider the meaning of this man's words.

Left standing beneath the mahogany tree, the deserted Mr. Gilbert called after her. "I only ask you to pray for me, Miss Hart. Please know I am praying for you—and *about* you."

When he added "about you," Anne began almost to run, trying to escape the meaning of those words. Her anxious mind swirled with questions with no good answers.

All evening Anne appeared preoccupied, shifting her supper on her plate, ignoring questions from her family. Waiting until they were dressing for bed, her wise, observant, and tender sister observed, "Something has disturbed you, yet you appear happy. Is there anything you have not told me about?"

This strong, confident sister who rarely cried, flung herself on their bed and wept. Elizabeth rubbed Anne's back with the slow, lazy circles reminiscent of their mother. Starting to relax, Anne rolled over and asked Elizabeth, "Have you ever longed for marriage, love, and a life apart from this house?"

Grabbing her sister's arms, Elizabeth peered into her eyes, still wet with tears. "Are you trying to tell me you have romantic ideas after all these years? Of course, I have considered the possibility that someday I might marry, as improbable as it might appear. Can you tell me who or must I guess?"

Anne bolted upright. "How could you guess? We never see anyone who would aspire to marry either of us."

Elizabeth grinned and waved her index finger back and forth, as she began connecting her observations. "I watched Mr. Gilbert the last several weeks at church follow every move you made. He is a widower, right?"

With exasperation, Anne stared at her sister. "You are too observant, and I fear someone else might have noticed too."

Elizabeth became exuberant. "He is an ideal man for you. He loves God, he appears kind, yet shy, and I imagine he is lonely. Would you expect him to choose a woman simply because she was white?" Answering her own question, Elizabeth continued. "Of course not. He would require a woman whose life is based on character. God might indeed have a plan that includes this man for you."

The following Sunday, after the morning service, Anne had conflicting thoughts about why she sat again beneath the splendid tree in the cemetery. Would John Gilbert consider her forward? Would he assume she waited for him? The week was crowded with imaginary conversations with him. She admitted to herself how she anticipated his arrival.

She turned at a sound, and there he stood. His eyes searching hers, she could not prevent the nervous smile betraying her. Elizabeth often said her face revealed a heart of peace and serenity, yet she was anything but calm as she gazed at him.

Unsure where this third meeting would take them, Anne silently pleaded, "God help me!"

"Miss Hart, you honor me by returning to my tree."

"How can you claim this tree in a public cemetery, one that stood for years before you were born, Mr. Gilbert?"

He plucked a blossom from the scarlet hibiscus hedge and began to twirl it between his fingers. "I claim this tree with thanksgiving, and I often retreat here to talk to God. I claim countless things besides this tree, things not exclusively mine—my church, my island. I thank God for those, and I thank Him you were drawn once again to my tree."

Trying in vain not to view the smile she knew would disarm her, she now stared at her hands. "Mr. Gilbert, please do not think I came to sit under *your* tree because I expected you." Her voice sounded almost as a plea.

"Did you?"

"Did I what, Mr. Gilbert?"

"Hope to meet me here. Did you pray for me this week? Did you think of me?" He teased her boldly, openly taunting her.

A heavy sigh escaped before she could stop it, bemusing them both. Again, this man and his persistent questions halted her ability to speak. Her jumbled thoughts and fears failed to match his confidence.

She would not cry. She must not give in to tears. A voice within her heart pleaded with her to be honest. Knowing Scripture well, a verse filled her thoughts. "God hath not given us the spirit of fear, but of power, and of love, and of a sound mind." She hoped she had not said it aloud.

"Mr. Gilbert, yes, I hoped to talk to you. Yes, I have prayed for you. I know few people on this island would be shocked if you began an illicit relationship with a mulatto woman."

She turned sideways not wishing to see his expression as she continued. "After all, such a thing is a common occurrence. Common, but wrong. You appear to be a man who follows God's heart, so I cannot imagine you expect to have an immoral relationship with any woman. Why did you wish to speak with me? Why me?"

John realized he must explain his background. "Some years ago, I read John Wesley's pamphlet about the need to end slavery. A quest developed in my heart to attempt whatever I could to abolish this oppression of people of colour and even the demeaning treatment for Jews."

Anne dared to speak. "Mr. Gilbert, have you heard of the changes taking place recently in Saint Domingue? I hear of reports of the progress of ending slavery there. Though the newspapers here omit stories about the continuing war against slavery, my father relays the news to me from friends who work at the paper." She stopped and stared up into his expectant face, while he waited for her to continue. "I pray we do not have a war here to end slavery. I also pray we live to see the end of the heartbreaking inhumanity practiced throughout this island and in other parts of the world."

"Miss Hart, do you understand the import of our shared ideals? We have a common faith, and we both want to see all men treated with respect. I sense you are more educated than I am. Neither of us is afraid to step up and do what we can to treat all men as Christ would. Can this be a start?"

"A start?" she whispered.

Now John laughed. "*Yes!* A lovely start of a friendship between two equals in God's sight. My mother gave me an insightful nickname as a boy, *Don Quixote*. Can you follow how the name fits me?"

Glancing at a nearby windmill that served to crush the sugar canes into cane juice, she swept her arm in its direction. "Do you see windmills as giants, Mr. Gilbert?"

He chuckled. "Since windmills are frequently linked with sugar plantations and slavery, I do see them somewhat as giants. My mother imagined I always strove to right wrongs. Though as a boy I was small for my age, I often attempted to do things that caused my older brothers to laugh at me. I am not afraid of a fight nor of what others think of me."

Anne tilted her head. "Don Quixote, a man who sought to bring justice to the world and to undo wrongs. A man who, even his partner, Sancho Panza, believed him to be a little crazy." She looked up. "Yes, the name still fits you."

"*Yes!*" He nearly shouted. "Don't fail to think of me as Don Quixote. I also promised my companion, Sancho, he could be governor of his own island."

With a graver tone, Anne added, "My father tells me many people, including British soldiers, have died in the fight for Saint Domingue. Toussaint appears to be able to give the island to any Sancho Panza enslaved there. His methods go beyond justice, but I want to do whatever I can here in Antigua. I suppose I am a bit of a Don Quixote myself."

They remained quiet as they absorbed these revelations about each other. John broke the silence. "Several years ago, a ship called *The Bounty* sailed to Antigua to bring breadfruit trees from the Polynesian islands with the purpose of planting them here. They planned to use the breadfruit to feed the slaves. The crew mutinied against the cruel captain." John handed the hibiscus blossom to Anne. "I do not wish for an accusation of mutiny, but I will not stand by and do nothing. I suppose I am rather a rebel."

Lowering her head, Anne's hat covered her eyes.

John dipped his head to peer into those eyes of startling blue.

The usually talkative girl replied with a single word. "Yes."

Resting his hands behind his head, John's transparent smile spread across his face. "Yes, meaning you will rebel with me? Yes, meaning you understand why I am not afraid to request you be my Sancho Panza?"

Anne was unable to say the word, but her eyes told him what he wanted to hear.

# 16

# Changes

*1798*

The following week, Anne's apprehension mingled with hope. The service had frustrated her. She treasured Sunday morning worship services. Today her mind reflected on the man who sat and spoke with her after church the last three weeks. She found herself unable to concentrate on the message. Soon, she would sit once again in the cemetery under John Gilbert's mahogany tree.

Being thirty and unmarried created a degree of humility. How could Mr. Gilbert be serious about a woman of colour? Was it possible she had imagined his flirtatious manners?

The service finally over, Anne greeted friends as usual. She tried to prevent her eyes from searching for Mr. Gilbert. From the corner of her eye, she watched her family leave for home. Today, she sought his mahogany tree and the hedge of hibiscus that created a measure of privacy, and pondered what they must discuss.

When John's cheerful humming filled the air, all her well-planned discussions vanished. Instead, unexpected anticipation and uncertainty surrounded her like the towering hibiscus hedge. Turning to greet him, she felt unwelcome tears drip on her modest Sunday dress.

This thoughtful gentleman rescued her tears with a handkerchief. "Joy or sorrow?"

"Maybe both." Anne wiped at her tears and watched to see his reaction.

As had become his habit, he picked a delicate scarlet blossom from a hibiscus and sat down next to her. For a few moments, they were quiet as she prayed for direction, wondering if he prayed too.

"Do you think about what will come of this, Anne? Please let me call you Anne." His soft, calm voice covered her with pleasure. "Do you doubt my sincerity?"

After wiping her damp face Anne relaxed, then gazed at him realizing here sat a man she could trust. Faith in God's providence crowded out the doubts plaguing her these last several weeks. John Gilbert offered a sense of security.

"Perfect love casts out fear." She realized she quoted the well-loved verse aloud.

His eyes turned moist, too, as he laughed. "Oh, Anne, you are the most refreshingly transparent person I know. I could never love a coy, twittering woman. You don't twitter, do you?"

A smile escaped at his attempt to put her at ease. "John Gilbert, where are we going with this? What could there be for the two of us? To persist in a friendship will be hard for me. I live in a house full of children, with a beloved sister, and yet I hunger for a life of my own." Her own words staggered her when she admitted aloud a yearning for change.

Marriage between coloureds and whites was not illegal, but rare and frowned on.

John picked a yellow blossom this time and began to twirl it in his fingers. "Could it be we could have a life together, the two of us?"

Anne pulled back. "I am unsure I am strong enough to endure the censure that would surround us. Sir, I may not appear so, but at times, I am fragile, resembling glass about to shatter. How can we have a life together, even if we wished it?"

"I plan to marry you," he asserted. "I know this is sudden, and we will be walking into uncharted territory. But the world is changing. I have already told you that I despise the degrading ways many people treat slaves, free coloured such as your family, and even Jews or the Irish." He dared to touch her chin, tilting her head up so she would see his expression. "When I behold you, I see gentleness, grace, and caring, while the shade of your skin is unnoticed. Then, viewing myself, I recognize discontent with a deep yearning to make changes, and to do what I can to show how God created all men and women equal. Resembling these two flowers, different—but equal. Together they are beautiful."

Wrapping her arms around her knees, Anne began rocking back and forth. "I warned you I could be fragile."

"Oh, sweet Anne, you are strong, and I have no fear. Together we can weather this storm of opposition and be happy. Together we can make a difference. You quoted, 'Perfect love casts out fear' because you trust in God. We can cast out fear together showing others this can work—a marriage to give God glory." He paused, letting his words sink in. "Not without a battle can we do this! Tongues will wag, many will reproach us. But, I repeat, I plan to marry you."

"John Gilbert, I don't enjoy storms, nor the idea of a battle. I attempt to walk by faith alone, not by sight. I prayed for a husband, yet I assumed God's answer remained no. Still, I want to do things I could only attempt as a married woman." She shook her head. "Have we both eaten of the manioc plant and become mad from its poison? I want to run from this folly, yet I also wish to embrace it. We are both crazed by something."

This man, undaunted by overwhelming consequences, whispered as he drew closer, "If this is madness, then it is the right type of insanity. Remember, they called me Don Quixote."

Having agreed John would come to call on Barry Hart in a week, Anne stunned her father the evening before John's visit. "Father, John Gilbert wants to court me, and he is coming to seek your blessing."

Finding it difficult to understand what she implied, Barry stood still, his head bowed. "I have always wanted the best for my children. You girls are a burden on my heart more than all the others. I have wondered if you had sacrificed any opportunity for marriage because of the needs of our household."

"No, Father, when we lost Mother, each of us experienced an altered life. I took my life changes as from the very hand of God, and you did not ask for my sacrifice. God is once again changing the path I will walk. Even so, I am both elated and frightened."

Her father waited a moment before saying, “My parents were a unique combination of two cultures and two classes. I explained to you how your grandmother, Fanny, became pregnant from her white master, John Hart. They were not married. If they had married, they would have experienced extreme criticism. This hard-to-understand, but sad fact remains.”

Anne tried to calm her escalating emotions. “Father, it is not fair nor right how men have chosen to ignore what the Lord himself decreed. Regarding one person above another is wrong! Grandmother Clearkley married a white man, and I am aware of the tensions such a marriage caused then and would now cause for me.”

“Anne, it is still seen by others as an unacceptable union for a white man to marry a coloured. I love you, and I admire how Mr. Gilbert seeks a godly woman, and I realize we have almost no available white women within our circle of believers. No one here can hold a candle to your virtue and goodness. but I must advise John to return to England to seek a wife.” Barry reached out to hold her hand, but she moved back.

Now she began to cry, unashamed of her emotions. “Please, Father, speak to John. Listen to him.”

With resignation, Barry answered, “I will talk to him. I want to see you marry a fine Christian man, a man resembling Mr. Gilbert, only coloured.”

“Father, I remain grateful. Yet, an education such as we experienced altered our lives and leaves us unfit for almost all coloured men. Without desiring to do so, we intimidate them. I have been content to remain a spinster, and I think Elizabeth feels the same. But I realize marriage would increase my ability to teach more than my siblings and our few slaves. I could do so much more as a married woman.”

Barry did not respond.

“Father, I will honor you, but please consider what I already must battle with continually. Being both coloured and female prove to be a barrier to much I could accomplish. John and I recognize there will be difficulties if we marry. We also remember God takes His children into impossible battles, and we have both come to believe God is bringing us together.”

Her father finally spoke. “I taught you to notice throughout scripture how God’s people fought against stronger enemies. With God on their side,

His children prevailed. You are both His beloved children. If God is in favor of this improbable union, then the battle is His, not yours and not mine."

Anne embraced her father. "Thank you for considering listening to John. You listen, and I will pray for wisdom for each of us."

Barry appreciated Mr. Gilbert. The man displayed a sense of humor and determination. He valued God's Word, desiring God's will for his life. Still, Barry advised him to consider returning to England to seek a wife. John explained he could not afford to travel to England and believed God had led him to Anne.

A mere shade of skin separated John Gilbert and Anne Hart.

Barry told this persistent suitor. "I will at least pray about your request to marry my daughter."

When Anne next saw John beneath their tree following church a week later, she observed the absence of his usual cheerful demeanor.

With a hint of discouragement, he said, "I am not defeated. I believe it will please God if I marry you. Reverend Baxter, though he admires you, said he thinks they will lock me up in the insane asylum if we pursue this. They are wrong. The Lord warned against exactly what they are doing. My fellow Methodists disappoint me, acting as respecters of persons. Can you sit beside me long enough for us to ask God for an answer?"

She was silent as she sat with her eyes downcast. He took her hand and lifted his voice to God, expressing a passionate plea for grace and a petition for divine guidance.

"Anne, the opposition has already begun. I am overwhelmed with disappointment because Reverend Baxter has spoken to all the pastors to advise them not to consider marrying us. He also spoke to all ship captains, counseling them not to perform a ceremony."

John crossed his arms over his chest and blew out a slow, deep breath. "You are quiet. Did your father say more about our request?"

Slowly Anne told him of God's provision. "There is a Mr. McDonald, a visiting missionary who has been living at our home. Father respects him. Bartholomew McDonald heard the pastors were discouraging anyone from performing our marriage. Though a frail man, he is strong in his own convictions, and he does *not* believe our marriage would be unlawful, nor does he believe we are crazy."

Anguish lingered in John's expression. More rapidly Anne said, "If you remain confident this is God's will for our lives, Mr. McDonald will go to battle for us. He will perform the ceremony *and* he has convinced Father!" Now a mischievous beam filled Anne's eyes.

Leaping to his feet, John grabbed her hands and dropped to his knees, "Marry me, Anne, as soon as possible, marry me! Bless McDonald. But did you say he is ill?"

"Yes, elderly and frail. Mr. McDonald preaches the gospel with strength, returns to our home, and takes to his bed. So soon is best. Mr. McDonald said he would read the banns when Father, Elizabeth, you, and I are the only people present. We will do this legally, but not quite the way most people do."

John said, "I have a friend in Montserrat who visited here this week. He invited us to spend a week there."

She hesitated, "Does he know I am ...."

John interrupted her. "I told him I want to marry a woman of virtue, intelligence, and yes, a woman of the loveliest shade of brown God ever created."

"Then we will marry on a quiet Sunday afternoon with only my family there as witnesses."

He stood, shaking his head. "Totally efficient. How do you do it?"

"John, I am the oldest, and when my mother died, I took over as the organizer. Father declares I keep the Hart ship afloat. Of course, he says it only to me to avoid hurting his wife, Liza. Will you mind if I keep us organized?"

"I told you once I cannot abide women who twitter. An organized home sounds delightful. Three weeks for the reading of the banns, but we must keep this quiet."

She lowered her voice, "So starts the calm before the storms of outrage engulf the island once people know we have married. I treasure you, John Gilbert."

His voice grew soft. "I love you, Anne Hart, and I will go through any storm to be able to claim you as my own."

Now, John kissed her for the first time—beneath his mahogany tree—complete with the promise of a love that would take them through storms and trials.

# 17

# Finding New Purpose

*1798*

Walking into church with John the first Sunday after their marriage, Anne sadly noticed the few white believers in the congregation stepping aside and turning away from John. Anne and John talked on Sunday afternoon about what their attitude must be towards those who shunned them because of their marriage.

The first trial already materialized before the wedding. They removed John as a Notary Public and dismissed him from serving in the militia. After the wedding, they discovered someone had painted John's office door half white and half black, and ripped down his Notary Public sign and threw it into the sea. They were ready for their beginning to include some steep challenges, but this opposition was hateful. Their breaking the conventions of society gave many an excuse to treat them as common criminals. John and Anne determined to turn the other cheek and allow time to heal this breach. They were thankful when a sympathetic shopkeeper hired John to keep the account books.

Aside from the caustic attitudes of some people, Anne found married life beautiful. John's personality harmonized with hers and marriage satisfied her. Suppressed desires of having an existence of her own became a reality. Their personalities complemented each other. John reassured Anne daily of his delight in marrying her.

Soon after they married, Anne awoke early to an unfamiliar noise. The sweet, rhythmic sound of John snoring made her content. Though never a late riser at home, she often awoke to the racket of crying or whining from younger siblings. This sound was a pleasant change. Fully awake now, she slipped away to prepare breakfast.

Anne was cutting up fruit when her husband came from behind and embraced her. "Good morning, my new wife. How did you sleep?"

"Fine, until this strange sound startled me," she chuckled. "You didn't advise me when you proposed that you snored." She relished this new adventure and delighted in teasing her husband.

"Do I snore? No one had ever told me before." He came around and kissed her.

"I found the sound rather a welcome change, since I often awoke to whining in my father's household. You don't whine, do you, husband?"

Anne gained a new perspective on sharing expectations for the day with John. As the oldest sibling, she had rarely considered it necessary to consult the others about her 'intentions.' Her position in her father's expanded family designated her to be the one who kept everyone in line, and her schedule turned into the Hart family rule. This would not be her role now.

She touched his cheek gently. "John, I want you to remind me if I try to instruct you or forget to consult you. I am afraid of treating you as if I am a sheepdog pushing you around, since I spent so many years herding my father's family."

John patted her abundant halo of hair. "You are such an agreeable sheepdog, and I doubt I would mind. Do you have a plan for your day?"

Staring out the window to the small space behind their rented home, she said, "Today I intend to dig up the small patch of earth behind our cottage and plant a few seeds I brought from home. Soon we will be able to harvest our own vegetables."

John straightened his shirt. "Only time for tea and fruit this morning before I report to the office."

Once John departed for work, Anne began to work in the garden before the day's heat grew more intense. As she planted seeds, her mind drifted to the word John had used. A plan. In her father's home, she had always had an idea, a list for each day, yes—*a plan.*

Sweet contentment came with marriage, and Anne found tremendous satisfaction in John's love. Yet, she realized she needed a mission in addition to being John's wife.

With no schedule, Anne one day read a book undisturbed for hours and then laughed at the rare occurrence. Reading offered pure pleasure, but as sure as blood flowed in her veins, having a purpose flowed in her core, and thinking of others gave her heart its beat.

Today she planned to walk about the town of St. John's with her eyes open to see what God had for her. Usually, she walked with her eyes down, feeling apprehensive about being a free black woman walking about St. John's by herself. A generous bergère hat shielded her from disapproving stares.

Remembering the satisfaction of teaching her father's slaves to read, Anne felt sure this was not her last opportunity to serve. As she planted the last seeds, she sprinkled water on them, then wiped the dirt from her hands. Excited about her day, she pulled off the smock covering her dress. Though her new life with John provided wonder and rest, the thought of searching to see where and how she could serve others filled her with direction.

John understood. Before she ever agreed to marry him, he knew she nurtured a goal to prepare slaves for freedom. Moving from her father's house transformed her. A brief glance at her looking glass revealed a garden dirt smudge on her face. She smiled at the thought of her complexion hiding some specks of earth, but she rubbed at the smudge and grabbed her hat.

As Anne shut the door and turned the key, she realized she had forgotten to take a basket to buy provision for her husband's supper. John came first since she was a wife now. Retracing her steps and taking up two baskets, her mind overflowed with thoughts of service. She walked down the steps anticipating what God had for her to do and stepped directly into the mud hole where a pig had been wallowing in front of her gate.

"Life is a balance," Anne said to herself. "I must scan down as well as up." She remembered her mother saying, "First things first!" Wiping her shoe on the weeds next to the mud puddle, she gazed up. "Yes, Mother, first things first."

Slimy mud still clung to one shoe even after she wiped it off. She could clean her sturdy brogans once she returned home. Most women wore dressier satin style slippers with leather soles, but the ever-practical Anne wore leather brogans except inside the house. Mud edged only the hem of her unpretentious brown skirt.

Tending to avoid new styles, nonetheless Anne was pleased because this skirt Liza had sewn for her included pockets, something new to dress styles. One deep pocket held her handkerchief, and the other stored her money. She wore the skirt and a light-colored cotton blouse over a thin slip-like cotton shift. The missionary women arriving from England often dressed in silks and satins, but Anne appreciated and wore cooler cottons. Reserving judgment about choices others made was difficult for her.

That day, instead of crossing the road as she neared the rum shop, she walked in front of the place she despised. An unkempt girl possibly ten years old sat perched on the steps of the shop. Anne stooped to her level.

"Hello, what is your name?" Anne asked. When the girl peered up, Anne noticed her bruised cheek, and eyes void of expression. Sitting down on the dirty steps outside the shop, Anne realized the girl's clothes needed washing and repair. The waif had failed to answer Anne's question.

"Do you need a friend?" Anne persisted. While the girl shook her head *no*, her eyes seemed to plead, "Help me."

Anne whispered, "I am rather hungry, and I smell fresh bread from the bakery across the street. Do you want to come with me, and I will buy you a sticky bun?" Immediately the child raised her head and nodded. Without saying a word, she took Anne's hand. They crossed the street, and Anne purchased a sweet bun for the girl and a plain loaf of bread for herself.

After handing the girl the sweet bun, Anne noticed her dirty hands, making her wish she could have washed them first.

The youngster now gave the answer to Anne's earlier question. "Amelia."

Again, bending to the child's level, Anne said, "Hello, Amelia. How old are you?"

She shrugged and looked away.

Anne continued, "Where is your mother, Amelia?"

The girl glanced across the street to the rum shop.

Never having stepped inside a rum shop, Anne now knew it needed to be her destination. "Please wait here, Amelia. I will be back."

The establishment was nearly empty this early in the morning. Several men were drinking at the bar, and a woman was sweeping up debris from the night before. When they saw Anne, the men stopped talking, and the woman gave a harsh glare.

"I want to speak with Amelia's mother," Anne announced to the room.

"Why?" the woman asked in a gravelly voice. "Who you are?" If she had been an attractive woman, her scowl made her ugly. There was nothing soft about her.

Having no idea how to answer the woman, she said the first thing darting into her mind. "I am Anne Gilbert. While I was doing some errands, I saw Amelia sitting outside. I hoped to hire her to help me carry my basket as I make my purchases. Would you allow me to take her?"

The woman eyeballed Anne up and down. "I needs her to run errands for the shop, but you can have her for an hour."

Anne answered, "Thank you."

She turned, exiting the room reeking of liquor, stale smoke, and vomit. The waif was standing outside the door, having failed to heed Anne's suggestion to wait at the bread shop. Anne had no idea what she would do with Amelia for an hour. Anne did know it was enough to remove her from sitting outside a rum shop, while showing her some love and attention. If Anne had asked and been granted a day, she would have taken Amelia home to give her a bath, quickly sewing her a new garment.

They walked away from the rum shop. Anne worried that the child went so quickly with someone she had never seen before. Her mother had not even asked about the total stranger who wanted to hire her child.

"Amelia, my name is Anne. Are you still hungry?" The child had a baffled expression, but finally nodded yes.

"When asked a question it is polite to answer," Anne told her. "You might say, 'Yes, thank you.'"

Staring at her as if she spoke a foreign language, the child at last said, "Thank you."

Anne took her hand. "Then our errand will be to go find someone selling meat pies." Amelia was dumbfounded by the kindness.

They had walked only a couple of blocks when they found a woman sitting beside the road selling meat pasties from a tin pail. "Good morning. I want to buy two, please," Anne said. The woman wrapped the purchase in paper and handed her the warm, savory pies.

For the first time Anne saw a smile emerge from Amelia's grave countenance. Taking her hand, they began to walk. "There is a bench nearby. We will eat our meal there." Anne noticed a wet barrel on the next corner and looked down at the girl. "Let's wash our hands here before we eat."

They walked up to the barrel, and Anne released some water. "I know we don't have soap, but rub your hands together, and I will give you my handkerchief to dry them." Anne handed the child a dainty cloth embroidered with a small plumeria and the initial *A*, and her expression went from marvel to hesitation.

"Go ahead, Amelia. You may use it to dry your hands." Embedded dirt soon spoiled the crisp white handkerchief.

"Amelia, since both of our names begin with *A*, would you want to have my handkerchief? I could take it home and wash it for you. Then I will return the handkerchief to you. Are you often at the rum shop?"

Amelia reluctantly handed the dirty cloth back to Anne. "I lives at the rum shop, and Mama works there." Seeing the child's guarded expression, Anne realized her own nervousness had caused her to ask too many questions.

They crossed the street to the small bench near the courthouse. "Let's eat our pasties now, shall we? I always pray before I eat, and I thank God for his provision. Today, I will thank Him for you, Amelia." Bowing her head Anne thanked God for leading her to Amelia. The girl devoured the pie. Anne held out her own partially eaten pie, and Amelia eagerly consumed it as well.

Leaving the courthouse area, they walked down Market Street. The hucksters sat on cloths with their wares spread out before them—small heaps of guineps, mangoes, or scotch bonnet peppers ready for the eager buyer. Anne handed one basket to Amelia so she might feel she earned the few coins she would receive when Anne returned her. Soon the basket held ripe mangoes and a few onions.

As she glanced down at the girl, Anne again noticed the bruise. Had someone in the rum shop hit the child? Could her own mother do such a thing? Did no one love this child? Anne wondered. Next time she would ask for a longer time with Amelia and try to do more for her. Anne was confident there would be a next time.

She had no idea what her plan would entail, but Anne would devise a plan. How many more children akin to Amelia sat outside a rum hall or cowering in a corner, ill fed, barely clothed, and desperately in need of love?

When her allotted time had passed, Anne returned the girl to the rum shop. Amelia held up the coin for her mother to see. "Thank you," said Anne. "Amelia was a help." The girl set the coin in front of her mother and for a brief second Anne caught the hint of a smile.

As she exited the dingy building, Anne considered this encounter and formed the beginning of an idea. Her mind raced ahead to a future time when she returned the hankie and asked if she could hire Amelia for the day. This should happen in such a manner as not to offend Amelia's mother. Later, when she told John her plan, he cautioned his wife of this very thing. He was both pleased and amused seeing her look of pleasure as she told him of her visit to a rum hall—and both knew it would not be the last.

# 18

# Sisters Still Bonding

*1798*

Though delighting in her new life as a bride, Anne yearned for Elizabeth's company. They sent letters via her father when he came to town for his visits at the newspaper, but it had been weeks since they visited. Written notes could not include the silent messages, conveyed by facial expressions, or a simple squeeze of the hand. She realized how much Elizabeth helped with frustrations. Often without a single word, her sister's glance reminded Anne of Biblical principles of patience or other characteristics she struggled to live out.

Of course, without the extended family surrounding her, Anne experienced fewer vexations. Yet, marriage to a white man brought about a new series of challenges. Some of these she shared with John. Some she withheld because to her it would be whining. Anne detested complaining.

Anne found it hard to be cordial with people who stared as if she committed a crime by marrying John. Anne made every effort to ignore the stares, and she attempted to extend a genuine greeting when she said, "Good Morning," when often it seemed anything but a good morning.

The first week after they married, Anne's husband came home with a dog. "I'd feel better if you have him with you when you go to town. People tend to be afraid of dogs."

Leaning down, she rubbed the shaggy brown mutt's head. "Hello there, Tippet."

John laughed. "Is that to be his name?"

"Yes. I read once about a dog named Tippet, and I always thought I would choose that name if I ever had my own dog. He is perky, John, and it is so caring of you. At home, I rarely ever had time to think of my own needs or wants."

After giving her husband a quick kiss, Anne returned to petting the dog, Tippet. John unsure how this self-assured woman would respond to the dog, sighed in relief. Anne prepared Tippet with all he needed for a trip to the shops—a collar and a leash. They didn't want him running after one of the stray goats or sheep often roaming the streets. Anne taught him to wait outside while she purchased her provisions.

John offered to take her to visit her father's household. The thought of a visit with Elizabeth brought her near tears. Anne rarely cried, figuring her sister, who cried over a dead bird or a fight between siblings, shed enough tears for both.

John chatted the entire ride to the plantation, while his wife pondered what she would do first on arriving. Father would be out working, and the noon meal would be a good time to visit with him. She wanted to see everyone, but she yearned most for a visit with Elizabeth. John always attempted to listen when Anne talked, but her sister had often known what she was about to say before she said it. Elizabeth understood Anne's simplest needs, like when she was overwhelmed and needed a walk or a cup of tea. Gathering their hats, Elizabeth would take her sister's arm and guide them out the door. Without a word, Elizabeth would crush her hat down over Anne's usually unruly hair. They would both laugh, and Anne would say, "Thank you." John loved her, but Elizabeth understood her.

Arriving at the Hart home an hour before the noon meal, Anne soon found herself surrounded by the entire household except for her father and brothers. The noise was overpowering after a month of quiet and uneventful days while John was at work. Before her marriage, she had often wished for the pure sound of silence. Now the cacophony of noisy greetings flooded her with delight. She wistfully remembered the sounds of questions hurled at her with no opportunity to answer.

Lifting four-year-old Mary up and holding her tight, Anne realized she pined for Mary's childish babble. She touched each of her half-brothers, kissed Sarah and Ruth, and attempted to listen to their rapid-fire remarks. Liza, pleased to see her stepdaughter, called across the heads of the children, "How long can you stay?"

With this reminder, Anne turned to John, who was rocking the wagon with his laughter. She had almost forgotten John!

Clapping her hands to gain their attention, she waited for a slight hush. "Everyone, please greet my husband."

John waved to all and called out to his wife, "We best start back by five p.m., or we will be traveling home in the dark." He told Anne, "I'll go and visit with your father."

Liza knew Anne craved a visit with Elizabeth. "Children, please come inside while your sisters take a walk before we eat." Waving at Esther through the kitchen window, the sisters took off down the path.

As they had done for years, they strolled to their favorite mango tree. Before they sat down, they swayed with a tight embrace. Elizabeth was crying. Anne shed a few tears too.

"What is this?" asked Elizabeth. "Crying over a stroll and a visit with your sister? John has brought out a more tender heart in my strong sister. Tell me marriage is not a disappointment."

Shaking her head, Anne wiped at her tears. "Indeed, marriage has made me gentler. John is an excellent husband, but I cannot begin to tell you how much I miss you."

"I never thought I'd long for the noise of this vast family, but I do. I even miss Liza. Oh my, what a low thing to say. Please forgive me. I left you with the care of all."

Patting Anne's hand while she talked, Elizabeth said, "God gave us Esther, and she is a tremendous blessing."

Anne asked the question she could not mention in her letters. "How is Liza coping? How is Father?"

"Liza appears to have rallied, having less foggy times," said Elizabeth. "I still cannot beat Father in chess, and he misses your games together. George, at twelve, is becoming a capable player. Jacob has asked for the afternoon off from his job so you can see him. I trust Charles and Gratianus will be with Father at noon."

"And Sarah?" Anne probed.

"Sarah is becoming more helpful with her siblings, so we manage."

Anne patted Elizabeth's jumble of hair. "*You*? How is it now for you?"

"I have tried to do what you did for so many years," said Elizabeth. "But honestly, I am delegating more, allowing Esther to mother me more. Liza somehow understands she can't be as needy as she was in years past. I am, by God's grace, finding a cadence in life. What about you?"

Anne leaned back. "Never did I imagine how many hours there are in a day when all the tasks formerly occupying my life shifted to you. Now, daily I go to the small shop for our vegetables, read, and work some in our garden. I must create a better fence to keep out the marauding goats and sheep. I am keeping my eyes alert as I go to town to see what purpose God might have for me, besides being a wife for John."

Elizabeth giggled. "And what about John? Tell me how it is to be a wife at last. Does he make you happy?"

Giving a teasing shove to Elizabeth, Anne lowered her eyes. "John is both patient and tender. At thirty, I finally know the pleasure of being cared for by someone whom I only share with the entire Militia!"

This surprised Elizabeth. "Whatever do you mean?"

"I suppose I was naive enough to imagine possessing John most days. The Militia has asked him to come back to train men, and he keeps the books for a business in town. He is mine only during our too-short evenings and on Sundays. I am a silly goose."

The afternoon discussions with Father and her brothers were about Anne's life in town. The children wanted to know all about Tippet. Elizabeth and Esther filled baskets with provisions from the plantation's bounty. When, at last, they sat alone in the wagon, Anne realized how exhausting the visit had been. The thought of a quiet night nestled in her husband's arms warmed her. She was going home.

Two months later, John again took Anne for a Sunday visit to her family.

Hoping to impress Barry, Liza gave Anne the silver candlesticks that had belonged to Annie. Beautiful clear glass shades kept the wind from extinguishing the candles when lit. They pleased Anne. This was a practical gift, and she was a practical woman.

Not long after the second visit home, John chose his own gift for his wife. He wanted to buy her something impractical, something she would not have purchased, but he questioned if his choice was foolish. Over the last months, John began to recognize her fixed opinions, her ideas of what she considered proper, and he hoped this gift might challenge her thinking.

As he came through the doorway, John held the box behind his back. "Anne, I was in town, and when I saw this in a shop window, I immediately knew I wanted you to have it." He presented the box.

"Whatever is this?" Taking the box and removing the twine, Anne was puzzled, as she pulled out the silken scarf. Her large family rarely exchanged gifts.

"John, I don't usually wear anything this colourful or cloth this fine."

"Exactly why I bought it. The scarf matches your eyes. You should occasionally wear something special, something beautiful."

Darker threads ran through the soft blue design. She touched the scarf as if it might burn her fingers. She had always avoided colourful fabrics, priding herself in not drawing attention in any way. She especially avoided blue because she was almost embarrassed by her startling blue eyes. Closing her eyes now, Anne allowed herself to run her fingers over the silky feel of the cloth.

Her voice softened as she pulled up a memory from years before. "When I was a girl, I wanted fashionable fripperies, but when I joined the church, I thought drawing attention to myself made me too proud. I gave them up, John. Do you not notice I choose to dress unpretentiously?"

John wrapped his arm around his wife and set the box aside. "Sit down, Anne. Let me tell you my thoughts."

Her expression made John apprehensive. This was going to be more difficult than he had imagined. "Tell me, dear. Those shells you collect from the seaside. Are they plain, or is each one unique and often colourful? The fish you buy at the market. Aren't some of them an amazing shade of blue, much as this scarf? The hummingbirds adorned in shimmering green coats. Who created all the beautiful colours?"

Anne hung her head. "I suppose God did create birds and fish and flowers, each with unique colours and design, but they aren't tempted to become puffed up and proud."

Her husband tried in vain not to laugh. "You are the most unselfish, humble woman I know. Consider this. Sometimes it is easy to become proud of our humility and to judge others because we are more guarded in our choices. We can become self-righteous because of what we choose to do or what we choose *not* to do."

Anne frowned and turned away. "Do you see me as proud and judgmental? Oh, John!" They had experienced few disagreements. This discussion distressed her.

He began to stroke her fingers. "Forgive me. I did not mean to accuse you of anything. I do believe Christ paid the price for our sins, all our sins. His sacrificial death covers sins past, present, and future. We must not take His sacrifice lightly. But we also must be careful not to feel we are adding anything to our position in Christ Jesus by our actions. Our actions should be joyful and confident, knowing they never change how Christ sees us."

"John, if I have added anything to my beliefs, it is a desire to be more holy than I was before, wanting to live with more of Him and less of me. I suppose I do tend to judge others who choose not to follow my path." She stopped and swallowed hard. "Some of the missionary wives shock me by how they dress with garish colours. I could never dress as they do. My choice of more modest colours is right for me."

"Precious wife, as we grow in our knowledge and understanding of God, we adjust some of the ideas we embraced as new believers. His Word helps us examine our choices."

Sitting with her eyes closed, she pondered what he said, while John remained silent. After a time, Anne smiled at her husband. "I had forgotten how often Elizabeth adjusted my self-righteous thinking. I will consider this, John, and be ready tomorrow to give the right response. Your gift is so thoughtful. I am unsure how I would feel wearing it, but please give me time."

John nodded. "Of course. When you are ready, we can talk about this."

The next morning as they read their Bibles, Anne glanced across the table at John. "I am ready to listen and consider if I have been wearing my pride instead of God's colours. God has given me a godly husband, and I do want to listen to your wisdom to help me see myself as I am."

John caressed his wife's hand. "I am reading Colossians. Paul wrote of the danger of submitting to traditions we have created for ourselves. The passage reminds us that some things have the appearance of wisdom, yet they become sacrifices of our own making."

Anne studied her husband's face. "At first, I will wear your lovely scarf at home. Soon I will wear it away from home, remembering how much God loves colour and how much my husband loves me."

There were no further discussions about the blue scarf. Slowly, over time, Anne realized how needlessly she had worried about many things.

Married life suited Anne. Nearly a week later as they lay in bed, she revealed the thoughts weaving in her mind all day. "John, are you still awake? I have been thinking about our first months together. I want to tell you what keeps coming to my mind."

John turned over and ran his finger down her cheek. "I think women manage to create their best communication when their husbands are at last at ease, with no distractions on their minds except slumber. Speak, lovely wife."

Without pausing, she crossed her arms under her head and began again. "I never anticipated marriage beyond joining forces, a pleasant partnership. Marriage has astounded me and delighted me with contentment."

He laughed. "Well, I am fulfilled by the pleasure you bring to my lonely life."

Spilling the thoughts stored all day, Anne declared, "As a new believer, I tried to live separated from the world, and I refused myself many small pleasures. Your outlook balances the rigid views I once held. You have revealed pleasures I saw as frivolous. With you in my life, John, everything is lighter, easier to endure, less intense."

"If less intense now, I can't imagine the intensity in your life before!" John declared as he kissed his wife's forehead.

"I know it is often the case that women soften men's views, but John, you have been the one to soften mine. My sister tells me I now laugh more often, even sometimes laughing at my set-in-stone ideals. I am amazed by the power of love."

"I am not surprised at all," John said. "I am sometimes intimidated by your intellect and challenged by your passion for helping others, but not surprised."

"A part of the amazement comes because I am fully aware now of the high cost our unique marriage brought into your life," Anne shared. "I realize some people who expressed friendship for you in the past now shun you."

He placed both hands on his wife's cheeks and declared, "We seek to please God alone, and God came to be a rock for each of us in the years before He united us. So together we seek His pleasure, and together we can make a difference. Those who spurned my friendship because of my choice of you would rejoice if they understood our shared joy."

Anne laid her head against John's arm. "You have become a gift that staggers me. I am sorry our marriage changed so much for you, but I am thankful for all the changes you brought into my life."

"My dear, the animosity toward me from the white community can be no different than the jealousy from other free blacks you experience. These indignities will keep drawing us closer to each other and increase our faith in a God who provides love amid hate. Without a doubt, anything altering the livelihood of the plantation owners will create opposition. They view the slaves as cogs in the great wheel moving their fortunes forward. Now we must sleep, my treasured wife, and rest this massive subject for another time."

Sleep came quickly for John, but Anne lay awake, reviewing their discussion as the tree frogs sang their midnight song.

# 19

# An End to Plantation Life

*1801*

To Barry's surprise Charles left the plantation before his other sons. Charles, always the adventurer, fell out of trees, attempted to ride the wildest donkeys, and kept his mother, Annie Hart praying he would survive childhood. Charles was only six when his mother died. His four older siblings and his father lavished love and attention on "baby" Charles.

The year his height overtook his father's, this youngest of Annie's sons approached Barry with his plan. The two stood on the veranda watching as a radiant glow in the sky marked the end of the day. Charles's declaration made it seem as if more than the sun had set. "Father, I need to leave the plantation. I am grateful for this place, but I am 21 and a man now. I need to make my own way in the world."

Barry stared at his son and finally smiled. "Did you fear I would try to stop you?" He touched his son's arm. "I recognize your time has come, son, but what is your plan?"

Charles responded with a half frown, half smile. "This may shock you, but I plan to marry Jane Hodge and work for her father in his shop in town. Are you disappointed?"

Barry answered, "Son, I never wanted you to follow my choices. Jane is a fine girl. I suppose you have spoken to her father?"

Charles nodded. "I spoke to Jane, and she agreed to marry me. Some months ago, her father approached me about working for him. Since he has only daughters, he has anticipated at least one of them securing a husband interested in the business."

That evening Barry told the family Charles had an announcement to make. As Charles disclosed his plans, his brothers slapped him on the back, teasing him about being the first among the three brothers to marry. Later, Barry spoke with Jacob and Gratianus alone. They sat out on the veranda where, over the years, the most meaningful conversations took place. Barry began what he knew to be one of the most challenging talks he had ever had with his sons.

"I suppose, boys … well, I will always consider you my boys, but now at 27 and 25, I should no longer think of you as lads. You are men. I have often told you how your grandfather thought plantation life resembled an insect entangled in a spider web. When a man senses he is trapped he should escape. Charles is leaving, and I need you both to tell me if you feel ensnared, but are staying to help me on the estate out of duty. I need an honest answer. When you feel the time is right, please tell me exactly what you would want to do with your life, if not caught in the plantation's muddle."

Gratianus answered first. "Father, lately I have been thinking about this. I will have an answer for you soon." He opened the ornate mahogany door leading back inside the house and left Jacob and Barry leaning against the veranda railing. Jacob rubbed his forehead as if he were bringing an answer to the surface. "Father, I can answer you tonight, but will you tell me how you will manage if both Gratianus and I choose not to remain on the plantation?"

Barry gazed at his oldest son. "I don't know the answer yet, but for a time I have experienced a restlessness. I am weary of working the land. I have always been distressed by the fact I own other men. If neither you nor Gratianus want to be a plantation owner, I have prepared myself to consider selling all this." Barry now spread his arms wide and gazed out over the land he loved. At times, he had also experienced a deep sense of regret he had inherited the estates.

Jacob sat down in one of the chairs nearby. "Then my answer is to sell it, Father, and Gratianus will agree. He is talented in music, and I know laboring with his hands cannot be a good choice for him as a musician. He dreams of someday owning his own newspaper, and I think he is almost as talented a writer as you are. As for me, I can't say much until I speak with someone tomorrow."

Barry scratched his head. "I thought this would be an inheritance for you boys, but it has become more of a burden. I want you free to choose your own paths. If we moved closer to town, there is talk of a new school to provide an education for the children. Thank you for your honesty, Jacob."

Barry laughed. "You have no idea how I have dreaded discussing this possibility with you. Now I see it was the fear of not knowing my own future."

Because his sons' plans did not include farming, Barry's thoughts now turned to Elizabeth. She was approaching thirty, and he had sincere regret over the few choices available to her. The same as her brothers, his daughter had loved and supported her father with sacrificial acts over the years.

Long ago, Anne acknowledged her extensive education lessened her appeal to most free coloured men. He knew her observation also fit Elizabeth's situation. She had no opportunity to see what she could accomplish if not tied to family responsibilities. On the other hand, living alone was neither proper nor safe.

Barry trusted John Gilbert's judgment. On Barry's next trip to town, he presented to his son-in-law the possible sale of the estate. Barry also explained Elizabeth's request to teach at the private Negro school in St. John's. John resounded with, "Yes! Yes! She must come to live with us! I can't wait to tell Anne."

Anne came out to the garden where her father and John had been talking. She placed her hands on her hips and smiled at these two men she adored. "Do I hear my husband shouting "*Yes*" loud enough for half of St. John's to hear? Whatever have you two men been discussing that has you both beaming from ear to ear? Tell me."

Her father cleared his throat. "We were discussing selling Harts and Royals. If I sell, John has invited your sister to live with you."

Anne hurled herself first into her father's arms and then embraced her husband. "Tell me what, why, when ... Oh, what a delight it will be to have Elizabeth with us!"

Barry explained the decision to sell was not as hard as he imagined. Family obligations came before ties to an inheritance. If the plantation was not serving his family, then it was time to sever connections to a piece of history. For all his life, the land supported him. However, the estate represented more bondage than freedom for his adult children. He must set them free.

He needed to tell Liza next. Barry waited several days to muster his courage to speak to her about his plan to sell the plantation. First, he took the time to explore homes they might purchase in St John's.

One house Barry viewed with a lawyer seemed to fit his idea of his wife's expectations, and the lawyer had a potential buyer for the plantation.

Barry approached Liza as she sat sewing in their parlor. "Could we discuss a matter I have been thinking about?" Barry sat down and took her hand as she lay her sewing aside.

"I don't quite know where to begin. Our life on this land has become more of a burden than a blessing. The plantation was my childhood home and my gift from my brother. *But* my lasting inheritance is not a piece of land, it is my family. The plantation has struggled financially over the last several years. The right buyer with money to invest could make it profitable again. Selling both Harts and Royals soon would be in the best interests of the family.

Liza gasped, then began to cry. Barry waited for her to compose herself. When she raised her eyes, instead of displaying her often unreadable expression, she was smiling. His wife was smiling. Barry asked, "Would you want to live closer to St. John's and be near where the children can all go to school? I can take you to explore available homes in St John's."

"Oh, Barry, I have missed living in town more than I ever thought I would. I miss my job as a seamstress. Here on the plantation, we are so far from the bustle of town life. Yes, sell the plantation. The children will miss the animals, but I will not miss much of anything. Can Esther come with us?"

Overcome with pleasure at her response, Barry told her, "The decision will be up to Esther, but by now she considers herself as a part of our family. The slaves will all remain with the plantation, but if the price is good, we will be able to hire kitchen help. We can take our favorite milk cow and some of the chickens. The house I saw has a small barn, suitable to serve as a stable for the horse, the cow, and the fowl."

Barry was thankful that his wife did not ask how he might find employment once they were living in St. John's because he did not know. He only knew he must provide an income somehow. Now he could speak to Elizabeth and then to Esther.

Elizabeth's expression was one of astonishment, as Barry explained his plan. She questioned, "John has agreed I can live with him and Anne? Oh, Father, this is beyond my dreams. And I can teach at the Negro school I visited. When will we do this?"

"John and Anne said you may move in with them as soon as you are ready. I am speaking to Esther next and hoping she will stay and help Liza prepare for this move."

His daughter asked, "Father, might I go with you now while you speak to Esther? She has become like a sister to me."

Her father understood the bond they shared. "Go and find her, and we will ask her now."

The family could never overestimate Esther's contribution to their lives. Sixteen years had passed since she joined them. When Anne left home, Esther's unique role expanded. The children respected this strict, Jewish woman who had no fear of being labeled a stickler. Often when Esther spoke, it came across in a snappy manner. Yet with her sternness, Esther also showed a tender side. She displayed her gentle character best when she sang bedtime songs to the children in Portuguese, songs she grew up hearing in Curaçao. Though they could not understand the words, the children saw her love so vividly the lyrics did not really matter. She would gather the smallest onto her ample lap and lift her sweet, soft voice in what sounded almost like a prayer. When she sang, the family marveled at how her entire personality softened and transformed.

Barry thought about the Bible story where Mordecai pronounced his cousin, Esther, to possibly have been born "for such a time as this." As he contemplated this change in his life, he knew Esther held a significant role.

Elizabeth soon returned with Esther. The woman seemed puzzled when Barry asked if she wanted to go with them when they moved to town. "Where else would I go?" Esther asked. "Have I not been grafted into your family? I love each of you."

With those details settled, Barry turned to more difficult matters. It pained him to consider selling his people. He insisted a sale would only be possible if the agreement included keeping the slaves on the estate. If they divided them up and sold them separately it would be worse for the welfare of the people.

Liza approved of the spacious home located at the edge of St. John's. Two generous rooms would serve well for the children, then one for Barry and Liza, and another for Esther. There was a fifth room to hold Barry's large desk and allow him a quiet retreat when he wrote. The veranda was not as extensive as the gallery at the plantation house, but there were fruit trees and space for a garden behind the house. The house had an outdoor kitchen that pleased the women because the heat from cooking need not add more uncomfortable temperature to the home.

Confident the plantation would sell, Barry purchased the house in town. Charles wasted little time arranging to marry Jane Hodge. Jacob purchased a fishing boat from a widow, and he found great freedom in his small but profitable business. To Gratianus's relief, he found enough open-minded students for him to teach music while also writing some for the newspaper. He and Jacob shared a small residence in St. John's.

Elizabeth moved into the spare room at Anne's home and began to teach at the nearby school for coloured students. Barry realized none of Annie's children would be under his roof, making him both sad and aware of his age.

Sarah, 16, requested they consider her studies complete. She wanted to learn more about becoming a seamstress. Barry thought it would be a help to have Sarah at home while the others attended school.

The new house gave Liza a zest she had lost over the last sixteen years. No one had imagined a change in location would transform her outlook. This was her home, not one inherited from Barry's family. His wife began to add all the touches her spirit had locked away during her childbearing years. Slowly she ventured out to the fabric shops in town. This was the woman Barry had found attractive after he lost his Annie.

After a fortnight, the plantation sale was final. The family said their goodbyes to the slaves, took cuttings of hibiscus, crotons, and other well-loved shrubs to root and remind them of their home, and they even moved Anne and Elizabeth's old bench.

Harts and Royals were now a part of the family history. Barry laid one last bouquet of flowers on Annie's grave. No longer bound by the plantation, the family was now united by love. All Annie's children had begun lives of their own.

Over the next few weeks, Barry began to realize he had missed an important truth about his marriage to Liza. For as long as they lived together with Annie's children, in what had first been Annie's home, Liza had imagined she was sharing Barry with his first wife. Now Liza appeared to have a freedom she did not enjoy while living on the plantation. The house in town was her home, and only her children surrounded her. Barry had never considered that Liza might struggle with the lingering essence of Annie.

After the move, Barry walked with his daughter Anne to see the progress on the Methodist Church addition. "Liza is more involved at church since we live so near Temple Street now. The distance from the plantation to town made it challenging."

Anne replied, "I pray you will find a new purpose. I cannot imagine your being idle for long after working so hard for over forty years, consumed every day with the needs of the estate. I know you want to go to the newspaper office. Go ahead, Father. I want to stay awhile."

As Barry stepped into the office to deliver an article he had written, Mr. Kelsick called to him, "Mr. Hart, I want you to meet Mr. Payne." Barry joined the two men. He learned that Mr. Payne, newly arrived from Britain, would soon travel to Trinidad to work. Mr. Payne motioned for Barry to sit and said with enthusiasm, "I set sail soon on my first journey to Trinidad. This fascinating country with a very mixed population recently became a British Crown Colony. Yet, it has a number of French and Spanish-speaking residents."

"I read it was a Spanish colony until the end of this last war with Spain, but during the years of the French revolution, did not many flee there from the French islands?" Barry asked.

Mr. Payne nodded. "You are correct, Mr. Hart. The island of Trinidad has Spanish laws, French speakers, and now a British government. Over the last year, they have had an enormous influx of settlers from the United Kingdom. New estates are being bought and sold daily. As a lawyer, I will deal with all the many legal transactions. Have you ever written legal transactions, Mr. Hart? I hear you are an educated man who writes well."

"I am humbled, Mr. Payne. Yes, I have written some wills, manumission papers, and legal documents here in Antigua. Why do you ask?"

Mr. Payne patted Barry on the back. "Ah, yes. They told me you were both humble and articulate. They also told me you recently sold your plantation. What are your arrangements for the future?" he asked. "Would you consider going to Trinidad with me as my secretary, Mr. Hart? For substantial pay, of course."

Barry closed his eyes, this offer seemed like a dream.

Mr. Payne repeated his question. "Will you work with me, Mr. Hart? All the documentation required in the changeover from Spanish to British rule has overwhelmed the government. I need a secretary with an eye for detail and a clear hand at writing. Completing the transactions will take months, at the least."

Barry cleared his throat. "I must give this some thought and speak with my wife before I answer you. When do you sail?"

"I sail in a fortnight. But I need your answer by week's end." A confident Mr. Payne extended his hand out to Barry as if he had already accepted the job.

Barry thanked the man and walked out the door in a daze, almost forgetting to leave his article. The lawyer called as Barry departed. "I am at the Seaside Inn. I look forward to hearing from you. Good day."

Barry sometimes used a cane. At age 61, aging troubled him, and today he needed it. If he took this offer, he knew it would only be for a year at most. To uproot his wife and his second family of seven children was unthinkable. Could Liza manage without him for the months he would be away? The toll of the physical work necessary for so many years on the plantation hung heavy. This job would require mental energy and allow him to learn more about legal transactions.

As he walked home, Barry considered how to approach Liza, she must be the first person with whom he discussed such a change. A teasing Liza curtsied as she met him at the door. "Welcome weary sir. Please come in."

Sinking into a chair, he exclaimed, "Liza, I welcome the return of your smile. I never want to do anything to take away your contentment."

Her answer pleased him. "I am happy with my new home. While the children are at school, I have hours of quiet to myself. Esther and Sarah are undemanding companions. Yes, I am content."

Barry declared, "Rest assured, I love you, and I love our children. But I need a purpose to my day. The plantation took all my energy and thought for so many years. Now I must seek employment. Do you understand?"

His wife appeared uncertain. "Of course, I understand. I will not keep you bound in a chair at home. You must seek your purpose."

He examined her expression. "And if it meant I needed to travel for months at a time, could you manage?"

Her smile stiffened. "What do you wish? To be away from me?" she asked. "I don't understand. What would take you away?"

"I received an unexpected, yet exciting, job offer this morning. I met a lawyer who stopped in Antigua on his way to Trinidad. He is in search of a secretary to write up legal documents for all the property transactions in the newly created British Crown Colony of Trinidad. The gentleman was given my name as a person who had experience in these matters. I would be gone for months, and if you object to the idea, I will not consider it."

Liza hesitated, then asked, "If you are away, might I use your office and desk as a sewing room?"

Bemused by this response, Barry laughed. "Of course, if I accept this position, and I am away, you may use my office for anything you like. This is your home, and when I return, we can build another room for your sewing. I would earn a good salary while away, and it would help us with expenses."

Not yet smiling, she answered. "If this is what you want, Barry. The children and I will be fine with Esther's help." With her response to his proposal, Barry recognized again how significant a transformation had taken place when he brought her back to St. John's to live.

The plans quickly solidified. As for the boys, George and Joseph at 15 and 14 could help with many of the chores, and Liza would manage. Daniel often joined the older boys but took time with Thomas, who at nine stayed glued to his father's library reading books. And the girls, Sarah, age 16, and Esther offered companionship for Liza. Ruth, at age ten, delighted in keeping her eye on seven-year-old Mary, who was inclined to be like her older brother Daniel—always eyeballing mischief. This might be the last piece of the puzzle.

His wife interrupted Barry's thinking by kissing him on the cheek. "Though I will miss you, this is an excellent opportunity for you to use your brain and not your muscles for a while. I should tailor you some new clothes worthy of a professional secretary."

Barry went the next day to the Seaside Inn and spoke with Mr. Payne. He accepted the offer but requested a fortnight to prepare himself and his family for the transition. His wife sewed a new travel outfit for him, and he purchased new shoes. The idea of going to Trinidad filled him with anticipation, though he regretted having to leave his family behind. A new adventure awaited.

# 20
# Grace Bestowed

*1801*

When her father had announced the sale of the plantation, Anne's words of 17 years before kept circling in her mind, reminding her how she declared that she wanted no money if her father sold her two slaves. Over the years, she tried to forget she owned Quano and Hercules. Quano proved an eager learner, attending her reading classes. Besides reading and writing, he learned to do sums. Anne would not have called Quano a friend, but they respected each other. She avoided contact with Hercules.

Since her marriage three years earlier, Anne made only short visits back to the plantation, where she rarely saw Quano and never saw Hercules. Realizing her father would soon sell his people, she speculated what to do about the two who were her responsibility.

John, who understood her so well, knew she was troubled. "Anne, can we talk about whatever has you frowning all day?"

Anne grimaced. "I have never been good at keeping my emotions from showing, have I?"

Her husband came closer, wrapping his wife in a gentle embrace. "You rarely scowl, but all day you have displayed a sour milk face. Talk to me." He walked over and patted their chairs.

She endeavored to smile before following John. "Remember how I told you about my despicable inheritance of two slaves when I was only 16 years old?"

Realizing the source of her distress, John grew sober. "So, now that your father is selling his workers, you feel responsible for the two you own. Have you thought of what you should do?"

Unlike many husbands who made most decisions for their wives, John thought Anne capable of deciding for herself. Getting up from her chair, she paced their sitting room.

"I do not know what I should do. Quano studied with me years ago, and he can do sums, as well as read and write. He is 34, only a year older than I am. If he were free, he could succeed." Anne cleared her throat. "Hercules is older, closer to Father's age and a greater concern, since most slaves at his age are unable to work in the fields all day. A kind master might find a position with less physical demand. But I cannot bear the thought of selling a slave. Sadly though, he might be considered too old for someone to hire him independently if he were free."

Walking over to Anne, John took both her hands in his. "Have you talked to your father about this?"

His wife hung her head. John dropped one of her hands and began to walk alongside Anne as he talked and paced with her, gently swinging their arms in rhythm. "We will plan a Sunday afternoon visit with your father. You can ask for his advice and have a visit with your family. For now, please allow me to help you share this load."

Anne embraced this man who had transformed her life. "I'm sorry, John. I should have asked you earlier about this. Explaining my complex emotions with these two men is so hard. Hercules seethed with anger towards those he saw as the enemy. He frightened me, and I am hurt that anyone should view me as his enemy. Owning people has always been intolerable for me. Quano was teachable, and it will not be difficult to ask my father to free him when he sells the others.

Once again, John wrapped his arms around her. "Let me guess the rest of this dilemma. You see Quano as deserving his freedom, but Hercules as undeserving. Is this the problem?"

Anne stammered, "No … Yes! Oh John, I want to do what is right, but my heart is cold towards Hercules. Maybe my concern about his age is an excuse not to give him his freedom, and part of me wonders if he even deserves freedom. I realize I am being judgmental. Ignoring the needs of Hercules and setting Quano free would be much easier. But I want to think as Christ would. Help me, John."

Anne experienced the peace of sharing her burden with this man who loved and cared for her. She sheltered her head on his chest, relief washing over her troubled heart.

"You know, God gives us guidance in His Word, instructing His children to love their enemies," John assured her. "Scripture reminds us He causes his sun to rise on the evil and the good, and He sends rain on the righteous and the unrighteous. If God blesses the unrighteous with his bounty, should we not be willing to do the same?"

He stroked Anne's back, and she leaned harder into her husband. "I feel better already. Why do I react as if everything is up to me to settle? Yes, let us talk to Father. He will tell me to treat both men equally, to free them, and entrust the outcome to God who specializes in grace for the undeserving. I know scripture tells me as I have received a gift to use it to serve one another." She looked at John and heaved a sigh of relief. "You are right. Hercules deserves grace as much as anyone else."

There were those of her father's people Anne had allowed herself to love. Old Molly, who had died years ago. And the children, how she loved the slave children! While she hesitated to become too attached to some of the other slaves, beyond providing food and clothing, she found satisfaction in teaching them.

The late afternoon sun played with her hair, turning it a reddish-brown. Anne leaned back. "I have always struggled with the freedom God gave to me as a black woman, extending privilege upon privilege to me," she admitted. "I have done nothing to deserve the blessings I have always had. I have worn guilt as a heavy cloak ever since Judge Blizard burdened me with owning two men."

"You were not guilty. None of us deserves the blessings bestowed on our lives," John told her. He lifted her chin as he assured her, "When your mother died, and your father was occupied with the plantation, many tasks fell on you. But now I can help you with this burden."

Anne stared at John. It felt as if he peered deep into her soul. Much of her life already came with her own share of heavy, heartbreaking burdens. But this trouble lingered under the surface festering like a splinter. She could not remember when the guilt had developed, yet she could not ignore that her freedom as a free black had generated a nagging sense of self-reproach.

Despite these heavy thoughts, it was a beautiful day. Anne examined the beauty she saw in the flaming flamboyant tree, and it reminded her of God's provision in all things. She paused to inhale the scent of the frangipani growing near the veranda and smiled at this man who had become such a gift. She slid her hand over his afternoon stubble, her fingers lingering near his lips.

"I never had anyone I could tell about my shock of finding out I owned two slaves. Elizabeth and I shared almost everything, but I kept this from her all these years. Father tried to relieve me of the burden, but I always knew someday I would need to deal with it. You are lifting this burden, and I am more peaceful. Thank you, John, for understanding me better than I understand myself. What a joy it is to be married to you!"

# 21

# Elizabeth's Painting

*1801-1802*

Liza embraced a fresh sense of freedom after the move to town. Elizabeth's independence meant no longer providing supervision for her father's second family. Their father no longer owned slaves, which was liberating for all of them. The plantation remained in the girls' memories as a connection to their mother, a link with their childhood.

With her teaching, Elizabeth discovered new responsibilities. In addition, living with Anne renewed a pleasure both sisters missed when Anne had left home three years before.

Anne continued developing her own sense of purpose, providing help wherever possible for a growing number of street children in need of care and love. Amelia's mother from the rum shop occasionally allowed her to spend longer periods with the girl. An equal number of times she cursed and told Anne to go away. Those were the occasions piercing Anne's heart and leaving her to wish for an orphanage. Of course, Amelia was not an orphan, nor were some of the other children she dared to help.

Both sisters tried to spend an occasional afternoon visit with Liza and her children while their father worked in Trinidad. They often borrowed books from their father's library and continued to share their love of reading with their father's second family.

Missing everyone, Barry Hart returned to Antigua from Trinidad before a year was up. The desk job provided a good change, a transition from life as a plantation owner. His assignment there required no long hours in the sun, no fear of how the plantation could survive another storm or another drought, but Barry was feeling his age. The ship bringing him home experienced rough seas, reminding Barry how his father's second wife had determined to never journey by ship again. Understanding how she had arrived at her decision, now he too reached the same conclusion.

When Barry arrived at his home in St. John's. Liza joyfully embraced her husband, "Barry, you are home!" But he appeared to have aged much more than she expected. "Come and sit on the veranda. You look tired after your long trip."

Almost leaning on his wife, he said, "It was a hard trip. I am glad I am home. I just need a cup of tea and then a rest. I will see the children after I have slept."

Barry did little besides sleep for the first two weeks following his return. Even during their welcome visit, Elizabeth and Anne were alarmed when he fell asleep while sitting with them. Anne motioned for Elizabeth to stop talking, because she did not realize her father had drifted back to sleep while she told of her experiences of teaching in the St. John's Negro School. Both sisters quietly stood up and went inside to say good-bye to their stepmother. Anne cleared her throat before asking, "Do you think Father is ill or merely exhausted?"

Liza told her stepdaughters, "He refuses to go to the doctor, and I believe it is exhaustion from the rough sea journey. I am questioning what he ate while he lived in the boardinghouse in Trinidad. He lost weight, and nothing fits him." She held up the trousers she was altering and frowned.

The sisters bade Liza goodnight and slipped out to return home. Anne was the first to speak. "Of course, he is tired. I can only imagine what it must be like sailing almost 500 miles on the rough sea. We will visit again in a few days. Surely, he must get over this."

Elizabeth said, "Sarah is doing well, helping with the children and sewing, and strange as it is, Liza seems to have benefitted from Father's absence. She appears comfortable in her new role. Though Father is ill, Liza appears calmer than I can ever remember."

"You are right," Anne agreed. "Calm is not a word I would have used to describe the woman we knew for so many years. Maybe it is living in town, her children beginning to grow up, or Father being home at last. But, yes, she is doing so much better."

On their next visit, the sisters found their father outside working in the vegetable plot. "Hello, my lovely daughters," he called out. Moreover, Barry was wearing his charming grin. The girls rushed to their father and hugged—not minding he was sweaty and dusty with garden soil.

"Father, you are well," they said almost in unison.

"Sorry to have scared you," said Barry. "Yes, I am back among the living and happy to take pleasure in working the earth once more, but let's go sit in the shade."

Anne led him to the old bench she and Elizabeth had claimed as their retreat years before. Elizabeth called out, "I will see if I can find a drink for us," as she walked toward the house.

Sipping the refreshing soursop juice, Barry assured his daughters he was his old self, telling them he had even asked at the newspaper if they would want some articles describing life in Trinidad.

Anne described Amelia for her father. She thought he might write an article about street children in St. John's and the need for an orphanage. "Father, I never realized we had so much to be grateful for when we lived on the plantation. I often thought about how blessed we were to be born free, but I had no idea how many unfortunate white children, as well as mixed-race children, existed in the town. What I see in St. John's on an almost daily basis makes me appreciate you and Mother even more."

Barry gave them a little extra to spend on the children who touched the hearts of these selfless daughters. "Tell me, Elizabeth, how are my children doing in school?"

Elizabeth patted his hand. "They do well. I try not to favor my step-brothers and sisters, and I am thankful for the time with them."

Knowing the privileges so many whites experienced, as a child, Anne had sometimes wished she had been born white. Before her mother died, she began to recognize how rare her parents were. They loved and cared for all their children. The values surrounding her childhood were often missing on the streets of St. John's.

The colour of one's skin did not dictate the quality of parenting. There were, of course, children of every shade in need of parents who could or would take loving care of them.

After losing her heart to Amelia, Anne grew to love more of these girls. This love drove her to action. In a few years, the options open to these girls would probably involve earning their living in ways that knocked the wind out of her. Now she began to consider how she could help create a better future for these girls.

The sisters discovered there were many parents who could not read themselves, begrudging their children the advantages they lacked. Anne and Elizabeth often chose not to ask permission to teach a child. They simply included them in classes. If needed, later they could always ask the parents to forgive them for interfering.

One afternoon Elizabeth withdrew from her bedroom and announced, "I do not wish to sound rude. I have plans to work on a project which I do not want you to see until I finish. Can I ask you, Anne, not to come into my room until I tell you I am ready to share it with you?"

Giggling was a rare occurrence for Anne, but now she did. "You sound like we did when we were 12 and 15. I remember you attempted to make me a birthday present, and I walked in our room without knocking. You screeched as if I had ripped out your hair. Of course, I promise not to peek in your room."

Elizabeth immediately shut the door, and after this, she often came home from school and shut herself away in her room until Anne called her for a meal. John teased her and began to call her "the mystery girl."

Elizabeth was thankful for the opportunity to have a private place to create this special project hidden away in her mind for years. While living in her father's home, there was neither time nor space for creativity. Here in her own room, there was little requiring her attention after school hours.

When the plantation sold, and Elizabeth moved to Anne's home their father gave his second daughter the colour box—his source of joy as a child. Years ago, Elizabeth dreamed of painting a picture showing her mother surrounded by her five children. After Barry remarried, Elizabeth set aside the dream, knowing they could not hang such an image in their home after Annie died and Barry married Liza.

Elizabeth knew the imagined painting would be a beautiful reminder of their beloved mother. Over the years, she tucked away small sketches in the colour box, viewing them now and again. The children would be sitting at Annie's feet with their backs facing those viewing the painting. Annie would be in her chair with a book on her lap. It was a reminder of the poor children Elizabeth taught whose mothers were unable or uninclined to sit and read aloud to them. She had been blessed to sit at her mother's feet day after day. Her gratitude for the years spent with her mother made this painting a joy to create. Elizabeth began to mix the colours and put her memories on paper imagining her mother smiling at the idea.

Elizabeth spent many hours in her room, frustrated with many false starts with her painting. One evening she emerged wearing a tattered old dress. She hid her hands behind her back as she asked, "Describe for me the colour of Mother's eyes. They were brown, but can you help me remember more?"

Anne did not have to think long before declaring, "Sparkling, soft brown, with flecks of gold. You must be writing a poem. How sweet to be writing about Mother. I anticipate reading it soon."

Turning, Elizabeth pulled her hands from behind her, so Anne did not notice the specks of paint. Peering over her shoulder, she called out, "Don't expect to see what I am doing anytime soon. Some things need time. 'Sparkly' helps, though. Thank you!" Elizabeth winked before shutting the door.

Anne's husband smiled at her. "We have a genuine mystery going on in our own house." "Your sister is a delight," John said, returning to the book he had set aside when Elizabeth darted into the sitting room.

Almost a month later Elizabeth told John and Anne, "I have something to show you. Shut your eyes until I tell you to open them."

Both obeyed her instructions and in unison said, "Ready!"

When Elizabeth told them to open their eyes, she expected to catch them unawares. What she didn't expect was for Anne to be speechless. Walking closer to the painting, Anne lightly touched the likeness of her mother. waving her hand over the children as if pulling up a memory of the many times they sat at their mother's feet while she read to them.

"Sparkling eyes and a halo of hair and all us children at her feet. Oh, how many years did you keep this memory alive? Yet it is just as I remember, and beautiful beyond words. You captured us perfectly— the boys with their darker brown arms because of all the time they spent outside and you and I are slightly paler with hair like Mother's own. Oh Elizabeth, how she would have loved to see this, to know how we all grew up still missing her!"

Elizabeth dipped in a bow, "Thank you. I was unsure I could remember all our youthful faces, so I decided to paint us with our backs to the viewer. But memories of Mother were so vivid, and I became confident I could capture her."

John studied the painting closely. "I can see your mother in both of you. She was a charming but strong woman. I know because she had such a part in what you both are today."

# 22

# The Move to English Harbour

*1803*

The French threat of an attack on the island escalated again. Antigua had been constructing fortifications for years. Against such invasions, the British now employed 1,000 troops in the English Harbour Naval Dockyard.

One summer evening Anne heard John running up the wood steps to their cottage. It was hours before his usual time to return home.

"Anne," he shouted as he burst through the door. "Anne! I have news! A fast schooner just arrived with news that the French Governor of Guadeloupe has dispatched 700 men in 13 warships for a direct assault on our Dockyard."

John bent over to catch his breath, then stood upright, beaming with pleasure. "Remember when we married, how they threatened to have me court-martialed? Because at the time I served in the militia in St. John's, they merely decided to dismiss me instead."

Anne handed him a glass of water, and he took a gulp before he continued.

"As a boy I served in English Harbour at the Naval Dockyard as an assistant to the storekeeper. Before we met, they had sent me to St. John's to train the militia here in preparation for any future attacks. Now with all this military activity, they need me and have forgiven me for marrying the most amazing woman on the island! They have asked me to take a position as the first clerk to the storekeeper. That means a move to English Harbour at once."

Anne clasped John's hands and looked into his eyes expectantly. "We discussed possible military activity escalating, but this is sudden." She patted his back. "I have never been to that side of the island. What is it like?"

John sat down after taking another drink of water. "The Dockyard is a superb military fortification like none other in the Caribbean, though the village of English Harbour is small. Nearby Falmouth Harbour has a few shops and dwellings as well. Britain has been at war with France for nearly 100 years. Our island needs a strong defense against pirates and the French, now more so than ever before."

Anne demonstrated to John her ability to handle adjustments by standing up and starting to prepare him a meal. "Since it takes over two hours on rough roads, it's too late for you to go today. Tomorrow you can go ahead to the Dockyard while I start packing up the things we will need to take from here." She had already tied on a smock and was busy setting a dish on the table for him. "I imagine they will provide lodgings for us. Once you have a place secured, send a note, and I will come to join you. Let's pack a few necessary items for you right away."

In a few days, a note from John advised his wife he had arranged for a cottage outside the large, rowdy military setting of the Dockyard. To Anne's relief, Elizabeth offered a fellow teacher a room in the house. She would not be alone. The women would oversee the house in St. John's in case this flurry of military activity subsided, and they sent the Gilberts back to St. John's.

The wood house John rented in English Harbour needed paint and a good scrub, but it had a peaceful view of Falmouth Harbour. Their home was a short distance from the area called The Middle Ground, where the King's Negroes lived.

When going to the market on her first day in English Harbour, Anne walked briskly and avoided eye contact as she passed by the noisy, often uncouth sailors. Her heart sank as she realized most of the women encountered outside the military facility were prostitutes. Her steps halted when she saw children reminding her of Amelia, ill-clothed with expressionless faces.

Her thoughts shifted as to how she could make a difference in helping those unkempt and ill cared for children. While the men and some women drank rum at all hours of the day and night, the children sat on the roadside waiting for their mothers or fathers.

As she prepared John's breakfast on her second day in this military village, Anne began to visualize opportunities. "John, I remember you told me about meeting a Mrs. Looby who lives nearer Falmouth Harbour. If you believe it is safe, I will walk there this morning, taking Tippet to protect me from any sailors."

An amused John smiled. "Good, you are already beginning to shape your life here. Mrs. Looby will be an encouragement, and I expect you will come home full of proposals about how to reform this town full of fallen women and disadvantaged children."

"I have some ideas of my own," he said. "The King's Negroes, though slaves, are also craftsmen with privileges unknown to most slaves. They can construct their own homes and have gardens on The Middle Ground. The authorities want someone to teach these men to read and learn basic mathematics." John patted her mass of yet uncombed hair and kissed her. "We will talk tonight about starting a Sunday Service soon, because you are not the only one trusting God to give you a plan."

As Anne bundled a bit of bread and cheese for John's lunch, the blessings of starting a ministry together wrapped around her like her comforting blue scarf from John. She finished her morning chores and made ready to walk with her dog, Tippet, to Falmouth Harbour.

Singing softly helped dispel the fear churning up as the sailors whistled and called out invitations. She ignored them. Holding tight to Tippet's leash, Anne asked directions at a small shop. She learned Mrs. Looby's brother-in-law owned it. Walking two houses past the shop, Anne found the widow, Mrs. Looby, who turned out to be everything John had described

The women sat under the shade of a generous avocado tree appreciating the tranquility of Falmouth Harbour as they visited. Immediately Anne sensed God's gift of a kindred spirit. Confiding in her gave a feeling that they had known each other for years.

When she learned one of Mrs. Looby's daughters occasionally worked in her uncle's shop, Anne blurted, "Mrs. Looby, do you feel your daughter Lily is secure working so near the sailors?"

"Please call me Mary," said Mrs. Looby. "And yes, Lily is secure. She keeps the accounts in a room behind the shop and no one sees her. You might be questioning why I remained here in this wicked part of the island. My husband built this home next to his brother's 20 years ago. My memories of him are here. Before he died, he asked his brother to watch out for me, so to be here was his dying wish. This was our spot to sit and talk."

"I do not mean to pry, but I am trying to know how to feel safe while John works long hours in the Dockyard. When I lived in St. John's, I considered myself quite secure when I went into town or for a walk by myself." Anne realized she hadn't even confided her fears to John after moving to English Harbour.

"Watch you do not allow fear to rule your heart. God has not given us a spirit of fear. But do take Tippet with you when you go out and carry your parasol for more than protection from the sun." Mary patted Anne's knee. "Your husband and I met when he came into the shop. John has chosen well. He is a good man."

Anne spoke of another matter on her heart. "Some of the poor children I see sitting outside the grog shops wear threadbare clothes. Do you know if anyone is caring for these waifs?"

Seeing where this was heading, Mary now said, "Your husband told me you would seek out a mission after you came here. Do you sew? We could sew for these children."

"As a girl, it was always a battle to keep our large family clothed. I learned how to defend our household with a needle and cloth. My wardrobe is small, but I can transform something of mine for one of the children. I frequently sewed for all my father's slaves. Sewing is a start. Thank you, Mary."

Mary smiled. "My Rosa, she is 15 and has recently outgrown a couple of dresses. Next week, could we get together to sew then?"

When she left, Anne thanked Mary for the advice as her mind whirled with ideas. Hope bubbled in her heart, but before the next week, a disturbing visit unsettled everything.

Months before, Reverend Baxter requested Anne and Elizabeth to compose a history of the Methodist Church in Antigua. Anne delivered her paper a fortnight ago. She thought she could now turn to other areas of service.

The knock at the door sounded urgent. Anne opened the door, stunned to see a grim-faced woman she knew as Mrs. Smith. Anne had met her only briefly when they were living in town. The Smith family had come as missionaries about two years before. Anne believed several of the missionaries, including Mrs. Smith, remained troubled by her mixed marriage. There was no time to offer a morning greeting before the angry woman held a rolled-up copy of the history Anne had written. "This is not right! Why should the Reverend Baxter ask you to write the history of the Methodist Church?"

Anne opened her mouth to answer. But the angry woman raised her voice and continued, her face turning a darker shade of scarlet as she interrogated Anne. "How did you convince them you could write as well as my husband or the other missionaries?"

Anne checked her emotions and quietly asked, "Will you come in, Mrs. Smith?"

Ignoring the invitation, the woman continued. "My husband is a missionary sent from England, and asking an uneducated woman to write the history is an insult. Do you imagine marrying a white man makes you qualified to write this?"

The woman shook the paper in Anne's face while continuing her unfounded accusations.

"I do not belittle your contribution to the church. I know you have been faithful to attend church and teach the children, but it is an affront they would ask you to write the history of the Methodist Church. Surely they don't believe you could do as well as the missionaries who have sacrificed to come here and who have experienced great trials."

Heat began rising in Anne, as she bit her lip to control her tongue. "May I interrupt, Mrs. Smith, to assure you I did not ask to write this history. My education might not have taken place in a formal setting, but my mother ensured I received an education equal to what she had acquired in England."

Mrs. Smith rolled her eyes as Anne told her of her mother's formal training. Finally, she blurted, "You need to tell Reverend Baxter he should find someone more qualified. Do not embarrass yourself and him by continuing with this task." The furious woman turned and nearly tripped as she descended the steps. She opened her parasol and stomped away, muttering to herself.

Anne plopped into a porch chair and began to laugh. She wanted to shed no tears for such an unwarranted and insulting slur, and she could choose to either laugh or cry. She was sure John would defend her right to create the history, but this offence would upset him.

Later that day, Anne described the tirade to John. He frowned. "How could she judge you? The woman has no idea of the articulate, educated, godly woman she boldly abused. I am so sorry. Scripture does tell us man views the outward appearance. She sees only your beautiful skin colour and deems your brain and heart are less than her husband's. What a fool!"

"John, be careful. We are to call no one a fool—though the thought entered my mind as she spoke."

John chuckled. "That woman may be so foolish as to underestimate the mind and talent of my wife. I am wise enough to know I could never be the writer you are—never. Will the day ever come when men and women do not judge others by the shade of their skin?"

"John, I was honored when Reverend Baxter asked Elizabeth and me to write the history. I am thankful all the missionaries are not as rude as Mrs. Smith. Most of them did sacrifice to come here to share the gospel. My anger bubbled up inside me at her unfair words, and I asked God to forgive my poor response."

John kissed her forehead and concluded their day by reading several Psalms aloud for his wife.

As hurricane season ended, a much more severe threat neared Antigua. The news had been circulating in the Dockyard that between 10,000 and 16,000 troops on French and Spanish ships sailed nearby. John avoided discussing the threat with her, but gossip, like the smell of salt fish, lingered in the air in the shops. Anne heard from John a few months before that Admiral Nelson had sailed past Antigua with a dozen battleships.

Now as John entered their home, Anne sensed his churning emotions even before he spoke. "I have news from England—both good and bad."

Anne led her beloved to their chairs and nodded for him to begin.

"The British fleet took a position in the Mediterranean against the Spanish and French fleets with Admiral Nelson leading them. The British broke through the blockade defeating Napoleon's plan, but Lord Horatio Nelson lost his life at Trafalgar."

Anne could see John wrestling with his emotions as he conveyed this news. She remembered him speaking of meeting Admiral Nelson years earlier. She responded, "Many will remember Nelson as a naval hero. He became Vice Admiral when quite young, didn't he?"

John nodded. "Yes, a hero, but he was also arrogant and blatantly bold. I remember him as short of stature and equally short of character."

His wife reached across and touched his face. "Yes, I remember hearing he abandoned his wife and took a married woman, Mrs. Hamilton of Nevis, as his mistress."

"I apprenticed as a naval storekeeper in the Dockyard when I was only 14. Horatio Nelson came in and out English Harbour at the Dockyard while I served. I remember when he first sailed as the captain of the *Boreas* in 1784. The man was ruder than most of the lower ranking sailors, often strutting like a peacock into the naval storehouse. Yet, I am sad for the loss to the British Navy." John patted his wife's hand. "Let's speak of happier things. I had an opportunity today to talk at length with a Charles Thwaites in the Dockyard who wants to join us for church on Sunday. He is distressed and weary of all the debauchery here in English Harbour. He was an educator before, but he turned out to be a shipbuilder. Charles thought life in Antigua might be an adventure. The man is lonely and searching for answers, so I am praying I can be a friend to him."

Anne sat quietly as John leaned back in his chair. "I did explain that most of the people attending our services are either free coloured or slaves, but it didn't dissuade him. He told me he was unimpressed by conversations he has had with a couple of the Methodist missionaries he has met here." John wiped his forehead. "If the Reverend Smith is as intolerant as his wife, then I understand why Mr. Thwaites has not been interested in the religion he offered. I told him all we offer in our small Methodist chapel is Christ alone and His sacrifice. Perhaps on Sunday, we can ask him to break bread with us. Charles is different from most of these rough shipbuilders, who curse every other word."

Reverend Baxter had started services in English Harbour years before, though the Dockyard did not consider Sunday a day of rest. Over the last year some people from The Middle Ground had begun gathering to sing hymns and listen to a brief message on Sundays. John invited Charles Thwaites to join them for a meal after the service. Their garden provided a few vegetables, and Anne prepared salted fish to add to the pigeon peas, okra, tomatoes, and eggplant. One of the church folk brought her a small pineapple and the sweet tropical scent filled the small house. The men visited on the veranda while she warmed the meal. Hearing John laughing with another man was good.

John worked all day with men in the Dockyard, but Anne knew he didn't consider most of those men as friends. Some made jokes about his choice of a wife, and Anne overheard coarse remarks a few times when passing the sailors on the street. But Charles Thwaites was different from most of the white men working in the Dockyard. As they ate, he asked Anne about her family and was particularly interested in her education.

"Mrs. Gilbert, you are aware I work as a shipbuilder in the Dockyard, but I am restless to return to life as an educator. Your husband told me you taught your father's slaves for many years. Can you tell me what method you used? Many don't believe the enslaved are capable of reading and learning mathematics. I count myself as one who believes in educating anyone with a craving to learn."

"Sir, I am most convinced all who want to learn should have the opportunity. Years ago, I noticed those denied the privilege of learning craved it more than those who wasted their education. Some of my father's people absorbed every bit of knowledge I could teach them. My father had a large library, and I took books for granted until I realized some slaves, who had no books, were more eager to learn than my own brother."

Charles's face radiated with excitement. "Exactly! Actually, I have asked some of the Dockyard sailors if they want to borrow some of my books, and they laugh at me. Yet, I believe books are treasures. I perceive a hunger in the eyes of some of the coloured men working in the Dockyard when they see me with a book. When I taught school, all too many uninterested students discouraged me, so I joined my father in building boats." He pursed his lips. "I must be fickle because now that I have built boats for several years, I find I itch to return to teaching."

Anne cleared away the dishes from lunch while listening from across the room. This man was rare, and it was clear he would be a friend to both her and John.

"I am thinking we could offer classes for those few coloured men who are eager to learn," said John. "We must be careful, though. Many scoff—even fear—the idea of educated free coloured people."

"I would welcome the chance to return someday to teaching," said Charles. "If you think we can begin evening classes here, I know of several men who would welcome the opportunity."

John glanced across the room. "Anne, come and join Charles and me. We have an idea to propose to you!"

Expectantly Charles asked Anne, "Would you help me teach a couple of men from the Dockyard to read? We could offer a weekly class, but I'm afraid it might need to be here in your home. His Majesty's Dockyard would frown on using my living quarters to teach."

Anne's eyes twinkled as Charles made his request. "John and I could both help with this. I confess I have envied my sister Elizabeth having her own school for free blacks in town."

She turned to John and he nodded to their guest. "Charles, bring two students on Monday evening with an interest in learning to read!"

Charles smiled. "Would it be possible to allow another man to sit and read one of your books while we teach two others? I can think of one man who has devoured every book in my small collection." He stood to go. "We will come after supper. Thank you for this support."

After Charles left, Anne turned to John. "What an exciting opportunity! You know I can sew for needy children, but preparing people for life beyond manual labor is important to me. Education frees their minds, and it appears even the King favors it. Oh John, thank you for bringing Mr. Thwaites home."

When Monday evening came, Charles appeared as Anne was clearing away the evening meal. She heard him introduce the men to John. When he said the last man's name, Anne spun around and gasped as Charles introduced Quano. She stepped closer, realizing the man Charles brought with him was indeed her former slave, inherited when she was 16. He was the young man she taught to read so many years ago, the man she gladly gave his freedom two years before when her father sold his plantations. Quano never knew he had belonged to a girl who not only despised slavery but had been burdened by guilt because she was free while others lived enslaved.

Anne stepped into the room. "Hello, Quano. I am pleased to see you again. You are working in the Dockyard?"

"Mistress, dis be your home? Me heard your father say you married, but me not know you be in de Dockyard. Me sew sails for de boats dat Mr. Thwaites builds. He be pleased when he find out he can write notes, and me can read dem to make sails de right size. Mr. Thwaites, he loan me books. Now me see he knows you, and he say maybe you will let me read a book because me done read all he got."

Anne shook the man's hand. "Welcome, Quano. Yes, I am sure I have a book for you to read. Who are your friends?" She relaxed some and turned to meet the other two men. "Welcome to both of you." Teaching again brought contentment.

Charles, taken aback said, "I had no idea you knew Quano. He told me a girl had taught him to read and do sums years ago."

James and Alfred were introduced to the Gilberts. The cottage was small, so Anne and Quano worked at the small kitchen table. Charles and James read on the veranda, while John worked with Alfred sitting in the two chairs in the front room.

Anne held her arm out to the full bookcase on the wall. "Quano, choose a book with me. We will send a book home with you, and when you return it, we will find another. Lowering her voice, Anne questioned Quano, "I am wondering if you know what became of the other man my father granted freedom when he sold the plantation two years ago? His name was Hercules?"

Quano paused and searched around as if someone might be listening. "Mistress, you ask plenty questions. Mr. Thwaites be so kind and loan me his books. He told me must treat them very carefully, and me do." Not wanting to be overheard Quano whispered, "Hercules he found work to care for some gardens. Me saw him a few months ago, and he is glad to be free. To be free not be easy. No one buy you food if you spend all your money on de rum, and Hercules he love he rum. But I married now, and me wife no want me drink de rum."

"Thank you, Quano. I want to meet your wife. Now, choose a book and read it aloud to me. I can help with any troublesome words."

Quano and Anne took a lantern to the table, and he read aloud. Anne later asked Charles to invite Quano and his wife to Sunday services.

# 23

# A Lesson in Love

*1805*

When Elizabeth arrived one humid morning at the St. John's Negro School, she noticed a small tan-coloured letter propped against the bottom of the door. She ran her fingers thoughtfully over the neatly blocked inscription to "Miss Elizabeth Hart, Teacher."

Elizabeth sat down and slit the wax seal to open the folded paper.

> *To*: *"Miss Elizabeth Hart, Teacher."*
>
> *"I am Charles Thwaites, an educator with a sincere interest in your school for Negro children. I hope to visit your school at 10:00 a.m. My plan is to observe quietly, and then I want to offer a small gift. If an extra chair is available, please place one near the door at the back of your classroom so I may observe without disrupting. Thank you for your consideration. Sincerely, Charles Thwaites."*

Elizabeth folded the small note hesitantly. Who was this Charles Thwaites? Elizabeth opened the shutters, letting in light and air, checking to be sure the floor did not need sweeping. Soon the students began drifting in, and chatter filled the room. There was no extra chair, so Elizabeth asked one of the older boys to place her own chair by the door.

Removing the delicate chain and watch from her pocket, she noted she was several minutes late calling the students to order. She clapped her hands, and her classroom grew quiet.

"Good morning, class."

"Good morning, Miss Hart," the boys and girls chimed in unison.

"Let's recite our memory verse together." Elizabeth raised her arm, and as she lowered it, the class quoted from Matthew 22:37. *Thou shalt love the Lord thy God with all thy heart, and with all thy soul, and with all thy mind.*

The rhythmic sound of the children lifting their voices in unison always gave Elizabeth pleasure. Standing in front of her desk she prayed, "Father, we thank you for minds grasping what it is to love you with all our heart. Help each child to be attentive and learn today. I pray for little Joshua who has been absent. Help his body to heal. In the name of Jesus, Amen."

As she glanced up, she noticed a man had slipped silently into the classroom while she prayed. He was sitting by the door. Recovering quickly from the surprise, she tried not to draw attention to the strange white man observing her class. "We will begin today by continuing to read the story I started yesterday." There was no need to tell them to listen. Her students loved the sound of her voice.

"As you might remember, this was a book my mother read to me when I was a young girl. In the story, the orphan girl Margery has become a teacher. We will begin where I stopped reading yesterday." Trying to ignore the mysterious man, Elizabeth took a deep breath and began, "*The History of Little Goody Two-Shoes*." Reading aloud with her siblings had always been an activity she loved, and she had the children's full attention.

"More, please," one boy begged as she came to the close of today's story reading.

"Tomorrow we will read more about Margery, little goody two-shoes. Now watch the board please as I begin to write some numbers." Turning her back to write on the chalkboard, Elizabeth wished she indeed had eyes in the back of her head as she sometimes joked with the students.

Why was this man here, and what was he thinking? She finished writing the numbers and began to call on students to tell her what number she had written. Then she asked one of her older boys, "Irwin, can you add those first two numbers together and tell me what they equal when combined?"

She noticed the man raised his eyebrows. Her mistake of stealing a quick glance at the stranger caused first one student and then another to turn. His presence now obvious, Mr. Thwaites moved with confidence to the front of the room. He was a short man with large ears and curly hair bleached by the sun. He had a dark tan—not stark white as were some British men. He perched himself on the teacher's desk since she was standing at the chalkboard. He smiled engagingly at the students and turned to Elizabeth.

"Good morning, class. Good morning, Miss Hart. I am Mr. Thwaites. Class, I envy you having heard the first part of the book your teacher read. Tell me, is she always as animated a reader as she was today?" He turned as if to tease her.

The room was silent for a minute before one girl asked, "What means animated?"

Mr. Thwaites replied, "Animated means you feel present, inside the story. Few people read with such lively expression. Is she always a good storyteller?"

Now the children chimed in, "She always be good with stories. Teacher be best storyteller ever."

Mr. Thwaites hopped off the table and walked towards their teacher. "Well, then I have brought your teacher a prize."

Elizabeth marveled at his actions. What white man would bring a prize for a coloured teacher in a Negro school?

Mr. Thwaites walked among the students sitting on their benches. He stopped in front of one of the boys. The man patted his pocket and said, "See if you can guess what I have here."

The boy's eyes filled with excitement, but he shook his head.

The tension rose in Elizabeth's mind as to why this stranger was here. She shook her head to discourage him.

Mr. Thwaites laughed. "May I present a short science lesson for your students, Miss Hart?"

Struggling to find her voice, Elizabeth nodded.

The man reached into his pocket, pulling out a flat object about 7 inches long and a piece of paper. Holding the paper on the blackboard, he used the strange flat object to write, *"An excellent teacher."*

There was silence, and then one boy read what Mr. Thwaites had written. "This not be ink. How you do dat?"

Mr. Thwaites motioned for the boy to come up to the board, and he held the paper up for him. "Young man can you please write your name on the paper?" The awed boy took the strange writing stick and crudely wrote *Alfred*.

Elizabeth found her voice. "I think it is a graphite stick!"

"You are right, Miss Hart. Ten years ago, a French scientist discovered when they mixed graphite with clay and heated it in a kiln the result was a writing tool. They wrapped the first sticks in string. This graphite stick has been encased in two thin pieces of wood to keep your fingers clean. I ordered several from England and decided to share one with your school."

Elizabeth covered her mouth and then lowered her hand to her chin. This unexpected offering left her feeling off-balance. "Mr. Thwaites, I don't know what to say. How do you even know about our school?" She leaned against her desk, for her knees seemed weak from the morning's strange events.

Mr. Thwaites brought Elizabeth's chair up to her desk and returned to a space beside one of the students on the front row of crude benches. He spoke directly to Elizabeth, ignoring the 27 students watching.

"I am friends with your brother-in-law, John Gilbert. We worked together at the Dockyard, before I began to do private tutoring here in town. I came to Antigua as a shipwright, but I am seeking direction now as my time of indenture at the Dockyard is ending, and I want to return to teaching."

"I see," Elizabeth said, struggling to understand where this was going. There was an awkward pause. Trying to gain control of the situation, Elizabeth clapped her hands, though everyone was already staring at her.

"Class, can you recite a poem for Mr. Thwaites?" She turned to him. "The class has few books, and the students are very talented at memorizing poetry and scripture by rote."

Irwin spoke up. "Can we recite *The Cost of Fish*?"

"Mr. Thwaites, the children love the sing-song rhythm of William Cowper's verse about fish. Go ahead, children."

With a delightful cadence, the children sang out the words in unison.

*Cocoa-nut naught,*
*Fish too dear,*
*None must be bought,*
*For us that are here,*
*No lobster on earth,*
*That ever I saw,*
*To me would be worth*
*Sixpence a claw.*
*So dear madam, wait*
*Till fish can be got*
*At a reas'nable rate*
*Whether lobster or not,*
*Till the French and the Dutch*
*Have quitted the seas,*
*And then send as much*
*And as oft as you please.*

Charles Thwaites doubled over in laughter. Elizabeth joined in his delight at the class reciting Cowper's poem with gusto.

When Mr. Thwaites had composed himself, he exclaimed, "Oh my! If only Mr. Cowper could have heard you children. He would have loved your recitation. Well done!"

She needed to speak alone to this man who had taken over her class and clear the muddle in her day's schedule. "Yes, it was delightfully fun. Class, you are excused to have a dipper of water or attend to anything necessary. I will call you inside in a few minutes."

Elizabeth took out her hankie and wiped the heat from her face. What a surprising day this had become.

Charles Thwaites stepped towards Elizabeth.

Before she thought about what she should say, she blurted out, "Tell me, Mr. Thwaites, why did you really come to my school today? Is there some trouble?"

He began to explain. "Your sister did warn me a visit to your school might frighten you."

Elizabeth rarely interrupted anyone, but she couldn't help declaring, "My sister! My sister knew you were coming to the school? You know Anne too?"

Charles held up his hands. "I must be going about this all wrong. Please forgive me if I startled you by my unorthodox visit. I only hope you will allow me to visit the school again. I came because Anne is delightful, and she told me the story about your school. I was intrigued someone had the gumption to start this school, and I wanted to meet you."

"Why did you bring me a graphite stick?" Elizabeth went to the window to check on her students. Unaware he had followed her, when she spun around, she stood face to face with Charles Thwaites and experienced a sudden shiver.

"I had two pencils, and when Anne told me about you, and well ... I wanted to share ... I wanted you to have one."

Such was a simple explanation, yet Elizabeth sensed this was anything but simple. Why did he want to share with her? What did he mean about visiting the school *again*? Elizabeth went to her chair and sank down. Without saying it out loud, she groaned, *"Oh, Anne!"*

Glancing up, she saw Charles Thwaites watching her. Then she giggled nervously. Composing herself, she asked, "Mr. Thwaites do you want to stay, or do you have important business in town?"

Yes, I have important business in town," said Charles Thwaites, "but I would prefer staying to observe."

With a teasing tone, Elizabeth replied, "I have time for a helper, but no one is allowed to simply observe." She raised her eyebrows, and before he could respond, she instructed, "You may listen to Irwin read—at the back of the class." She handed him a book and turned to write something on the blackboard.

Charles wondered whether this was a positive response or a dismissal. As the children came inside, she clapped her hands, and they all quieted and took seats on the benches.

"Irwin, you may go and read with Mr. Thwaites. He has offered to assist me." She cleared her throat. "Who wants to come to my desk and write their name with the graphite stick?"

A chorus of voices called out, "Me, teacher, me. Please, me!"

"Starting with the first bench, line up in an orderly manner." She had considered refusing to keep the writing stick, but seeing their excitement, she would allow this unusual gift.

Since most of the children toted water for their mothers or worked to help their family in other ways, the school day was only three hours. Elizabeth thought her watch must be broken because the time passed so slowly. As the children left, Charles volunteered to sweep the floor. Everything this man said and did unnerved her. He knew Anne, he worked as a boat builder, he recently became a tutor—and he wanted to return to teaching full time. He built rapport easily with her students, stayed to sweep the floor, and he was charming. All these thoughts and more churned in her mind.

Bemused by her thoughts, Elizabeth watched him sweep. Anne had encouraged him to come! Elizabeth could not help asking herself what was happening, and why was she thinking about him?

Turning from cleaning the blackboard, Elizabeth told Charles, "Thank you for the writing stick. This generous gift excited the children."

He stopped sweeping. "What about you? What did you think?"

Placing her hands on her hips, Elizabeth calmly replied, "You make me uneasy, Mr. Thwaites. Thank you for sweeping the floors, but perhaps you best leave."

"I want to walk you home."

Grabbing her school satchel, Elizabeth said softly, "I think that is unwise. People might get the wrong idea."

Charles Thwaites turned to close the shutters. "I think I have the right idea, but I see clouds indicating we should hurry, or we will get wet on our way home."

How could she argue with someone who would not take *no* for an answer? She added *determined* to the list of all the qualities this puzzling man revealed over the morning.

The clouds were turning dark, and both knew rain in Antigua came abruptly. They met at the door as they closed the final shutters. Taking up her parasol before locking the door, Elizabeth could not help but smile.

Charles Thwaites relieved her of her bag, as she struggled to lock the door while balancing her parasol. She added *kind* to her list of thoughts, turning to leave the school as the first heavy cloud unloaded on them.

The two hurried through the downpour. Elizabeth's rushed pace caused her to slip in the mud, and Charles instinctively took her arm to keep her from falling. Her face flushed, and she feared eyes must be watching from every window. They arrived at her cottage, and she invited Charles to wait on the veranda for the rain to stop. She pointed to a chair as she unlocked the door to the cottage. He bowed slightly before sitting down.

"I will make some tea." She hurried inside, leaned against the closed door, and tried to breathe normally. Occasionally a man had mildly flirted with her, but she had never experienced this reaction. Charles Thwaites openly showing her attention made her both pleased and uneasy. But Anne had guided him her way, and her sister always protected her.

As Elizabeth arranged teacups on the tray, she said to the empty room, "What now, Anne?"

She placed the steaming cups of fragrant bush tea in front of the man waiting on her porch and sighed. Apologizing, she said, "I am sorry if I appear rude. This has been a most unusual morning."

As Charles Thwaites sipped his tea he asked, "Do you think me brash to show up in your classroom as I did?"

Elizabeth counted honesty as vital. "I am not sure what I think. Who are you really, Mr. Thwaites?" She lowered her head, studying her tea.

"I appreciate you are direct and to the point. I want to tell you my story."

She raised her eyes, and nodded permission for him to continue.

"My father was a builder of boats and my mother a teacher. When I finished school, I taught for a few years in London but was discouraged by the students who were not as eager to learn as I was eager to teach. For two years I helped my father with his craft. One day I read a notice in the newspaper asking for shipwrights to immigrate to Antigua. They provided my passage and quarters and in exchange it required I work as a shipwright for six years. That is how I came to this tropical island. A few months ago, I started attending the services John Gilbert began in English Harbour. I heard the gospel, and the Lord became my Savior and I, His servant."

Elizabeth interrupted, "You are a believer, Mr. Thwaites?"

Charles continued, "Yes! I heard the gospel as a youth, but I managed to avoid church and God's Word until I met John Gilbert. He explained the gospel, and God began drawing me to Himself. I came to know your sister through John. We worship together on Sundays."

Sipping her tea slowly, Elizabeth placed her cup down and turned to Mr. Thwaites. "I have never attended a service in English Harbour with Anne and John, but I understand it is mainly the free blacks or slaves who attend."

Charles protested. "When you call me Mr. Thwaites it feels oddly formal, since Anne and I have been talking about her sister Elizabeth for some time now. Would you consider it too bold if I asked to call you Elizabeth and you call me Charles?" He quickly added, "I trust we will become friends."

Elizabeth's eyes grew large and straight away disbelief marred her expression. "Oh, no, Mr. Thwaites, this is too sudden. I am unsure why you visited my classroom today and even more unsure why we are now sitting here sharing tea. Perhaps you should go since it would appear the rain has stopped.

Charles rose. "Thank you for the tea, and I do look forward to our friendship. I cannot imagine Anne's sister will not become my close friend. Both she and John are the dearest of friends to me. Why don't you ask Anne what she thinks if you and I become friends?"

At the bottom step he turned back. "You are an inspiring teacher, and your students impressed me. Until next time, Miss Hart …."

As he walked down the street, she thought she heard him quietly say, "Elizabeth!"

Elizabeth took the cups inside, gathering pen, ink, and paper to write a note to Anne. This would be a long note with many questions!

Dear Anne,

How are you, my full-of-wonders darling sister? Why have you not told me about your friendship with Mr. Charles Thwaites? The gentleman says he is good friends with you and

John and attends church with you. I know John believes English Harbour is not a place for me to visit as a single woman, and you are busy most Sundays with the church. But why have you failed to mention Mr. Thwaites to me? On your visits here and in your letters, you mention people you have met in your new setting. You also told me about Father's former slave, Quano. Yet you have never mentioned a Mr. Thwaites. Is there something I should know about this mysterious man? He visited my classroom today, acting as if I should be expecting him, and indicated a possible return visit to my class. I had the strangest sensation he has an interest in developing our meeting into something more. You married a fine white man, but contrary to your experience, I have almost no dealings with white men.

Oh, how I miss you, and I long to go sit under the mango tree on our bench with you for a long uninterrupted chat. So please write to me soon and tell me why I am anxious. I love you, and I have always trusted your judgment.

Pray for me, Your sister, Elizabeth.

Elizabeth waited for the ink to dry and then addressed the note, sealing it with a wax stamp. She walked to a shop in town that traded with the shops in English Harbour. No formal arrangement for local mail to go from St. John's to English Harbour existed. Once a month, the ships took letters between Antigua and England, but no postal system served the island. People must entrust someone to transport mail when making a journey to deliver goods. There was little guarantee someone would not open mail or dispose of it. This note was of such personal significance, she prayed only Anne would read it.

# 24
# Plans to Prosper

*1805*

A week later, when Elizabeth arrived at school, she discovered Charles Thwaites sitting on a rock humming to himself. "Good morning, Miss Hart. I trust I did not startle you, this time." He held out a note from Anne. "Your sister gave this to me because she knew I was coming to town to do some tutoring this morning. May I hold your parcels while you unlock the door?"

Elizabeth measured her words. "Good morning, Mr. Thwaites. Thank you for delivering Anne's note." She glanced to be sure the wax seal was unbroken. The presence of a white man outside her school unnerved her, and Elizabeth fretted she might fumble the key and drop it. She reminded herself, after all, he was there for good intentions. With the door unlocked, she set about opening the shutters to let in light and air.

He began to assist her with releasing the shutters on the opposite side of the room. "What time do your students arrive? I thought we might have a little time to talk before I leave to tutor my student."

Her words now nervously tumbled across each other as if standing in too tight of a line. "My students will arrive within the next twenty minutes, Mr. Thwaites. How are my sister and John? I wish Anne could come for a visit soon."

With a disarming grin Charles bowed. "Your wish is my command, and if you open the note from your sister, you will see she plans to visit your classroom later today. Anne misses you as much as you miss her, and she asked me to bring the note first thing so you will expect her after she has completed her shopping. John is also in town on Dockyard business, and they rode in early with me."

Elizabeth relaxed. "Sir, you are very kind and generous to deliver this news. I will have a hard time concentrating on the lessons knowing Anne will be here soon. I suppose they will return to English Harbour later today?"

The gentleman brushed away the dust on his trousers. "We will start back by half past three, so we can arrive in English Harbour before dark. I have made the 10-mile journey in two hours, but John has supplies for the Dockyard, so the weight of the load will slow us down. Anne thought we might all have lunch together after John finishes. She packed some bread and cheese and suggested we could either go to your cottage or eat together here in the schoolroom."

This man took charge and arranged things with ease. Did he have any idea how his presence unsettled her? After straightening the books on her desk, Elizabeth gave a tentative smile.

Charles said, "I will go teach a Latin lesson with my student and return about noon. I remember your pupils leave by then, and you will perhaps have had a chance to visit with Anne. She told me that you two have always shared freely."

He turned and waved, leaving before she could answer. She had no idea how to handle the emotions churning inside. Anne had revealed to this stranger the closeness the two of them had always experienced. She felt a sense of envy because this intriguing man had spent so much time now with her sister and John!

Elizabeth unsealed her sister's note.

Dear Elizabeth,

What do you think of the courier I sent? I need to make some purchases of things unobtainable in English Harbour shops. Charles comes once a week for a time of tutoring, so John and I asked to accompany him. Trusting you won't mind, we invited him to share our lunch. I know the men will be hungry. All your questions will be answered when I come to school this morning.

Trust me. Anne

Elizabeth realized several students slipped inside. If the pupils had not been watching, she might have wadded up Anne's note with what might be misunderstood as anger. Elizabeth didn't feel angry, but a prick of unease caused her to shudder when she placed the note inside her book on the desk. Her experiences with white men were limited to the missionaries and her brother-in-law, John. Many white men outside of the church thought of mulatto women as easy prey. She knew extremely well her own father came from a background of a white man taking advantage of his housekeeper. However, she could not think of Mr. Thwaites as such a man.

Spelling and mathematics filled the next hour, yet Elizabeth found concentration difficult. The moment she noticed Anne approaching the door, she clapped her hands. "Class, please read while I leave the room for a few minutes. I will be outside the door, so remember to read in silence."

Embracing her sister, Elizabeth motioned to the rock Charles Thwaites sat on earlier. Elizabeth rehearsed her questions, but once she saw her sister, all she could ask was, "What?"

"All you can say is *what*?" said Anne. "Do you mean what am I doing here? What a lovely day? What is happening in English Harbour? Or do I guess you want to know *what* I think of Mr. Thwaites?"

Elizabeth shook her head with enough force to dislodge a hairpin. "No … I mean, yes. What does that man want?" She pushed a stray bunch of curls away from her eyes.

"You charmed him, sister. He could talk of little else Sunday at lunch, and it appears he wants you to consider being his friend."

Elizabeth jumped up. "Friend? I know what most people believe when they see a white man with a coloured girl. A friend is often considered by many to be an intimate friend—a mistress."

Anne rose. "Elizabeth, we both know you would never consent to anything improper, and I know Charles would not consider such a relationship. He is a man you can trust—faithful and God-fearing. I can't speak for him, but I feel sure he will never ask you for anything of which God would not approve."

Hands on her hips, Elizabeth stated firmly, "You and God might be the only ones who approve of a white man marrying a coloured woman!"

"He asked you already?" Anne exclaimed. "This *is* sudden!"

"Stop!" Elizabeth pled. "Of course, he hasn't asked me. I have been thinking about you and John encountering the taunts and ridicule after your marriage. Would you do it again?"

"How can you ask?" Anne sat back down on the rock. "Elizabeth, if I have learned one thing over the last seven years, it is how God has blessed my life with John. I learned what others think is unimportant. What is important is what John and I share in a ministry, and it is unlikely he would have started a church in the Dockyard if he had remained unmarried."

"What are you saying? Most white men make me uneasy, yet I am thankful you have John. To be truthful, I have a sensation of falling, and there is no secure place to stop my fall."

"Dear sister, you have trusted God in so many difficult situations, and now you say the shade of a man's skin makes you nervous? That my husband possesses a lighter shade of skin is unimportant. I trust you have not judged Charles because he is white?"

"Charles and I … we are so different. This is so sudden." Elizabeth began to wring her hands, denying what her sister was trying to tell her.

"Elizabeth, Charles wishes to return to serving as a teacher, and you are an educator. The Dockyard will not always have a position for John, and Charles has almost finished his job there. God could do great things with the four of us as a band of like-minded people, set apart to help train more slaves than those we helped when we were girls." Anne stopped to let her words settle. "Charles has noticed what John and I share as a couple. When he met you, his mind began to swirl with the possibilities. No one will rush you, but because of public sentiments, if God brings you two together, then it should happen without delay. I remember how John and I needed to act before tongues began to wag."

Elizabeth resolved not to cry, and she needed to return to her students. But her tears would not obey her. She sniffled. "So, the three of you will be here at the schoolroom for lunch? I can compose myself by lunchtime. Do you have other errands, or can you help one of my students with her reading?"

Handing Elizabeth her handkerchief, Anne teased. “It has been a while since I had to carry what I always thought of as my *Elizabeth hankie.* Come on, dear, I hear your students starting to get rowdy.”

They turned and entered the classroom as Elizabeth put away the handkerchief. “Class, please welcome my sister, Mrs. Gilbert, and show her how polite you can be.”

“Good Morning, Mrs. Gilbert.” The class chanted in perfect harmony.

“Now class, I will prepare some equations on the board, and Sarina, please go to the back of the room and read for Mrs. Gilbert. My sister is also a teacher.”

Shortly after the students left for the day, John and Charles arrived at the schoolroom. Elizabeth greeted the men, as they began pulling out some of the students’ benches to use as chairs, leaving Anne to clear her desk. John asked Charles to thank the Lord for their lunch.

Charles’s rich deep voice spoke to the Lord with a warm ease. “Heavenly Father, we thank you for this beautiful day, made more delightful by the blessings of friendship and fellowship we share. Thank you for bringing John and Anne into my life. Thank you for Elizabeth and what she does here in this classroom to bring honor to you. May this food nourish our bodies, as friendship nourishes our souls. Amen.”

He sounded so sure of himself whether talking with the Lord or with her. Yes, she was nervous, even as she listened to Charles Thwaites’ calm voice.

Overwhelmed by the camaraderie the three shared, Elizabeth listened to the others talk as they relaxed together, but her heart was anything but relaxed. Did it show? She knew Anne saw it. Her primary friend had always been her sister. Friendly conversations with men took place mostly with her father, her brothers, and John after he married Anne. Greetings with pastors and missionaries were brief and impersonal.

Anne asked a question and waited for Elizabeth to answer. Elizabeth stared at her, “I’m so sorry. My mind was flitting here and there. I am listening now.”

Anne repeated, “We were saying we will return in two weeks and come on a Saturday so we can go visit Father and Liza. Will you go with us for a short visit with the rest of the family?”

Charles spoke hesitantly as he watched Elizabeth, "I want to meet your family if it is all right?"

Elizabeth heard him, but her answer had to fight past her nearly paralyzed throat. The words came haltingly, "Yes. Of course."

Anne knew she must come to the rescue. "We really must go. We will stop and leave a note with Liza telling Father what time to expect us two weeks from now."

John turned to Elizabeth. "Charles and I have been discussing the future, and what we desire to see in English Harbour."

Charles added, "I remembered how God told us in Jeremiah, *For I know the plans I have for you ... plans to prosper you and not to harm you, plans to give you hope and a future.* I have clung to the verse, waiting for Him to show me His plan."

John added a quick, "Amen." The *future* lingered in the air with many questions.

"Thank you for coming." Elizabeth added as the Gilberts climbed into the wagon. When Charles hesitated, Elizabeth lowered her head. "Goodbye, Charles." For the first time, she had allowed herself to use his given name.

"Until next time," he responded. He started to walk away, then turned and said, almost in a whisper, "I am waiting on His plans."

John called to the horses. The loaded wagon stirred up a cloud of dust as they pulled away. Charles glanced back at Elizabeth, and she responded with a timid wave.

A fortnight later the wagon approached Barry's home with Elizabeth, Anne, and her husband, along with a white man whom the girls' father had never met. Elizabeth was surprisingly silent as they emerged from the wagon while Anne gave her father a kiss and John shook Barry's hand.

John spoke first. "Mr. Hart, may I present my good friend and colleague, Charles Thwaites." As Charles stepped forward, Barry reached out his hand with a confused look on his face.

"Hello, sir. Pleased to meet you at last. Anne and John have shared so much with me about your family."

Barry blinked several times, as if the sun were troubling him. Elizabeth nervously rubbed the toe of her shoe in the dust.

"Hello, Father," said Elizabeth. The only other sound was the faraway cooing of a dove.

Not any time too soon, Liza stepped outside, and Anne stepped up to greet her. "We have missed the family and decided to bring a new friend along on our visit. Liza, this is Mr. Charles Thwaites. He works in the Dockyard with John, helping us with both church and the reading classes we have started with the King's Negroes."

Liza raised her eyebrows. "I see." Then she asked, "And how are you, Elizabeth?"

Barry rescued the awkward moment by inviting them inside for refreshments.

Esther came bustling out of the kitchen, but quickly realized something was amiss and went about trying to change the cool atmosphere. "Excuse me, I'm Esther. I was adopted into this family twenty years ago. I'll go fix tea, and there are some coconut buns fresh out of the oven. Come help me, Elizabeth."

Esther often used a commanding voice. In many ways she *was* in command. Often left in charge, she became accustomed to acting as the family authority now that Anne and Elizabeth no longer lived at home. Almost from the beginning, they considered Esther more as family than hired help. As the door to the pantry and dining area closed behind them, Esther rested her large hands on Elizabeth's shoulders. "Tell me. Who is this man?"

"I don't know." Elizabeth said, her eyes downcast. "I mean, I don't know what to tell you. I think he has an interest in me." Esther wrapped her ample arms around Elizabeth and then stepped back and lifted her chin so she could see Elizabeth's eyes. "Is he a good fellow, this white man?"

"Of course, he is good. Do you think my sister would encourage a man who was anything but thoughtful and honest? But what will Father say?"

Esther turned and gathered cups and plates from the pantry, and she cleared her throat. "Your father will say this is about time some kind, generous man saw what a prize you are. You are over 30 and wise enough to know your own mind and heart." Esther patted Elizabeth's hair into place. "Now, pour the tea, and see if you can steady your hands enough to carry it to those folks sitting in there waiting for you. I will bring the coconut buns. We are fortunate George took all his siblings for a sea-bath at Fort James. We will have a quiet house to welcome this gentleman of yours."

Elizabeth batted at Esther, pretending she was angry at her last comment, but smiled as she pushed open the door.

Charles stood to help Elizabeth with the heavy tray of cups. "Elizabeth, this is a fine home. Your father took me outside to see the cows and chickens in the barn." Elizabeth searched her father's expression to see if Charles had been so bold to ask for time with her father, so he might question him about courting her. Barry attempted to light his pipe, something he seldom did inside the house.

Anne began to tell her father how the Dockyard officers encouraged them to teach the slaves who belonged to the King to read and write. "Father, you remember your former slave Quano, from the plantation? Quano is employed at the Naval yard as a sail maker, and Charles has been bringing him to our home to continue learning when we teach in the evening. Could we choose a couple of your books to take back with us?"

"You girls know I am always willing to share. I am pleased Quano is doing well. What is it you do in the Dockyard, Mr. Thwaites?" Barry looked puzzled, like he wanted to ask *what is it you really do? What is your interest in my daughter, Elizabeth?* Once more, it appeared a white man had chosen another of Annie's daughters. Barry could see how Charles watched Elizabeth, and it became obvious the purpose of this visit was to ask if he might court her. A weary Barry did not consider discouraging Elizabeth from choosing the same trials her sister had experienced with a mixed marriage.

Barry held up his pipe. "I am quite low on tobacco, and I need to take a short walk to the tobacco shop. Would you care to go with me, Mr. Thwaites?" Charles glanced at Elizabeth, and she smiled her approval.

"I would be pleased if you will consider calling me Charles. When someone asks for Mr. Thwaites, I still find myself searching to see if my father is in the room." They all laughed, and the two men left. Liza excused herself to lie down, leaving only Anne, Elizabeth, and John in the room. Esther chose to stay in the kitchen.

Elizabeth regarded her sister. "I remember when a violent storm was about to hit our little island, and how I both dreaded it and was in awe at the power of God. I feel the same anticipation now, as if something powerful is about to send my life swirling." She bit her knuckle to keep herself from laughing or crying. Her sister came to sit next to her and nodded towards John, who was reading one of Barry's books.

"Having a good man at your side is worth the storm, Elizabeth. You know I would do it all again, even knowing how hard it might be at times."

"He hasn't asked me yet!"

"Of course not, you silly goose, he will speak to Father first. But since he lives in English Harbour, and you live here in town, sooner will be wiser than waiting. I know you will want to finish teaching this term, but it ends in eight weeks, right?"

"Eight weeks? Do you think I will know by then what to do?"

"I imagine you know now, but my advice is to give the school your notice you will not teach after this term. Just think, we could work together again! The King's Negroes were chosen because they are intelligent, hard workers, and they are making terrific progress in their reading and mathematics. When freedom comes, these men will be ready for anything, and we can be a part of it, Elizabeth. Teachers of the King's Negroes! What a foursome we two couples will make!"

"Stop. You are getting ahead of me." As Elizabeth stood, she noticed her stepsister Sarah peeking into the room. Sarah, Liza and Barry's oldest, was a shy, quiet 20-year-old girl, and an accomplished seamstress. Elizabeth assumed she had gone to the sea with her other siblings. Yet in this noisy bustling household, Sarah often retreated to her sewing room for hours at a time. Sarah had not yet ventured out to greet them but she did listen at the doorway. Now she shyly said, "Elizabeth, I want to make your wedding dress."

Elizabeth rushed to Sarah. "Please do not speak to anyone what you might have heard. We have not decided … I mean … Mr. Thwaites has not asked me to marry him."

Sarah was not given to emotional displays, but she said with full assurance, "He will ask. I saw him watching you, and it is exciting. I know you must wait three weeks for the reading of the banns in church. That will give me enough time to make your dress." She was a fair mulatto, so Elizabeth could see her blush. "I would marry him if he asked me."

Elizabeth playfully tugged on the long braid hanging down Sarah's back, and the girl retreated to her sewing room, giggling as she went.

Sometime later, Charles and Barry made an entrance, laughing together at something one of them had said. John stood. "We don't want to travel back in the dark, so we must be on our way. Anne and I were able to convince Elizabeth it is time she comes for an overnight with us and meets the folks in our church. We will bring her back to town tomorrow after our noon meal. She collected a travel bag when we stopped for her at her cottage, so we are set now to start for English Harbour."

Elizabeth realized at once that this would be much more than a ride to English Harbour.

# 25

# Dealing with Prejudice

*1805*

The four jostled along in the wagon as they headed back to English Harbour. Only this time, John sat in the bed of the wagon while Charles sat up front on the bench with both sisters.

John began to softly sing as they bumped along the dusty road that afternoon. John sang to give Charles some privacy to speak to Elizabeth. Charles held the reins while telling Elizabeth about the conversation with her father. She tensed, feeling her head whirling at the awkward discussion.

"I enjoyed your father, Elizabeth. His story of falling in love with your mother the first time he saw her is sweet, and he says you are as lovely as she had been. Although your father describes how you remind him of your mother, I wonder, since he said your mother always voiced her thoughts and was something of a chatterbox. I find you rather silent much of the time, or perhaps you only become silent when I am with you?"

"Charles, my mother had a way with words, and she always knew what to say. I write words better than I say them. Yet, I have no idea why I find it difficult to speak much when you are around. I suppose that other than John, I am unaccustomed to speaking my mind to white men."

"Please, stop speaking of me as a *white* man!" Charles spoke louder than he intended, and John intensified his singing to match. "I am a soul, same as you are a soul. Do not define me by my colour. Define me by my habits, my faults, my quirks, my character—*not my colour*. There are good men of colour in this world, as there are evil men of colour. Some men happen to share with me a lighter shade of skin. But some pale-skinned men are good. I want you to think of me by who I am. Can you do that?"

Elizabeth let out a long slow breath. "I am guilty. Seeing past the outside is harder for me than I thought, and I know it is wrong. You are making me start to see you. I can see patience, kindness and thoughtfulness."

Charles grew silent, with only the sounds of the wind blowing the palms and John's soft humming in the background highlighting the absence of further words. Elizabeth turned to Charles. "Mr. Thwaites ... Charles. Forgive me for judging you by your whiteness. Though my father was quite light skinned, he regards himself as a black man. I fear I have regarded most pale men as rather unattractive and sometimes frightening. This is so fast I feel caught in a groundswell and washed out to sea. I do not look at *you* as pale or unattractive or frightening. I have been unaccustomed to men in general, and I am beginning to think of you as someone I can trust."

Charles attempted to make Elizabeth more comfortable. Most of the remainder of the journey to English Harbour continued in silence except for John's singing. As they approached the Gilberts' cottage, Anne invited Charles to stay for dinner before returning to his own room in the Dockyard. "Esther knew we would return late, and she sent a savory lamb stew back with us. Please stay, Charles, it smells delicious."

Charles's expression seemed hopeful, and Elizabeth indicated her approval. "I appreciate the invitation and I will accept. Then I must return home and finish preparing the Lord's day message for tomorrow."

"Lovely. You two shake off the dust of our journey while I warm the stew." Anne dashed into the house while John carried in the pot of stew. She turned and called, "You can watch the sunset from our veranda. This is our favorite spot this time of day."

Elizabeth and Charles stood taking in the beauty. Charles took her hand and led her to the two chairs facing the setting sun. "Miss Hart, Miss Elizabeth Hart, put your mind at rest. Your father did not refuse my request to court you, but I can wait. I desire to protect you, to honor you, and yes, to marry you. But now I need to hear from you that you are not entirely opposed."

Elizabeth began to laugh. "My half-sister Sarah said she would gladly marry you!" Her teasing encouraged him.

"Charles, I am becoming more comfortable with the thought that we are sitting here discussing a serious commitment. Not merely as two people joining their lives, but as two people heading straight for a storm of opposition, a possible fiery trial. I am apprehensive, but I am not opposed, and the thought of living once again near my sister is thrilling." She eyed him wistfully. "I had imagined I would never marry."

"If you are willing, Charles, you could take me back to St. John's tomorrow following the service and noon meal with Anne and John. That would give us more time to talk."

"Elizabeth, I consider myself honored to take you back to St. John's tomorrow. I also request that I may come visit you each Friday when I tutor in town if you find it agreeable?"

"Yes, I can bring some bread and cheese for us to share after my students leave on Friday."

John brought a basin of water and a towel onto the veranda. He swatted away a few mosquitoes hovering near the door. This was the time of day for those pests to gather in anticipation of a meal of fresh blood. "You two should wash the dust off and join us inside. Anne tells me the stew is warm. I'll go help her cut some bread."

The two washed up then Charles took the towel and wiped at a smudge of dust adorning Elizabeth's cheek. They stared at one another, missing the beauty of Falmouth Harbour as the sun faded fast, and the air filled with the flurry of birds returning to their nests. "We best join your sister and John."

Elizabeth spent a restless night attempting to sleep on a pallet in the main room of Anne and John's cottage. Was Charles a gift from God or was he a distraction that might keep her from teaching the students she loved?

Preparing for the Sunday service, Elizabeth had brought along a clean but plain dress to wear. As she placed the hat over her mass of curls, her sister tucked a bright red hibiscus blossom under the plain ribbon adorning the hat. Elizabeth was surprised.

"Dear Elizabeth, the few women who attend our services love colour. They have nothing elaborate to wear, but they often tuck a flower in their hair. So, I thought we might do it too. I am learning from these women even as I teach them." She plucked off one more flower and tucked it into her own hat. She then patted Elizabeth's hat and gave her a reassuring smile.

The service was not long. The people sang with joy and enthusiasm. Most of them stood. However, there was a crude bench for the oldest people. Though not eloquent, Charles gave an uncomplicated message delivered with passion. Elizabeth considered herself honored this ardent man had asked her father if he might court her. The thought of becoming a team such as she and Anne had been was slowly changing from worrisome to agreeable.

After greeting many of the people attending the Sunday service, Elizabeth noticed Quano waiting to greet her. "Hello, Quano. I hear splendid news that you are married now and doing well working here."

"Yes'um, when you come again, I'll bring my wife and son. You will come again?"

Elizabeth glanced out over the people gathered to worship and saw Charles. "Yes, Quano, I am sure I will come again and look forward to meeting your family."

Though she had feared to come to English Harbour in the past, her confidence deepened that God might have a place for her here, joined to a man intent on marriage. He was a good man, a godly man, a man whom she was beginning to value. The thought of returning as Charles's wife hovered as a possibility.

During the meal after church, she was quiet as John and Charles discussed the people who attended the service. Anne kept glancing at Elizabeth, not wanting to intrude on her thoughts. Anne slipped from the room and returned holding a small square sheet of paper folded, sealed with wax, with Elizabeth's name written across it. "Read it later," Anne said cryptically as she handed Elizabeth the note.

"You two should start for town, so Charles does not have to return after dark." John said. Anne linked her arm through her husband's and handed Elizabeth a small tin. "A ship arrived last week with tea grown in Malaysia. Knowing you often make bush tea, I thought you might appreciate a change. John is right. You need to be on your way. I'll be praying for you, Elizabeth, and I'll see you tomorrow, Charles."

Elizabeth realized she wanted to see him too. On the way back to town she began humming the hymn they had sung that morning. Charles joined her by singing the words. When she remarked what a beautiful voice he had, he countered with, "If you spend more time with me, then you might discover other things you would like about this strange *white* man."

"I am learning to forget you are white and perhaps not as strange as I first thought. I enjoyed the church service this morning. You did a fine job of sharing God's Word with the folks there. How many do you suppose can read?"

"Ah, ha! The teacher thinks she might want to teach the King's Negroes as well as the others who are eager to learn. I must advise you English Harbour also has plenty of rowdy sailors. Many have little interest in anything other than the women of the night and the next bottle of rum. You saw the best of the folks today, those whose hearts are set on higher things."

Elizabeth began thinking what new experiences English Harbour might bring into her presently well-ordered life. The location was not the issue. This man sitting so close to her as they bounced over the rough road to town was whom she must consider. Anne's peace in her marriage was so vibrant. Would marriage add a missing aspect to Elizabeth's life? She thought back to her parents and knew theirs was a blending of strengths and personalities. Was what her father had experienced with her mother, Annie, the reason Barry gave approval to Charles?

"You have gone silent again, Elizabeth. May I ask what you are thinking about, or is that being too bold?"

"Charles Thwaites, you *are* bold. I was thinking about English Harbour and my mother and father. My mother died when I was not yet 13, but she is always present in my memory. I am wondering what she would say to me today. I still miss her."

"Anne mentioned you painted a picture of your mother surrounded by her children. I want to see it sometime. I wish I could have known her."

"I have not done much with my art for the last couple of years. Teaching keeps me occupied, and I love to read. My father gave me his colour box. Except for my Bible, it is my most treasured possession."

"As a shipbuilder, I deal with sketches of boat shapes, but they are rather lifeless things. Someday I might try my hand at painting a landscape. Could you teach me?"

"Charles, I can't imagine having you as a student, but I would gladly share my colour box with you."

"Friday I will be back in town to tutor. Expect me at noon, and we can go to scenic Fort James." Charles smiled. "You can bring your colour box for my first painting lesson."

As they neared her cottage, Elizabeth spoke up. "Friday will be good, Charles. Now, if you will set my bag on my veranda, I am tired and need to rest. I did not sleep well last night. My life was progressing rather slowly until a fierce wind blew you into my classroom, sir, and I am trying to consider what is next."

Charles helped her down and bowed. "Thinking of you unable to sleep because I have planted thoughts of possible changes is good. However, it is selfish, so sweet dreams, sweet Elizabeth. Sweet dreams."

With a jump into the wagon, Charles waved and began the long ride home. Elizabeth opened the door and sank into a chair, pulling the note from Anne out of her pocket.

> Dear Elizabeth,
>
> Thank you for finally coming to spend a night and a Sunday with us. I thought Charles gave a challenging message. Please give the school your notice soon. I am trying not to push you, but marriage to Charles will be not only fulfilling for both of you, but will allow the four of us to serve together. I am praying as you seek God's answer to Charles's petition for you as his wife. Do send a note back to me when Charles next comes to visit.
>
> Love, Anne

Elizabeth imagined she could sleep on the chair, but she changed from the dusty dress into a sleeping gown. Crawling into her bed, she wondered if she would dream of Charles and Friday.

Elizabeth spoke to the school administrator and told them she might not return for the next term. She had been instrumental in the formation of this school, teaching there for four years. She declined to give a reason for her possible departure.

Charles continued to visit each Friday. Elizabeth listened for the sound of the wagon approaching as she tidied her classroom. Today was the fourth Friday, but he was late. Elizabeth closed the school and sat waiting on the flat rock. She missed him. This must be love because Charles filled her heart and mind with dreams of what life might be as a married woman. Strong hands touching her shoulders startled her. Turning, she saw Charles. "Where is John's wagon? I worried. I missed you."

Charles dropped his hands to her waist and lifted her off her stone perch. "If I had known it would cause you to miss me, I would have planned for a wheel to come loose last week. The wagon is at the blacksmith's shop for repairs, and I arrived late to tutor because of it. Thus, I was late to come for you. Why did you miss me, Elizabeth? Can you tell me why?"

Elizabeth blushed. "I suppose it is time to tell you, Charles, I think I finally know how love must feel. I missed you because you have become a necessary part of my life."

Giving a loud whoop, Charles fell to his knees, "Marry me, Elizabeth! Marry me! As soon as we can post the banns and arrange things." Charles barely stopped for a breath. "Can we pack a bag for you and go tell Anne and John? They have prayed with me for this day. I spoke to a naval chaplain based in English Harbour who will perform the ceremony since we are certain to experience the same opposition from the clergy that Anne and John faced."

"You already spoke to a chaplain?"

"Yes, and John suggested since we are meeting in his home, we may post the banns there because it serves as the church. No one in our congregation will protest our marriage. I spoke to the naval chaplain as soon as your father gave permission. I prayed it would be soon. I love you, Elizabeth." Charles bowed his head and prayed, "Thank you, Lord, for giving Elizabeth into my care. I will cherish her, Lord, protect her, and love her."

As they left her cottage, Elizabeth pulled on his sleeve. "Charles, might we stop by my father's home on our way to English Harbour?"

When they stopped at the Harts', Elizabeth asked to speak to her father in his study. Charles accompanied her, and Barry spoke before they could explain. "Well, my brave and bold daughter, you are choosing I perceive, to follow your sister's path of shocking the island with marriage to this fellow?" Barry stood, and reaching across his desk, shook Charles's hand. "When will this be, and whom will you convince to perform this marriage?"

Charles cleared his throat. "I have met a naval chaplain who is based in English Harbour, and he has agreed. He has not met Elizabeth, but he took my word she is an honorable choice for me. We will post the banns at the Gilberts' home when we have our Sunday service, and read it again the following two Sundays. The wedding will be in three weeks, sir, and we will be pleased if you could bring your family."

"Indeed, we will plan to be there. You will live in English Harbour?"

Charles took Elizabeth's hand. "Yes, sir. I will continue with my position at the Dockyard, but we pray someday we will be able to devote our lives to teaching."

"We must be on our way, since I have asked Elizabeth to go with me to stay with Anne and John while the four of us make plans. We have only a couple hours to reach English Harbour before the sun sets. Thank you, sir."

Elizabeth shifted from one foot to the other. "Will you please tell Esther we wish for her to be there too? I will send a note to tell you the time of the ceremony, and I will send notes to my brothers as well. Thank you, Father. I have no doubt now this is God's direction for my life."

Barry watched the two drive away. He shed a tear for his Annie, who could not be there to watch Elizabeth radiant with expectation of a life including a husband. As he shared the news that evening with his family, Esther chortled, and Sarah whooped with excitement.

Three weeks later, when the family arrived a few hours before the ceremony, Sarah grabbed Elizabeth's arm, dragging her into Anne's bedroom. She unwrapped the muslin covered package she held in her arms and expectantly watched as Elizabeth unwrapped the dress.

"Sarah, this is lovely." The delicate pale cotton was a soft shade of green. Small, embroidered flowers adorned the bodice and the hem.

Sarah knew she would not wear anything elaborate or bright, but this was subtle in its beauty. There were layers of cloth covering the skirt, and each edge ended with a row of pale flowers. Touching the beautifully rendered flowers, Elizabeth smiled at her half-sister. "Thank you, Sarah. Will you help me change?"

Elizabeth loved the dress even though it was more elaborate than anything she had ever worn. This was her wedding dress after all and special. Sarah had spent every day over the last few weeks creating this dress. Elizabeth would return the dress to Sarah after the wedding and tell her to save it for her own day, a day she hoped would come to this shy sister she loved. Elizabeth experienced a giddy pleasure as she slipped the dress on.

There was a knock at the door, and Esther and Anne entered. Elizabeth watched her sister form her brows into a frown as she saw the dress. Both sisters took pride in the simplicity of their lives. When Sarah turned to help Elizabeth fasten the dress, Esther placed her finger to Anne's lips and shook her head. Esther had become rather protective of Sarah. Anne knew Esther was right. Elizabeth must wear the beautiful dress. Only the family and the naval chaplain would be there for the ceremony anyway.

Esther excused herself from the room. "I am going to prepare a meal for the family while you girls have some time together."

Elizabeth's brothers Jacob, Gratianus, and Charles along with her father, Barry and his wife, Liza as well as Sarah and Esther traveled to the ceremony, requiring renting a second wagon to hold all seven of them. The younger Hart siblings stayed home.

They were a dozen in all by the time the chaplain joined them. John presented a short charge to the couple. The naval chaplain gave the exchange of vows, pronounced them husband and wife, wished the couple well, and said he must return to his duties.

Esther prepared a meal of goat stew, seasoned rice, and a dessert of chocolate she had made at home for the celebration. The chocolates had melted slightly but were relished. After the meal, Barry offered a prayer of thanksgiving for these two daughters he loved so much, and it brought an ache to his heart. Weary, he wondered if he would live to see his second family married. He felt old as he gave one last embrace to Annie's girls.

Barry rubbed his hip. "Please come and visit us in town when you can. This road to English Harbour is getting too rough for my old bones. I am happy for you, Elizabeth and Charles. Farewell, until you can come to town. You are always welcome."

Charles secured a small cottage only a few houses beyond where John and Anne lived. Over the last three weeks, he thoughtfully chose an assortment of needed furnishings and acquired a mongrel dog he named Brownie to help protect Elizabeth while he worked. Elizabeth brought a few kitchen items and linens from her cottage in town on her trip two days earlier. Yesterday, she and Anne stocked the small pantry with necessary provisions from the nearby shop. Tonight, Charles and his bride walked home together arm in arm to the beginning of a partnership, a union blessed by God, despite what others might say. The night was full of salty sea air, the sounds of tree frogs, and a glow wrapping this unlikely couple in a love bright with promise.

# 26

# The King's Men

*1805*

On the first Sunday after her marriage, Elizabeth rejoiced to see Quano again at the worship services. She looked at the small woman standing next to Quano, whose large expressive eyes glanced first to Quano with affection and admiration. Elizabeth said, "Quano, please introduce me to your wife."

"Me happy for you to meet me wife, Molly."

Elizabeth gave a curtsey. "I am glad to know you, Molly. I am Elizabeth. Anne told me about your coming to her class. Quano was one of our best students."

"Quano, he told me you teached him how to read. Now he teach me to read."

Elizabeth knelt to greet the child who hid behind his mother's skirt.

With obvious pride Molly told Elizabeth, "Quano be one good artist too, he tell me you be first artist to show he how to draw."

Taken aback, Elizabeth was trying to recall when she had shared with her father's slave how to draw, and Quano could see she was trying to remember.

"Mistress, it be long time ago you try to show me how to make my letters, and you draw a picture wid charcoal on de walls of de drying shed. Me neber forget how dat stir de longing to draw. Mr. Charles, he call what I do mo-saic. He get permission for me to have small bits of scrap when I cut de sailcloth for de boats. I sew dem scraps together and draw on dem with charcoal. Den I cover it with de juice dat comes from de tree, and de charcoal it not smear."

"Quano, what a wonderful thing that you create beauty from something discarded. I would love to see your art."

"Mr. Charles, he tell me you gonna say dat, and me make one for you, mistress." Smiling, Quano tapped his wife on her arm, and she took from her bag a small frame with a creation unlike anything Elizabeth had ever seen. Carefully pieced together and shaded with charcoal, the scene was the Dockyard, a mosaic of many small bits of sailcloth, replicating one of the large ships with many sails.

Regarding him with wonder Elizabeth exclaimed, "This is beautiful Quano! So skillfully pieced, and then covered with sap to preserve the drawing. This is an amazing work of art. Thank you. You have rare talent."

Quano lowered his eyes. "Mr. Charles, he make de frame. Your husband he say de sailors might buy."

Elizabeth smiled at her husband. "Charles, you have kept some secrets from me. You told me you worked with Quano in the Dockyard. I didn't know you were helping him develop such a skill."

Charles nodded and smiled at Quano. "We men enjoy surprising the ladies. But Quano has all the artistic talent. I only made the frame."

When Elizabeth and Molly were in a quiet spot, Elizabeth asked, "Molly, do you live in The Middle Ground?"

"Yes'um, Quano he built me home dere."

"Are there many women living in Middle Ground? "

"Der be de bum boat women, two dem dat lives in Middle Ground."

"What is a bum boat woman? I have never heard about them."

"Dems be de womens what row der boats out to sell de produce to de sailors in de big ships. Dem no can go into de Dockyard to sell, de gate and de guards would stop dem. But dey row de boats out and can sell all dat dey grow to de big ships."

"Molly, I want to meet some of the women living in The Middle Ground."

"Jane Lake, she be friends wid me. I bring she someday to meet you. She be one smart bum boat woman."

"Please do. I want to meet Jane and the other women. Now we must go back and join the others before the service starts."

Not long after, the two sisters sat on Anne's veranda sharing the cool early morning sea breeze and the view of Falmouth Harbour. They met together most days for tea, served in Annie's dainty blue and white cups.

Elizabeth put her cup down, "I missed our talks together after you married, and especially after you moved here to English Harbour two years ago. I understood, since both Father and your John thought it was too arduous a trip and perhaps not a safe place for me to come visit."

Anne cleared her throat. "I confess I am not a very good example for you to follow as far as household accomplishments. Yet John and I could not be happier—unless God should bless us with a child of our own."

With a wistful look Elizabeth said, "During those years on the plantation, you and I were never involved in the laundry or much of the cooking. After we lost Mother, we were concerned with raising the boys and teaching the slaves. Others handled the domestic aspects of life."

"Yes, but even after I married and moved to town, I was never particularly interested in domestic undertakings. Thankfully, it satisfies John I have found goals to give me fulfillment. Our cottage requires little time to clean. The meals I prepare are little work, and I do our washing once a week."

A slow breath escaped as Anne said, "My husband totes water for drinking, bathing, and laundry from the large tank supplying the village. John had to remind me water is a luxury, and to use only as much as necessary. I weed and water our vegetable garden in the early mornings."

Elizabeth interrupted her sister's listing of chores. "But now you and I can set out to accomplish more challenging tasks. John comes first for you, as Charles comes first for me, but there is so much we can do here."

Elizabeth rose, stretching her arms apart. "Imagine the opportunities waiting for us. I am quite sure our husbands will join us as much as possible. I am looking forward to see what lies ahead for all of us." To sit idle for long would never suit these women. After tea, they would set off to the market to purchase food for dinner before their husbands came home.

Many days they assisted in the Negro hospital located in the hillside area above the Dockyard. Because there was an orderly there to tend to the men's physical needs, Elizabeth and Anne spent hours reading to the men or feeding them. Both John and Charles insisted the women always walk with either Tippet or Brownie to protect them. John drove a strong post into the earth outside the hospital, where they secured a tether for the dogs. The hospital had a generous veranda facing the Dockyard. Once a man had recovered enough to sit on the veranda, the ladies would bring the dog up to keep him company. At first the matron frowned at this, but came to understand it helped the patients.

The men also learned to amuse themselves during the long days as they recovered. One man recovering from a foot amputation often sat on the veranda. He had constructed a banjar made from a large hollowed-out calabash gourd covered with goatskin. With a few braided horsehairs stretched across a narrow neck, he could play a rather lively tune.

Daylight and sunset remained much the same year-round. Most people rose with the first rays of light near six a.m., and the sun descended about 12 hours later. The evening hours after the sun went down and the heat subsided made a productive time to read, study or write.

Sundays found both couples serving the believers gathered in the small Methodist chapel that Rev. Baxter started years before, and where John, and eventually Charles, shared God's Word. Elizabeth continued with her poetry and hymns, while Charles wrote notes for teaching or sermons. Anne often read aloud to John, or he wrote in his journals.

Several months after Elizabeth and Charles married, they sat reading side by side when Elizabeth set her book aside. "Charles, remember the Bible story of Mordecai saying to his cousin, Queen Esther, *who knew if she had come into the kingdom for such a time as this*? And Esther bravely went before the king even though she knew it was dangerous. I am aware how being here in English Harbour could maybe be unsafe."

Charles moved to kneel at her feet. "Do you think your life is in danger here in the Dockyard, Elizabeth?"

She looked deep into her husband's eyes. "No … no, Charles, I do not fear for my life, but perhaps something larger than I can see is happening here. I am elated to be with Anne again, trying to make a difference somewhere. I know the men in the hospital appreciate us reading to them and bringing food."

She ran her fingers through Charles's sun-bleached curls. "I remember how Queen Esther did not ask for anything right away when the king promised her up to half his kingdom. She waited and allowed the king to offer a third time before she told him what she wanted. God miraculously stopped the evil planned for the Jews. Esther waited for God's timing to accomplish what she desired."

Charles lay his head on Elizabeth's knees. "I would give you up to half of my kingdom. What is it you want, my dear Elizabeth?"

She touched his cheek. "God must surely grieve to see all the evil surrounding the lives of so many of the people here. He knows I want to do all I can to stop the injustice I see and feel. And the guilt. The guilt I have by being black and yet free. I wonder if it is like Queen Esther's secret guilt of being Jewish. I sense the men watching me as I read to them and maybe they wonder why I am free, and they remain enslaved."

"Elizabeth, I want you to feel free to do those things God has given you to do and I will never stop you. I do want to protect you. Please tell me if you ever imagine you are unsafe."

"The evenings when we teach together give me so much pleasure. I am striving to wait as Queen Esther did for the right time to prepare more of the slaves for the day their freedom finally comes."

Charles stood up and stretched his legs. "I, too, want to be building lives to glorify God instead of crafting vessels to sail the seas. When I asked you to marry me, I told you my goal was to join you as an educator, but when the Dockyard wanted me to continue—well, I thought it was good to do so. Let's pray and wait on God for direction."

Charles tousled her curls. "Almost anyone can feed patients at the hospital, though not all can read to them as well as you do. I know you have so much more you want to do than reading and feeding."

"I have no regrets. We will wait on God. Meanwhile, Anne has promised to take me to meet her Mrs. Looby, and we will begin to sew for some of the women from The Middle Ground I have seen visiting at the hospital."

"The commander has spoken to me about the King's request for reports on the progress of his slaves. The King allows most owners to prohibit their slaves from becoming educated, yet he expects those here in the naval yard to be well-trained. Many of the men are the same as Quano with unrecognized abilities. I want to train as many as I can who have an interest in spiritual understanding as well. I have heard the King is soon to emancipate his slaves serving in the West Indian Regiment stationed here."

# 27

# Loss and Gain

*1808*

Anne's knees felt weak when she saw her brother's expression as he stood at the door. He was silent, but his hands trembled as he reached out to her, and she knew at once her father was dead.

Jacob seldom visited them in English Harbour, and his arrival was a foreshadowing of news Anne did not want to hear. Though a loving brother, Jacob was not given to demonstrative acts. Now he held his arms out and wrapped Anne in a tight embrace before saying a word.

Though her mind was prepared, her heart was not ready to let her father go. Anne became all she was because of her parents' influence and support. After her mother died 24 years earlier, Anne grew to be even more dependent on her father's loving counsel. Although she was 40 years old, in that moment Anne felt childlike and orphaned.

On his way to Anne's house Jacob thought about how telling Anne would not be necessary. Still, he had not spoken a word. Knowing Anne would read his expression as she had done over the years, words would be unnecessary. Never able to disguise his guilt or sorrow, he was like an open book to her, and it was no different now. His face reflected his distress, and he appeared as if he had not slept.

"Does Elizabeth know?" Anne thought first of her sister.

At last, Jacob managed to say, "I thought it best if you tell her. I will let Charles and Gratianus know, but I wanted to tell you first."

"Of course, I will go to Elizabeth, and we need to be with Liza." Her brother responded with another tight embrace. Anne took a handkerchief from her pocket and blotted her brother's tears. "I need to wash my face before I go to Elizabeth. Can you take me?" Always efficient, Anne had already removed her apron, rinsed the tears and put on her hat while Jacob, quiet Jacob, sat in a porch chair staring ahead.

His father had been Jacob's advisor for so many years. Now he was adrift, in a sea of grief that threatened to drown him. As they walked down the path, Anne took Jacob's arm and squeezed it. No words had passed between them as they rode the short distance to their sister's house. When they stopped and Jacob helped her down, he regained his voice. "Father enriched our lives with countless things. God blessed us beyond measure with our father."

Anne realized Jacob had been storing up his words to summarize his thoughts, and he had said it well. He left to tell the sad news to his two brothers.

Elizabeth came down the steps and saw Jacob driving away. Her hand flew to cover her mouth as she tried to hold back her tears. Her eyes held the question she could not express. Anne rushed to embrace her sister, and the two rocked back and forth. Again, Anne took out her handkerchief. Jacob's tears had not yet dried on the thin linen, but she handed it to Elizabeth.

"Father?"

Anne began to rub comforting circles on her sister's back, over and over, tenderly comforting her. Anne believed it somehow brought the memory of their beloved mother into their sorrow. "Yes, Father joined our Lord last night, and Jacob has gone to tell Gratianus and Charles."

Stepping back, Anne spoke brokenly, "I can picture their reunion in heaven with Father and Mother sitting at the feet of Jesus. Mother has been gone so long, but we have never stopped missing her. We should go to Liza and the children. Can you be ready in an hour? We should go to the naval yard and tell our husbands first."

Having obtained permission to take his wife and Elizabeth to town, John did not talk on the ride as he listened to the sisters sharing stored up memories of their father. He always admired Barry Hart, and now John realized even more the privilege of having him in his life.

When they arrived at the Hart home, John asked Anne and Elizabeth if they wanted him to wait, while they sat with Liza and her children. Anne smiled. "Can you please return for us in an hour?"

Elizabeth and Anne needed time with all of them, the seven younger children, Liza, and Esther. George, at age 22, was the oldest of Barry's sons from his second family and he began taking charge of the arrangements. The family had known this day was coming. Barry himself, as his heart weakened, gave George a list of all the necessary things to do when he died. As John prepared to drive the wagon away, Joseph caught up with him.

John held out his hand. "I am sorry to hear of your father's passing. All who knew him feel your loss. I am included on the list of those who cared for and admired him. Is there any way I can help?"

The young man patted John's horse. "Thank you, sir. Father arranged with the chapel for many of the necessary things, and I have just spoken with the preacher. The funeral will be tomorrow at 10 a.m. I'll go and give Mother the details."

As John left, his sorrow for the family who loved this generous man weighed on him like a heavy cloak. Over the last 10 years of marriage to Anne, John's admiration increased as he gained insight into Barry's character. Anne told John that Barry had even purchased the land where the leadership had built the church.

The next day the Methodist church in town overflowed, and many stood outside waiting to pay their respects. Even Esther, who never yet attended the chapel, wanted to go to the service. She sat between Anne and Elizabeth, her arms encircling the sisters who took her in many years before.

The mourners' pure, sweet voices sang with joy about heaven, lifting the spirit of the solemn event as they sang, "*We're Marching to Zion, Beautiful Zion*." Anne stretched across Esther to grasp her sister's hand, remembering the day Father had shared news of William Wilberforce, and Elizabeth had danced around them, singing about *marching to Zion*.

As Barry had requested, his seven sons sang Charles Wesley's hymn, "*Oh, for a Thousand Tongues to Sing*." In Barry Hart's life he had not only lifted his voice to sing God's praise, but he had also lived out his faith before his fellow man.

The next day Elizabeth anticipated helping in the hospital. Work would ease the sorrow of losing her father. A familiar guard at the entrance to the Dockyard greeted Elizabeth and Anne as they asked permission to visit the patients. Sergeant Dorsett saluted the two ladies. "God bless you. I know the men in the hospital are grateful for your time spent reading and helping them."

Sergeant Dorsett respected and appreciated their untiring work. Occasionally sailors spoke rudely when they passed, but the Sergeant always spoke politely. Elizabeth sometimes took him an extra coconut bun they baked for the men in the Negro hospital. The buns were usually fresh out of her stone oven behind her cottage. The sweet smell of coconut filled the air as they walked past the entrance.

As Elizabeth and Anne entered the hospital, the matron called Elizabeth aside. "Henry is close to death and is asking for you. Start with him since he might not last much longer."

"I'm sorry. Of course, I will see him first. Thank you for telling me."

"Hello, Henry." Elizabeth knew not to ask how he was doing. His appearance made it obvious he would not live long. His cheeks were sunken, his lips dry, his hair matted. There were not many chairs, but Elizabeth spied one and brushed it off, pulling it near enough she could smell Henry's stale breath. She put out her hand, and he took it.

"I understand you asked for me. Is there something I can do for you?"

Henry cleared his throat, "You remember you once try tell me de story of Joseph from de Bible and how he become a slave?"

"Yes, Henry, I love that story. And like your life, Joseph's life had many difficulties, perhaps the worst when his own brothers sold him into slavery. Many wrongs took place through no fault of his own. Joseph told his brothers *you meant it for evil, but God meant it for good*. Henry, you have had many difficulties in life, and perhaps it seemed everyone meant evil against you."

"Yes'um. You can no tell me what it feels to die, you don be dere yet. Me be 'fraid, Mistress Elizabeth."

Elizabeth stroked his hand. "I know since you have believed on Jesus and turned to Him, you are my brother, and heaven is our home. Do you want me to stay here with you?"

Henry struggled to pull a string from his neck, revealing a single dark blue bead. He placed the worn-out string with the single bead in her hand. "Dis be Africa bead. You told me you don' never been dere, but me be a child of Africa. Dis is all me have left of me home, and now I know heaven soon be me new home. So, me give you dis part of me home, to give you a memory of Henry."

Elizabeth clutched the bead in her hand. "I will treasure this. Neither I nor my parents ever lived in Africa, but my heart aches for those ripped from their homeland. Jesus waits for you with a new heavenly homeland. Thank you, Henry."

He turned calm, and his breathing grew shallower as sweat dripped from his body. Elizabeth went to ask the matron for a cloth for Henry's face, and when she returned to Henry's bed, she saw only the remaining empty shell. The slave was truly free. Elizabeth wiped the weathered face and went to find the matron.

Over the next year the scene was repeated several times. Both Anne and Elizabeth sat at the bedside of other slaves who belonged to the King, but men who often had no family.

Elizabeth did not wear jewelry much, but she strung the blue bead from Africa on a fresh piece of twine and hung it around her neck. The bead reminded her to pray for all the Henrys whose lives crossed paths with hers.

# 28

# The Birth of Sunday School

*1809*

Surveying the morning from her front window, Elizabeth watched people carrying water from the nearby catchment. Often it was young children toting heavy buckets, or women gracefully balancing a full bucket on their head. While observing these people eagerly collecting water necessary for their day, she spotted Anne briskly approaching their home. Anne usually strolled, but today her steps indicated purpose. Noticing her sister, Anne removed her sizeable hat and waved it in the air, a sure sign an interesting conversation would follow. Stepping onto the veranda, Elizabeth raised her eyebrows. Anne was almost running, and she rarely ran.

"Good morning! Clearly you have come with news."

Out of breath, Anne gave Elizabeth a quick embrace. Dropping into a rocker, she fanned her overheated face with her hat.

"I'll get the tea, and then you can tell me what has you in such a state." Elizabeth turned to go, but Anne put her hand out to stop her. "Let the tea wait. I am ready to burst with news!"

Elizabeth's quiet morning brightened with her sister's enthusiasm. "Serious news always requires a cup of tea first, so this must be wonderful news. Tell me."

"I met this morning with Mr. Light, the Moravian missionary who arrived last week. He told me of a movement that is working in South Carolina that effectively teaches slaves. What he told me may very well be the answer to our prayer to share more of God's Word with those who desperately need help. They call the movement Sunday School."

"Is Mr. Light going to begin an endeavor like they have in South Carolina?" Elizabeth slipped a question in while Anne paused to take a breath.

Anne shut her eyes to arrange her thoughts. "He believes English Harbour to be the right location for a Sunday School, and he believes we are the right people to start it! We would start the first Sunday School in the Caribbean."

Her mouth dropped open. Finally, Elizabeth managed to sputter, "You and me? And what is a Sunday School?"

Raising her hand as if she were requiring silence from a classroom, Anne sprang from her rocker and began to pace while continuing. "In America, some plantation masters have realized that teaching the slaves does not incite them to rebel. Rather, Biblical teaching helps the slaves have purpose. You see, the teachers come from the churches and use the Bible as their basis for teaching reading, doctrine, and Christian character."

An amazed Elizabeth ran her hands through her hair. "Why us?"

Words Anne had been preparing as she walked to her sister's house tumbled out. "So many reasons make us well fitted to take on this endeavor. He learned of our years of teaching our siblings, and he told me he has heard others talk of the efforts we made to help the slaves on Father's plantation. He also knows about the school you helped start in town for Negro students. Mr. Light believes John and Charles will add credibility when we speak to the plantation owners." She paused. "I need some tea now."

"We both need tea now and time to consider and pray about this. What will Charles and John think about such a bold idea?" Elizabeth shook her head to let Anne's words settle down and take root as she began to grasp this challenge and opportunity.

Anne followed and began to set out their mother's teacups. When Elizabeth returned with the kettle, she smiled at Anne's choice of cups. "Mother would be so pleased to know we are fulfilling the dreams she had for us. Though she has been gone nearly 25 years, I still miss her daily. How will we begin?"

Anne gave a knowing nod. "Exactly why I came to see you, because I have no idea how we will do this. Even so, I believe God will allow us to do this together with our husbands. Just think, if Mr. Light is correct, no one has attempted such an effort in the Caribbean. He believes we should follow the pattern of Robert Raikes. He is a generous British gentleman who began a school for boys in the London slums. His idea was to have schools on Sunday since they worked all week. The concept began in England and has now spread to America."

Elizabeth interrupted with one of the many challenges swirling through her mind. "How could one man make his idea work in England and then succeed with the example going to America?"

Bursting to explain, Anne raised her teacup and smiled. "Providentially, Mr. Raikes is a printer and a publisher. England had no system for teaching the masses. Thirty years ago, Mr. Raikes began to distribute small printed manuals for teaching the alphabet and spelling." Anne paused and sipped the fragrant soursop-lemongrass tea.

Elizabeth's excitement grew as Anne described Mr. Raikes. "Yes, I read that Britain only recently enacted a law limiting the hours a child may work to 12 hours a day. That sounds rather close to the slavery we have here."

Anne agreed. "Yes, for many, the Sunday schools are their only opportunity to learn to read and write. Parents who don't go to church are insisting their children attend. Raikes uses the Bible as a textbook, and his pattern for these weekly schools spread to the shores of the former colonies, where it is now established. I believe we can follow his plan, Elizabeth!"

"Will the plantation owners allow this?" Elizabeth sounded skeptical.

"We will propose to owners that this kind of teaching will actually improve the behavior and increase the productivity of their slaves."

As she sipped her tea and rocked, Elizabeth spoke with excitement. "Thanks be to God for all those who have prepared the way. Our grandfather Hart ensured Father receive a superior education, and Grandfather Clearkley sent Mother away to England to university. Then Father and Mother instilled in us a love of learning. Dear Anne, we must extend our education as far as we can. How blessed we are, both then and now." Anne set her teacup down and began pacing again as ideas of how to accomplish this undertaking crowded her mind.

The couples sat together that evening. The men listened with delight, watching their wives hatch their plan.

"You girls resemble the chickens in the pen behind our cottage, laying more eggs than both families can eat. Charles and I both enjoy the eggs those chickens lay, and the ideas you two hatch have clearly been from God." John patted Anne's hand approvingly. "Time for us to head to our own cottage and feed those wonderful egg layers."

As Elizabeth and Anne thought of what lay ahead, they realized they could not exert pressure on those powers that kept slavery operating as a system, but they could give the enslaved people hope and encouragement for a day when slavery would end. They would prepare them to live productive, independent lives, transformed from within.

The next Sunday, after a hasty departure from the services in English Harbour, the four traveled to Lyons Estate, having already developed a relationship with the management there. John assured the estate overseer, Mr. Westfield, that teaching slaves to understand and follow the Word of God would not result in rebellion. Instead, it would produce better workers. Charles explained they had learned of the system used in other countries. The results held promise for both the owners and the slaves.

Mr. Westfield conveyed his approval, "I would certainly welcome workers who have an understanding about God, and I trust you will encourage them to be obedient."

Anne smiled at Elizabeth.

The men made plans and shook hands. Charles reassured the overseer, "We will encourage them to follow all of God's Word."

They returned the following Sunday. Charles had prepared a board to mark with marl. Antigua had an abundant supply of marl, the soft chalk-type limestone that could serve as a writing instrument on a dark painted board. Much of what they could teach would be by rote memory, and many of the slaves were very apt in remembering and reciting whatever they heard.

John addressed the workers who had quietly gathered under a shelter. "Brothers and sisters, we are here to share the Word of God with you. We have permission to teach each of you to read and understand God's written word for yourselves. How many of you desire to learn to read?"

There was confusion among the people. The silence of only moments before was now a cacophony of voices.

A large man who appeared to be the spokesperson called out, "Who you be?"

"I am John Gilbert, and this is my wife, Anne." He directed their attention to Anne, then nodding toward Charles, he said, "This is my friend Charles Thwaites and his wife, Elizabeth."

Again, the noise of the group rose. "If you will give us your names, we will write them on this board. Each Sunday we will come and teach any who want to learn. Form a line and give your name to Mr. Thwaites."

The first Sunday, 35 workers lined up, gave their names, and stayed to watch as the alphabet was written on the board. The following Sunday, the group swelled to almost 80. Charles had prepared for more students by bringing an additional three dark painted boards and several pieces of marl. They divided the group according to ages, and all four began to teach.

The following week, upon their arrival, Anne tapped her sister's hand and pointed to a large nearby rock. Someone had used the marl left the week before to write names on the rock. They were learning and retaining all that was being offered.

Elizabeth clapped her hands to gain attention from her group, a cheerful assortment of young adults. "Please follow me. My class will sit under the beautiful flamboyant tree while I teach you Psalm 100."

The weary but eager faces of the young shone with anticipation. "I imagine all of you enjoy singing. This is God telling us to come to Him singing. These verses include all of us because it says all the lands. God takes pleasure in hearing you lift your voices. These verses remind us we belong to Him. I have never been enslaved, but I too have a master, and He is Jesus. So, I want you to say after me, '*Make a joyful noise unto the Lord, all ye lands*.'"

In unison they repeated what Elizabeth had said. "Again," Elizabeth repeated, and they followed her words. "Again."

Elizabeth recited the first ten words of Psalm 100. Only a few were unable to remember them. "Beautiful. Well done. You have learned a verse. Now we will learn the second verse that tells us to sing." Elizabeth repeated the next 11 words, "*Serve the Lord with gladness; come before His presence with singing*." She thrilled as she witnessed the enthusiasm spreading. They were learning scripture, and she prayed they would soon grasp not only words but the truths within those words. She hoped many would come to place their trust, their hope, not only in learning about, but also in understanding the One who had given these words of hope to all people.

As they lay in bed after an exhausting day of teaching, Anne turned to John. "When my father owned slaves, I never saw what I am experiencing at these other plantations. The inconceivable darkness of the world that many slaves inhabited was difficult to understand. Now, I also better understand the diabolical superstition they have learned and believed. The magical rituals … the sorcery of obeah and witchcraft … is firmly rooted in the hearts of so many, adding to the thievery and other evils. Only God could plan what we are doing, John. My dreams are taking shape, and I have hope for the future. I never imagined how many we would be able to teach. Colour makes no difference in the mind of a soul wanting to learn. I pray many of these have their names written not only in our earthly ledgers but also in the Lamb's book of life."

John kissed the tip of her nose. "What an arduous but rewarding day. Those mosquitoes tonight had a feast on your lovely face."

Anne rubbed at a bite. "The bites on my face are not bad, and I can manage most of the vermin, but I loathe the chiggers nibbling between my toes. I wish we did not need to teach beside the chicken coops with all the creatures waiting for fresh blood to feast on." Anne rubbed her feet together, scratching the many bites on her toes and legs from chiggers that liked to burrow under the skin. "The chiggers are worse than the mosquitoes!"

Elizabeth's excitement radiated from her smile as she visited Anne. "Charles has decided we need to purchase a second wagon! He received permission to teach at the Horsford Estate." Month after month the number of slaves learning to read increased. Year after year their enthusiasm grew as they watched God at work.

Two years later Elizabeth proclaimed to Anne as she held out her ledger, "Charles says that in our eight separate Sunday schools we have taught more than 1,800 scholars. I never dreamed we could reach so many who could not read."

The two couples never seemed to tire of long dusty wagon rides to the numerous estates where they had permission to teach. Anne looked out one morning to see her sister waving a letter in the air. Elizabeth was out of breath, "After four years of teaching slaves Sunday school, the Church Missionary Society has at last hired Charles. He resigned his work at the Dockyard yesterday. Now we can increase our evening schools."

Soon over 1,200 were learning in the evenings on 26 estates scattered across the island. Only a few years later as the foursome sat together, Elizabeth focused on adding all the columns in Charles's ledger. She shut the journal and wiped happy tears. "Our journals indicate over 3,000 students, and Charles has hired 21 different instructors to help." John softly said, "God be praised. He has blessed beyond measure all our hopes and dreams."

Charles concluded, "The teachers include 16 free blacks, four coloureds, and one white man. I am thankful they continue to do this with a pay of only a mere three to four dollars every month. Our mighty God has blessed His work."

One Sunday, as they arrived early to a new estate, they saw a christening of slaves taking place. The four climbed from the wagon and watched while slaves, all dressed in clean frocks, advanced one by one to the front steps of the plantation master's house. There the priest placed a few drops of water on their foreheads as each received a new name.

John gritted his teeth. "I see no instruction. I see empty ritual. I could believe the master believes christening them might prevail when the whip has failed. They resemble cattle being driven to a pond for water."

Anne tightened her grip on her husband's arm. "Perhaps it is by the same reasoning they have allowed us to teach. We know there is no merit in this ritual, but we will teach the Word in its fullness, and pray God transforms hearts. I pray they are drawn to someone much greater than a master granting a new name, along with new clothes."

*1813*

One evening Charles called when he came home, "Elizabeth! I have news. We are building a proper school!"

Elizabeth had been preparing their supper in the cook shed outside. She stepped inside their cottage with a steaming pot. "Good evening, Charles. Come, sit down, and I will give you some supper—breadfruit and yams."

Charles washed his hands in the basin she set out for him. He flung the towel over the chair as he straddled it. "Elizabeth, will you thank the Lord for all his provisions, for food, and for the promise of a school building … a proper schoolroom. My heart is racing, thinking of how excited I am." Elizabeth prayed and then handed Charles a plate of steaming vegetables.

"Where will we build this proper school, Charles?"

Charles blew on his breadfruit and set his fork down. "We will build it halfway between Lyons Estate and English Harbour." He took a paper from his pocket and held it up. "They have granted permission to build a room that will hold at least 50 students. We can start preparing the wood this week. We have permission for some of the slaves to help build it, when they are not working!"

# 29

# A New Ministry

*1816*

The graceful blue teacups rested on the small table between Anne and Elizabeth as they sat on the veranda overlooking English Harbour. The sisters met daily to consider their work.

Anne sipped the aromatic ginger tea, then abruptly set her cup down, sloshing tea onto the small table between them. As Anne mopped up the spill, she looked at Elizabeth. "Years ago, Mother told me to speak for those who had no voice. Elizabeth, it is time we begin to expand our vision."

Elizabeth leaned forward, "I agree. The training is going well with the men. We both keep talking about the needs, yet perhaps we now bravely enact a broader plan. Society seldom gives women approval to be involved in organizing relief for those in distress. How can we dare to think the public will accept our ideas?"

Anne touched her sister's hands and stepped inside the house. She returned to the veranda gripping something behind her back. She dropped a book on Elizabeth's lap. In bold letters on the cover Anne had written, *Records of the Society for Relief of Orphans and Destitute.* Elizabeth picked up the large green book and ran her fingers over the title. Opening it slowly, she read the first entry and then gasped, "You have already received support from Lady Grey? When did this happen, and why haven't you told me?"

Taking the ledger back and clutching it to her chest, Anne declared, "Yesterday, John traveled to see the governor, and I rode along with him. I planned to walk about town while they talked. But Lady Grey, who heard about our work, came out to greet me. I shared with her some of our ideas for relief at English Harbour. Lady Grey went inside and returned with this blank ledger. She had tucked a generous contribution inside to begin the Society for the Relief of Orphans and Destitute. She suggested the name and told me she will write to others asking them to support our organization. Think about it, Elizabeth. We have a beginning!"

Elizabeth clasped her hands tightly. "Only God could have met this need! He granted you an opportunity to meet with a thoughtful benefactress, who has caught our vision for a relief society, which lacked only the funds to begin. What do we do next?"

The wooden floorboards creaked, as Anne paced the room. She resembled a general marching while planning an attack. "Lady Grey advised that first we search for a suitable house, second we assist children ages 12 and younger, and third we help destitute women too ill or old to work. I agreed."

Plans were formulating for both sisters, but they needed a pattern to follow. Their ideas went beyond what they had been able to accomplish so far.

Elizabeth soon saw an article in the newspaper about Mrs. Joanna Bethune's work. She started the first society to help the poor and destitute of New York. Many ridiculed her efforts and jested about her worthy cause. Elizabeth wrote asking for suggestions about establishing such an organization in Antigua. The contact resulted in Mrs. Bethune becoming a supporter of the Society for Diseased and Destitute Slaves of Antigua. Her father had been stationed in Antigua years before, giving her an interest in their little island.

The very name of the society stirred up anger from most of the planters. They would be even more upset once they realized the organization in New York supported the sisters by sending books, clothing, and funds. British women's groups soon joined in the efforts.

Months after writing Mrs. Bethune, the sisters glanced up from their usual tea as Charles pulled up in the wagon and wrestled with a large crate. Elizabeth ran down the veranda steps. "Let me help, Charles."

Anne called out, "Dear Mrs. Bethune. Is this another crate from her?"

Charles shook his head. "This crate appears to be from an Anne Gilman of Alexandria, Virginia. News of you girls is spreading. The crate is addressed to Elizabeth, but I imagine by its size it must be for your Orphan Society."

Their anticipation made them as eager as children. Elizabeth implored Charles, "Please, open it, while I fix your tea." Charles affectionately ran his hand across his wife's cheek to calm her and went for the pry bar.

The nails screeched as Charles pried open the wood slats. Both sisters shrieked with delight when they saw the open crate filled with children's clothing. Anne lifted an elegant note nestled among the treasures and handed it to Elizabeth.

Unfolding the lavender-scented note she read aloud.

> Dear Anne Gilbert and Elizabeth Thwaites,
>
> I am a friend of Joanna Bethune of New York. We met when she traveled to Washington, D.C., speaking on behalf of her Benevolent Society. I learned her organization was the first to organize women to provide humanitarian aid to poor women and children. The Washington Times had published an article about her work, and I was delighted to meet her. I mentioned to her that my husband is a ship-merchant who sends his ships to the islands for molasses. Mrs. Bethune spoke of your worthy endeavors and the organizations you have begun. Since meeting, we have been corresponding and I know she has sent you books and clothing, as well as funds. At her suggestion I prepared this crate of children's clothing to send when my husband sent a ship to Antigua.

Elizabeth paused to examine the items. "Anne, here are precious baby things."

Holding up a small baby wrapper, Anne exclaimed, "These appear to be new and of high quality. How thoughtful of this woman whom we will probably never meet. Keep reading!"

Elizabeth clutched a tiny blanket in her arms as she finished the note from Mrs. Gilman.

The Lord has blessed my husband Ephraim and me with three healthy children, but we also lost several infants shortly after birth. I was unable to bear touching the things I sewed with such expectation for those babies we lost. I trust you will find mothers of infants that need these on your island. My prayer is these mothers will have babies who thrive. Included also are some clothing my girls have grown past being able to wear. My daughter Malvina, who is nine, wanted to include one of her favorite dresses.

Sincerely,

Mrs. Anne Gilman, Alexandria, Virginia

Delving deeper, Anne pulled out some colourful dresses for the girls. Elizabeth joined the search. "I will write and thank Mrs. Gilman for this generous donation and tell her more about our society. How thoughtful of Mrs. Bethune to encourage Mrs. Gilman. What joy to have wonderful, generous women who want to help those in need!"

Anne stretched deeper into the crate and caressed a lacy white baby gown. "I know of several expectant mothers who will be overjoyed by the baby clothes."

At age 49, Anne, who could be a grandmother at this point if she had married when young, tried not to think of how much she wished to be the one expecting an infant. The thought often came to her how God had blessed her with many little ones to aid over the years. Still, they were not her own children. Seeing these beautiful creations revived the longings. She did not hear Elizabeth approach with a fresh cup of tea.

Setting the tea down, her sister kissed her cheek. "The longing is still there for me too. Charles often reminds me we could never do what we do for hundreds of needy children if we had our own to care for. I know you know this, but God allows us to mother so many who need us."

Lifting her cup, Anne reflected, "I need this tea now. As always, you are the thoughtful one, reminding me God's plan is greater than my own desires. Do you ever wonder if you and I would have become as close as we have if Mother had lived? When we lost her, it was as though God joined the two of us to become a mere part of what she was. Now, let's decide to whom we will give these lovely gifts."

Anticipating the Dockyard's downsizing, Anne and John would soon be moving to St. John's. Still, Elizabeth determined she would carry on with the ideas she and Anne had begun. The need in English Harbour to help those in want of food, shelter, and clothing was immense. The funds supplied from women's organizations in Britain and Lady Grey made possible the purchase of a house, setting in motion a haven for those women and children in desperate circumstances. The Women's Refuge started as an elusive dream, but with the house's provision, it emerged a reality. The sisters created a home offering security and hope.

As Elizabeth took her daily walk, she felt compelled to talk with a young girl she saw beside the boats. Her tangle of matted hair both repelled and drew Elizabeth. Even from a distance, her appearance spoke of neglect, and Elizabeth could guess how an army of critters had easily established residence in the girl's hair. For years, Elizabeth and Anne had inspected their siblings' hair each morning. Once a month, they spent a morning trimming everyone's hair, even their father's. She knew all too well the challenges, even when keeping vigilant.

The girl appeared to be about nine years old with a tattered dress that was far too large for her small frame, most likely a cast-off from an older child. Elizabeth came close enough to notice her large but vacant brown eyes. Neither sadness nor anger were present. She appeared empty—alive, but dead, breathing but hardly aware of life. Love, food, then a bath, and a sturdy comb to untangle the child's natty hair might restore some measure of life to the waif.

The next day Elizabeth noticed the child sitting under the same tree as the day before, but she seemed skittish. She must approach her carefully. Elizabeth needed a way to attract her interest and win her trust without scaring the girl. A stray cat ran out from behind a rubbish barrel, and an idea came to Elizabeth. Perhaps Patches, her calico cat, might create a bridge between them. She was precisely the sort of child the newly formed Women's Refuge Society intended to help.

Returning later the same day, Elizabeth carried Patches. She approached slowly, holding the cat in view. The waif was startled, yet at the sight of the cat, the girl's mouth opened, and she drew in a relaxed breath, her eyes displayed a flicker of life.

Gently Elizabeth moved Patches closer. "She is fond of children. Do you want to hold her and feel her purr?"

The child stroked Patches with her small hand, glancing at Elizabeth.

Shyness evaporated. As the child held the calico cat, her dark eyes shone with pleasure.

Patches seemed to sense how important it was that she not squirm away but give comfort to the girl with her rhythmic purring. Now, Elizabeth thought she could begin to question the girl without frightening her. "I'm Elizabeth, and this is my cat, Patches. What's your name?"

"Dems call me Gloria."

Elizabeth knew she must be patient. "Who calls you Gloria, your mother?"

Gloria stopped petting Patches. "Me no got no mudder."

Elizabeth asked, "Who cares for you?"

Looking blank, the child blankly asserted, "Don' needs nobody. Some dem people gives me food for to eat. Me sleeps 'pon canvas down by dem boats. Me got blanket an' so."

With her heart burdened by the thought of the child surviving alone in the world, Elizabeth's words tumbled forth. "Gloria, come with Patches and me to my house."

An expression of disbelief changing to fear crossed the soiled face. Then she pursed her lips and sucked her teeth, making a rude sound.

At home Elizabeth's brothers had occasionally used the disrespectful teeth-sucking noise to display their annoyance. Both sisters had forbidden the offensive gesture.

"Wha mus' me do if me goes wid you?" The child looked skeptical.

Ignoring the rude sound, Elizabeth ached at the thought of those who may have taken advantage of a girl who lacked a protector.

"Well, you might help me feed Patches. She is always hungry. Are you hungry, Gloria?" Elizabeth would not believe the child if she denied being hungry. Her skeletal arms and legs proved otherwise.

"Me hungry bad now. Me wan' hold Patches."

"Patches would love for you to carry her home. I don't live far. Follow me and hold tight to Patches in case we pass a dog. She is not fond of dogs."

The girl followed Elizabeth. She was thankful Charles was away speaking to a plantation owner. A white man might frighten her.

Pondering a plan, Elizabeth knew food must be the priority. She hoped Charles had not eaten all the banana cake. Offering her a sweet food first resembled a bribe, but it might keep her interested.

"Bring Patches into the house, please, Gloria. I will see what we can feed her and what you might eat." Elizabeth smiled with relief to see some banana cake still on the table. Cutting a good-sized slice, she placed it on a plate, resisting the urge to ask Gloria to wash her hands before eating. Elizabeth placed a bowl on the floor with some goat milk for Patches. Then she sat down adding some bread and cheese to the plate which her guest devoured in minutes.

"Gloria, Patches usually takes a nap after she eats. If I put a blanket on the floor, she would curl up beside you."

Elizabeth pulled out her favorite quilt and placed it in a corner on the floor. Patches padded over to the quilt, circled three times, then curled up into a tight ball. The child followed the cat and lay beside her, also curled in a protective ball. Both needed a bath, but nothing was as important as giving security first.

Unexpected tears of both hope and joy ran down Elizabeth's cheeks. Patches had bridged the way, bringing the girl closer to accepting help. But what would help the most? What should her next step be? Elizabeth lay down alongside the child. Charles found them asleep together when he came home, recognizing instantly the girl as the one Elizabeth had been seeking to assist.

He smiled noticing Elizabeth's well-loved quilt, the one her mother had made for her many years before. Charles had never known Annie Hart, but he imagined this use of her handiwork would please her. He gazed towards the picture Elizabeth had painted years before of her mother, Annie, and her children. He whispered to the painting, "A beautiful sight, isn't it, Annie Hart?"

Seeing Elizabeth asleep, Charles decided to visit a sailor he wanted to invite to church. Soldiers and sailors overflowed the small community, men whose morals were as absent as the wives they left behind in England. Charles also wanted to reach out to these men.

When the child woke from her nap, she rubbed her eyes and began to finger the quilt. "This be pretty, and me tinks me dreaming. Where be Patches?"

"Patches will be back shortly," said Elizabeth. "My mother made the quilt for me when I was about your age. How old are you, Gloria?"

"Me no know how old me be. How you know how old you be?"

Sad the child had no idea of her age, Elizabeth answered, "I was born in 1771, so I am 44 years old. I can add numbers, so I know my age. Do you want to learn how to add numbers? I know children can learn to read and to understand numbers if they go to school. Would you want to go to school?"

Elizabeth suspected this was too many questions. She watched as the child stood up and began to make her way towards the door. "Mama done told me not to talk wid people, an here you be makin' me talk."

"Gloria, wait. I'm sorry I asked so many questions. I thought you told me you don't have a mama. Do you?"

Her eyes darted back and forth between Elizabeth and the door. Elizabeth knew she must recover any trust gained earlier. "How about a cup of tea, Gloria? While the kettle boils, we can go together to search for Patches."

"Me like Patches, and me like tea, but me no wan' read or know 'bout numbers."

Realizing the love of reading comes with the rhythm, and the rhyme with the beauty of words, Elizabeth knew it might not work today. But she would not give in to her setbacks about reaching this child and so many others.

"The kettle is on. Shall we go look for Patches? You may call her." They stepped outside, and the girl shouted, "Patches! Patches!" Thankfully, the cat came bounding over the fields right up to Gloria and began rubbing against her leg.

"You made a friend, Gloria. I must cook some dinner. Do you want me to tell you a story while I prepare dinner? The water might be ready for tea now, and you could have another slice of banana cake. Can you please bring Patches into the cottage for me?" Elizabeth turned, hoping Gloria would follow her.

Elizabeth stood with her back to the door, praying the girl would stay while the cat purred contentedly. "Thank you for bringing Patches inside. Do you take sugar in your tea?"

Turning, Elizabeth set the cup on the table. "If you want to add sugar there is a spoon." The child edged towards the table and took a seat as Elizabeth placed a slice of banana cake beside the tea. Amused, she observed the girl adding heaping spoons of sugar into the cup until it overflowed.

Petting Patches while she drank her tea, Gloria sat mesmerized by Elizabeth's storytelling. Elizabeth cut up vegetables to add to rice for their evening meal while continuing the story. Soft words linked in an imaginative tale might be almost as powerful as the purr of a loveable calico cat.

Soon Elizabeth noticed the little one's head drooping. She stopped the story, picked the child up, and laid her back on the quilt. How tired Gloria must be, and the thought of her sleeping under a canvas sent cold chills down Elizabeth's arms. What was next? How long before she could offer the child a bath without her bolting?

The cake had worked as a bribe. An offer of a new dress might entice the child to bathe. Elizabeth remembered a piece of soft pink fabric she had set aside when sewing dresses for the Refuge. Measurements were unnecessary. The dress could be small because the child was painfully thin.

Charles stepped through the door, and Elizabeth cautioned him with a finger to her lips. He pointed to the quilt on the floor, nodding he understood. Since it would soon be dark, he walked into the front room to light a lamp. Elizabeth joined him and whispered, "I'm not sure she will stay. Can you imagine only nine or ten years old, and she is all alone? Charles, it is so tragic she has no idea how old she is. I am planning to sew a dress for her. Your dinner is ready, and I will bring it to you in here." Filling their bowls, she tiptoed into the front room, and they ate in silence.

Finally, Charles whispered, "What should you do with her? What can *we* do for her?"

Elizabeth answered softly, "I am trying to build some trust with her. Gloria might not stay, but if she flees, I believe she will come to see me again." When they had eaten, Elizabeth returned to the kitchen. The door was open. Gloria had vanished.

"Charles, come. She is gone!" Charles gathered his wife in a reassuring embrace. "I will help you look for her tomorrow. Tonight, she might have gone anywhere."

Elizabeth kept herself from crying. Gloria was akin to so many children who concerned both Anne and Elizabeth, and the child was precisely why they had started the home for destitute women and children.

"Oh, Charles, she told me she sleeps under a canvas down by the boats. I trust none of those rough-necked sailors trouble her. How can people not care when they see a child on her own? I pray I can find her in the morning."

Placing his hands on her shoulders, Charles looked into his wife's eyes. "There is the possibility her mother was a runaway slave. You know they often try to disappear here at the Dockyard, where they might escape notice because there are so many people."

"Charles, I noticed how nervous she was when I asked about her mother. I should not ask her too many questions. I will take her to the Refuge and be careful not to probe too much. We do not need to report what we do not know."

Charles took off his jacket. "Let's call it a day, dear Elizabeth, and begin your quest tomorrow. The Lord is watching over the child tonight. I am thankful you found the older woman, Lucy, as your first resident at the Refuge. I pray you find Gloria in the morning, and she is agreeable to joining Lucy. Indeed, it is a wonderful thing you have begun."

# 30

# A Refuge for Gloria

*1816*

Elizabeth found Gloria waiting under the same tree the next morning. Holding the new dress behind her back, Elizabeth slowly approached, then held it out. A smile almost crossed the small face. "Will you go home with me and try the dress on, Gloria?"

"For me? De dress be for me?" The girl's eyes grew large. Venturing closer, she ran her hand down the soft cotton fabric, and then pulled it to her nose and inhaled the smell of clean cotton. "Where it come from?"

"I made it yesterday while you slept at my house. Come now, and you can try it on."

Again, the child asked, "For me? You done do dat for me?"

Elizabeth dared to reach out and pat her on the head, hoping no head lice attached themselves to her hand. "Let's go now. Are you hungry?"

"Me always hungry."

"And I always have food for hungry little girls. Do you want to help me make something for you to eat?"

"Me jus wan eat all de foo dat you can make."

Elizabeth wanted to laugh, but it would turn the girl's seemingly selfish response into a joke. Smiling and holding out a hand, Elizabeth hoped Gloria would take it. Tentatively the child put her hand in Elizabeth's and walked alongside. Thinking it best not to mention the bath right away, Elizabeth began to tell her a story as they walked. When they neared the cottage, Elizabeth stopped the story. "I will finish it after you have had a bath and put on your new dress."

"Me nah go in de water. Me nah fish."

One of the supportive women in England had sent a bar of lavender soap. Elizabeth went to the cupboard and removed the sweet-smelling bar. Inhaling the aroma, she gave a satisfied "mmm."

"What it be?" Gloria asked, "Can me eat?"

"No, but if I give you some nice warm water, you can smell the same as this soap, Gloria."

As the child took the bar of soap, hope blossomed for Elizabeth.

"You can wash your hands with the soap and see how the smell lingers on them."

The child touched the dress, asking again, "Dis be dress for me?"

Elizabeth laughed this time.

"This dress is for someone clean. You must have a bath first, and then the dress is yours. I want to wash your hair, and it will smell like the soap, too."

With a slight nod, while holding both the soap and the dress, the temptation to flee disappeared. But the girl's expression revealed caution. "Me be 'fraid."

Elizabeth knelt so she was looking right into the girl's eyes. "God loves you, Gloria, and I want to show you His love. After I heat some water and place the tub in here, you may wash, and I will prepare some food for you. Then I will help you wash your hair."

Fright made her eyes as big as saucers, but the child was not running away. Elizabeth placed the tin tub on the floor. The tub was not large enough for an adult to sit down to bathe. They usually stood in the pan and poured warm water over their skin, but the small child would fit in the tub.

When Elizabeth entered the bedroom with the warm water, the child stared at the washtub. Again, Elizabeth knelt. "Go ahead, sit down, and hold the soap, Gloria." Still dressed in her filthy dress, she sat down.

"Hold your arms up, Gloria." As the child lifted both arms, Elizabeth quickly pulled the garment off, leaving the girl naked—she wore no undergarments. Dipping the cloth in the water, Elizabeth rubbed it over the bar of soap clutched in the girl's hand.

"See how lovely the soap smells? I will show you how to use it." Slowly, she placed the warm cloth on the girl's back.

Giving a startled "Oh, me!" The girl gripped the sides of the tub.

"Is it warm enough, Gloria?"

Elizabeth began to pour more water into the tub. "You may dip the cloth in the water, rub soap on it, and rub your skin clean. To be clean is a good thing. Go ahead. I will bring fresh water as soon as more heats, then we will wash your hair."

Elizabeth knew she would need to cut some of the child's hair to untangle it.

As the dirt from the child's skin darkened the water, Elizabeth noticed multiple sores on the malnourished body. Closing her eyes, Elizabeth thanked God for the recent start of the Women's Refuge. Girls like Gloria needed this shelter for so many reasons.

"Gloria, I wonder if sometimes your head itches? I am going to wash your hair now, and it will feel so good." While Gloria played with the soap, Elizabeth slipped her scissors from her apron pocket. She began to snip some of the worst tangles, knowing a comb could not undo the neglect. As she tried to untangle the remaining hair, she began to sing.

Elizabeth handed Gloria a cloth. "Now the tangles are tamed, I am going to pour some water over your hair and use the lovely lavender soap to make it clean. Cover your eyes since you do not want water in them. Do you want a story or a song while I wash your hair?"

"Please miss, me loves de stories. Where you hear dem story?"

There had always been stories in the Hart home—oral stories and then so many books with stories. Elizabeth could not imagine a child's life untouched by stories, oral or written.

"As a child, I learned to read words in books, and my mother often told me stories. You can learn to read, Gloria, but I will tell you a story I read when I was a child. Now, I need the soap."

Elizabeth began the story. After she reminded Gloria to shut her eyes and mouth tight, Elizabeth poured the warm water over the child's head. Gloria gasped as the warm water flowed down her back, and then there was the pleasant sound of a little giggle—a giggle from this child who only the day before seemed unacquainted with merriment.

"I know it tickles, but it is wonderful to be all clean, and you will feel good in your new dress." Elizabeth continued with the story as she massaged the girl's hair with soap and rinsed it. When finished, she told Gloria to stand up. After she climbed out of the murky water, Elizabeth wrapped her in a large piece of soft cloth to dry her.

"I have a surprise. I saw pictures of a new clothing they are calling pantalettes. I have made some for you. You can wear it beneath your new dress. Let's dress you now."

Nodding her head, the child looked at Elizabeth. "Will you tell me more of de story?"

Elizabeth eased the dress over Gloria's head, but it hung loosely on her fragile frame.

"I will continue the story after you slip on these pantalettes, and I tie the drawstring. Oh, look at you! I will comb your hair again, and then we will find something to eat."

The story calmed the child while she sat still as Elizabeth unsnarled what remained of her hair. Much of her hair ended in the dustbin since it proved impossible to manage. Gloria's hands kept feeling the dress. How long had it been since she had someone to care for her? The transformation was thrilling.

"I have some goat meat I prepared early this morning. Will you eat some?" Charles and Elizabeth rarely ate meat, but they thought the malnourished girl needed it.

Another time Elizabeth would try to teach her something about manners. She prayed there would be another time to talk about things such as manners. Many other times. After she ate, Elizabeth dared to ask Gloria to go with her on a short walk. As they walked, Elizabeth began another story.

"Many years ago, I lost my mother. She died when I was a few years older than you are. But I had a father, a grandmother, and an older sister who loved me. Then some years later, God gave me a husband to care for me."

"You got you a man?" the girl interrupted.

"Yes, a good man. You might meet him later. He and my older sister have helped me build a shelter for girls and for women who have no one to care for them.

"What be a shelter?"

Elizabeth stopped walking, again getting down on Gloria's level. "A shelter is a safe place, a place with food, and clothes, and books like the one I read to you. We have beds and blankets, too." After looking down at Gloria's dirty feet, clean only an hour before, Elizabeth added, "And shoes, so your feet don't become dirty or injured. And they have a cat!"

Gloria fell silent, and Elizabeth feared she had again said too much.

They stopped outside a medium-sized wooden house, elevated on rocks to prevent damage during storms and heavy rain. The shutters were a lovely shade of blue, with red hibiscus planted beside the path leading from the road to the house. Elizabeth waved to Anne, sitting on the veranda reading a book.

"Good afternoon, Anne. I want you to meet my friend, Gloria." Elizabeth took Gloria's hand. Almost afraid the child would flee if she knew the plans forming in Elizabeth's mind.

"Gloria, this is my sister, Anne."

"Your mama done dead, too?" Gloria questioned Anne.

Anne opened the door, and Gloria cautiously entered the house while clinging to Elizabeth.

"Yes. We lost our mother when we were girls. Come, let's find Lucy and our cat, Bentley. Bentley adores little girls, and so does Lucy."

Bentley swaggered up to Gloria, and the child plopped down on the floor to play with him.

Elizabeth motioned for Anne to step away and whispered. "I have not told her I want her to stay. I am hopeful but unsure she wants to live in a house. She is fiercely independent for one so young."

Lucy finished laying laundry outside in the sun to dry. As the old former slave entered the house, Gloria got up and moved behind Elizabeth's skirts. "Gloria, this is Lucy. She lives here with Bentley," said Elizabeth.

Lucy was the first woman to live in the shelter. Lucy did not know her age. "Me reckon me be old, me hair white and me bones don work good."

Both Elizabeth and Anne prayed God would bring them in contact with women and children in need. Two weeks before they completed the house of refuge, one of the plantation owners asked Charles what he could do with a slave unable to work anymore. Once a slave became unproductive in the fields, many owners thought of the older slaves as a liability.

The sisters secured a house to use as a shelter, and three weeks ago Lucy was the first to come to them. Since she ate better food, her strength to do small chores was restored. She cooked for herself and washed the clothes donated for the shelter. Elizabeth brought a rocker to the home, and most days Lucy sat singing in a clear, strong voice as she rocked. Lucy reminded both sisters of Old Molly.

Now, propping her feet on the small stool in front of her rocker, Lucy began to hum. Elizabeth explained she hoped to bring children in need to the shelter. Lucy held her arms out. "Come here, child. Let Granny Lucy rock you. Dis be my favorite place." Her arms outstretched, she continued humming in a rich contralto voice.

Gloria timidly approached, watching Bentley leap onto the lap of the old slave. Moving closer she began to pet Bentley but avoided joining him on Lucy's lap. "Tis all good, deez be such kind womans. Dems trying to teach me to read. We be safe here," Lucy told Gloria.

The girl repeated the word "safe" as if it was foreign. Looking back at the sisters, Gloria asked, "Why you bring me here? What dis mean?"

Kneeling, Elizabeth took the girl's hands. "We made this home for Lucy and for children who need food, a bed, and clean clothes. The Refuge is a safe place—a good place. Will you stay today?"

Gloria's eyes darted all around, looking at Bentley and Lucy. She walked over and fingered a bed with fresh sheets. "For me? Dis be for me?" She sat on the bed, smoothing the crisp white sheet, and leaning over she sniffed the linens. She almost smiled.

Elizabeth nodded. "Yes, Gloria, this is for you. Come see the books and the garden. Lucy makes delicious Johnny cakes." Elizabeth was thankful her sister could see this beginning of the Refuge before she moved to town.

When a second and then a third girl came to the home, the sisters realized the truth anew. They could clean up the outside of a child, but until God ruled their hearts, inner struggles would cause problems beyond what they had faced with their brothers or with the children from their father's second marriage. Dealing with all the habits that came packaged with desperate needs took grace and patience.

Judith and Betty joined the home next. Judith had survived by thievery since abandoned by her mother. Like so many, she never knew her father. After Lucy complained that food kept disappearing from the pantry, they caught Judith filling her apron pockets with uncooked rice. Elizabeth confronted her as she was about to go out the gate. The girl's look of defiance was a dagger to Elizabeth's heart.

"Oh Judith, why would you steal from those who only want what is good for you?"

"Dem's make me do work here. Weed de garden, wash de dirty pots, scrub sheets and nobody don pay me nuttin—it don be fair."

Elizabeth swallowed the lump in her throat. She yearned to reach not only the girl's physical needs but also her emotional and spiritual needs. "Doesn't everyone help here at the Refuge? We work together for all who need food and clothing. If *you* take the rice, then perhaps one day we will need to turn away someone else who is hungry."

Societies such as Mrs. Bethune began in New York, sent funds as well as barrels of clothing. Of course, some of the well-meaning women from Northern regions had no idea what would be appropriate in a year-round warm climate. Some days they had to laugh rather than cry at the unsuitable offerings of clothing shipped from England and New England to Antigua.

As more funds arrived from Lady Grey, Mrs. Bethune, Anne Gilman and later the benevolent societies in England, Anne and Elizabeth discussed how they must be careful in keeping records of the money for both relief societies they had started. Releasing a contented breath, Elizabeth said, "I will keep the books."

Since Anne found numbers tedious, she was relieved when Elizabeth offered. "Thank you. You are so much better at writing the letters to thank these faraway women." They understood how important it was to give a picture of the good the contributions accomplished.

"We are blessed to have husbands who encourage, and assist us, but we also need to feed them." Elizabeth smiled. "Let's cook a large pan of pepper pot for those men. We will feed the others tonight."

On a sweltering day, they used the outdoor kitchen to simmer the stew over a coal pot. Then the women cut green papaya to make a treat for the children. If they added enough cinnamon and sugar, the flavorless green papaya reminded them of the apples they had tasted once when they were young. Their mother cooked apples that came by ship from the Carolinas. After two months aboard the ship, they were wrinkled and soft, but when cooked with cinnamon and sugar they proved a delightful treat.

Charles raved about the green papaya pie and remarked how much it reminded him of apple tarts he had eaten in England. Elizabeth appreciated that Charles never complained about the simple fare she prepared for him. He understood that when the aroma of seasoned meat filled their kitchen, most of it was intended for children in great need of a nourishing meal. He loved Elizabeth's giving spirit, so he shared her with the neglected and orphaned children of English Harbour.

He was also thankful his wife did not complain about the unsanitary and uncomfortable situations they found occasionally when they taught too far away from English Harbour to return the same day. Perhaps if Elizabeth had been white, the estate manager would have offered them a room in his home, but there were nights they spent attempting to sleep on an oversized table after an evening of teaching.

They prepared in every way they could. Usually, they traveled with mosquito netting, but it was not always possible to use it. Elizabeth was embarrassed to admit it frightened her when the bats began swooping down in the room where they slept. Even though the net made them feel more secure from the flying creatures, the persistent mosquitoes nibbled on their arms resting against the netting. After a fitful night, they usually arose and left at first light. Frequently a thoughtful slave brought them a still-warm bowl of porridge sweetened with cane juice and cinnamon, or a ripe papaya cut and left in a calabash bowl. On one trip, Elizabeth was pleased to see a slave had cut his name into the calabash bowl, a hard gourd-like material that he carved as if wood.

Charles and Elizabeth also placed their Bible in a metal box to protect it from curious and hungry rats and mice. Elizabeth usually packed a loaf of bread and some cheese for them to eat, securing it in the box from the varmints.

Elizabeth brought a knife and a spoon in her leather travel bag that also held their flasks of water, a candle with striker, and the very important nutmeg ointment to help with the pain from the chigger bites. She bought some nutmeg in the market after a ship traveling from Grenada transported the lovely aromatic nuts. The ointment was reported to have a variety of medicinal uses. Elizabeth had learned from her mother years before how to mix the grated nutmeg with beeswax to create a salve that gave some relief from insect bites. The aroma of fresh lemongrass discouraged mosquitoes, but nothing dissuaded the troublesome chiggers.

Charles and Elizabeth were always back in English Harbour on Sunday. The church was thriving. Lately they had been joined by some of the men from the 1st West India Regiments. These black soldiers, entrusted with more privileges than many experienced, lived in The Middle Ground Barracks at the top of the ridge. The influence of William Wilberforce and others had persuaded the King to treat his regiments with more civility. Freedom had been granted to the King's soldiers several years before, and many remained on the island.

# 31

# The Gilberts Move to Town

*1817*

Learning of the defeat of Napoleon Bonaparte and his forces, John knew the French ruler's era was over when they exiled Napoleon to the island of Elba. For almost a year, England still displayed caution about reducing its naval forces in the Caribbean, but with strategies in place to reduce the Royal Navy and the Dockyard, John knew they would eliminate his position soon.

His steps were light as he walked home, and he called out to Anne as he saw her sweeping the front veranda. "Put away your broom, Anne, and get ready to pack for a move back to St. John's. With the abdication and exile of Napoleon, the need to keep Antigua on a war footing has changed."

Anne gave a little shout as she set the broom aside. "How soon, John? Are you released as naval storekeeper? When do we go?"

John sat down to catch his breath. "My organized wife, you can't wait to start packing, can you? I have asked some of the men to bring some small crates tomorrow. We will move in a week."

John leaned back in his chair. "How is it possible anyone can secure a position for more than sixteen years such as Napoleon created, with his domination covering much of the world. I am so thankful the years of Napoleon's reign are over, but I am also thinking someday we may return to English Harbour."

They sat on the small veranda as the evening breeze began to cool the day. John squeezed his wife's hand, "Do you remember how we talked of the day coming when France would no longer be a menace, and what might be next for us? We can leave English Harbour and go forth to the next plan brewing in your keen brain. So out with it. What adventure happens next?"

He imagined she would begin to walk the length of the veranda as she discussed her thoughts. Anne did not let him down. Delightfully predictable, John tried not to laugh as Anne stretched, kissed his hand, stood up, and began pacing.

"Yes, I have several thoughts I have been pondering. Elizabeth and I have discussed what we could do if we returned to living in town. We have also spoken with our cousin, Elizabeth Lynch, about launching an organization to help women in St. John's."

John listened carefully, following her ideas. He knew few navy men as persistent and determined as his wife once she set her mind on a problem, and she could move mountains to get to a solution. Life was difficult for women who suffered because of the men they chose or because of an unexpected illness or hard times. Men could almost always find work, but children narrowed the possibilities for women.

"Anne, I have spoken with Charles. He and Elizabeth will continue in English Harbour so they may carry on the ministry of the church, the Women's Refuge, and the Sunday schools. Who knows how long peace will persist in the islands? The Dockyard will continue, but not as large or in need of my services for now."

"How I will miss Elizabeth and our daily cup of tea together. Even so, there will be a ministry for me in St. John's, so I must wait to see what is next." She sat down and tenderly asked, "Do you ever wish, John, you had married a wife whose biggest concerns were baking the next loaf of bread, or wondering if the rains would soak the laundry she had taken outside to dry?"

John lifted her chin so she would see the admiration filling his heart. "I continue amazed how you never tire of thinking of others. Yet the poor, the downtrodden, will always be there. I can advise you to consider taking a rest yourself, but I will not force you. I could not convince the rain to stop falling from the sky, and I will not attempt to stop your charitable deeds."

Anne always avoided compliments. "I continue amazed with a husband who seldom complains. Many projects take me away from our home, and you could have married a woman who only sat and knitted socks."

"While I would enjoy some new socks, many women can knit socks. However, who else equals the energy and vision you and Elizabeth consistently devote to those in need? The number you have helped is beyond counting. Nearly 20 years ago, I suspected I married a prize, but I now recognize I wed a rare jewel. I am so blessed to have you as my wife."

Anne looked at her husband. "John, stop. You know I loathe pride. I choose not to focus on what Elizabeth and I have accomplished in past years, and I want only to think about what is next for us. Now, I will begin to pack for a move to St. John's."

John nodded. "God will lead us in His time."

Anne added, "I will write to the London Society because I am impressed with what I recently read of a John Pounds in London. He established the Ragged School to help the poor working-class children where the poorhouses sounded identical to prisons. Women begin most of the charitable societies."

John reached for her hand and held it to his cheek. He kissed Anne's hand, as she shook her head at this man she loved more now than she could ever have imagined. The comfortable silence between them turned lighthearted.

"I could use gray socks. After you have completed one pair, I expect to hear your full idea for restoring the lives of downtrodden women in St. John's." John winked good-naturedly.

There was not much to pack except for a few kitchen items and the ever-expanding collection of books. They would share with others whatever they decided to leave behind.

Over the last ten years, John marveled at how well the two couples had worked together, and he would miss the companionship he shared with Charles. He needed to ensure that Elizabeth and Anne could continue to have time together.

Conflicting emotions ran through Anne's mind at the return to St. John's. Living close to the thousands of soldiers and sailors in English

Harbour had proven a difficult challenge over the last 12 years. Of the women living near the Dockyard, the majority were "opportunities for ministry." Nevertheless, Anne would miss Elizabeth, Mrs. Looby, and Quano's wife, Molly. Anne valued the ministry she had shared over the last ten years with Elizabeth and Charles, and her own, dear John. Without question she would miss those times. Elizabeth would do well operating the Women's Refuge, with Charles at her side.

John had put aside some funds during his years working at the Dockyard, enabling them to buy a small home in St. John's. While he made plans to return to bookkeeping, Anne looked forward to helping the underprivileged children and women in town once again. The Female Refuge Society in English Harbour could do nothing for women living in St. John's. She knew the same type of organization was certain to be a need in town. Anne would begin sending letters to those women overseas who had helped establish the refuge in English Harbour.

On the first day in their new home, they unpacked the necessary items to prepare a meal and arrange a bed. Anne turned to John, sorrow etching her expression. "I will miss Elizabeth. She encouraged me almost daily, but God orchestrated this move. I know it was not you, John, who chose to downsize His Majesty's Naval Dockyard."

They had been in town only a day when John came home with excitement written all over his face. He had barely removed his hat before he revealed his news. "There is an announcement in today's *Daily Register* asking for workers to help organize the registry of slaves. Someone must compile a ledger for all the island's plantations, recording the name, age, and sex of each slave and how they came to be in the possession of their owner. The government wants to ensure no one breaks the new law prohibiting the further importing of people. I signed us up for this job. We will meet the folks on all the plantations, and we can determine which overseers might be willing for us to come and start a Sunday school."

A surge of excitement at John's news thrilled Anne. This might be the start of a ministry to plantations closer to town. "Can we purchase a small wagon so we can travel between the plantations? We will also need a journal to record all this information."

Before Anne could continue, John pulled a journal from his bulging jacket and tapped it on her hand. "I just came from purchasing a wagon and horse and arranging for a stable down the street. The government gave me a map showing all 250 plantations. They want someone whom they can trust not to take a bribe or report wrong information. They want us to be the ones taking this census. When do you think you can be ready for this next venture?"

Anne smiled. "Well, you certainly executed this with haste and efficiency. I can go with you next week." She was so grateful he understood her need for involvement and pursuit of a goal.

John led her towards the partially unpacked crates. "Have you unpacked your mother's teacups? I think we should celebrate, but first let's pray." John's words comforted Anne. *"Dear Lord, thank you for this assignment to meet all the enslaved, those without a voice on this island. Please give direction regarding which plantations will be willing for us to begin teaching on this side of Antigua. Thank you, Lord, for this clear direction and opportunity."*

The next week John and Anne began to visit the plantations. John spoke to the owners or overseers, showing them the documents that gave permission to question each of the slaves. Most owners were agreeable and made way for Anne and John to interview and record the information. John spoke to the men, while Anne recorded statistics from the women and children. They tried to establish rapport with the person in charge, and hope grew about obtaining permission and returning soon to teach those interested in learning to read on Sundays. The first plantation owned 320 men, women, and children, so the survey took all day.

At day's end, Anne voiced. "John, this is a more demanding task than I anticipated. The rough ride and heat have left me exhausted. The overwhelming smells make the task harder. Many slaves probably have little water for bathing. My body is weary and my heart heavy, but worse was seeing the anguish written on their faces."

John knelt before his wife as she collapsed into a chair. "Anne, if this is too hard for you, I can go, and you stay here. I had not foreseen what a distance we would need to travel each day, or how rough the roads would be. It's difficult to question each slave while observing his needs, and yet be unable to help with something as necessary as water to bathe. I am sorry."

Kicking her shoes aside, Anne stood and rubbed her weary, aching feet. "No, John. You know I detest whining, and yet here I am complaining. Unlike the people we met today, I can come home free and ask my husband to prepare water so I can bathe." Anne gave him a playful nudge, and John bowed as he left to draw her water that would wash away the dust of the road and lingering odors of the day.

That evening Anne made her own copy of all the names she had recorded. She could not get away from the realization of the unearned blessing of counting herself among the free blacks on the island.

The task was arduous. Visiting the first four plantations spread across the small island took five days, miles apart on rough, dusty roads. The sugar plantations were generally on hillsides to catch the trade winds turning the sails on the mills that crushed the canes. Rain or diminishing daylight often halted their day before they completed the count. Some plantations were such a long way from town, that it meant they must stay overnight on the plantation.

Not all overseers cooperated, so John carefully exercised diplomacy while explaining the required counting and listing of all slaves. The workers responded well to Anne's kindly manner. Perhaps it was less intimidating to give all the necessary information to a woman of colour than a white man.

On a plantation that had 210 slaves, Anne recorded in her journal that the people were better cared for there, and it seemed a potential location for a school. Noticing a woman close in age to herself, Anne felt reassured to hear the owner call the woman, Betsy, by name. When the woman's child fell, the master himself picked the child up and dusted him off.

Anne needed to concentrate on the task at hand, but her mind flitted to her own father, who but for a generous master could have been a slave himself. A familiar guilt surfaced again when looking at the woman who, but by the grace of God, could be her. Pausing, she shut her eyes as if to suppress the thought. Sitting beside her as they recorded the names, John observed her momentary angst and passed Anne a bottle of ginger drink. She appreciated his quiet attention and care. The hot sting of the sweet, pungent ginger drink restored her. She cleared her throat and focused on the task.

"What is the child's name and age?" The child looked mulatto, with lighter skin than his mother, but Anne was to record only the child's name and age, not his lineage. She patted his head as he walked past her.

Later that evening John asked her. "Are you going to be able to endure this?"

Anne slipped off her apron and turned to lay it down, stroking her husband's chin. He needed a shave and a wash after the day's dusty ride. "I am troubled because so often the thought … *but by the grace of God, there go I* … keeps sounding in my head. Why have I been so blessed, John?"

"You have been blessed so you will make a difference in the lives of many of these people. Together we will seek a way to teach, prepare, and to give them hope. A man can endure almost anything if he has hope. This listing of the multitude is not our main goal. We are on a quest to discover where we can begin to teach on this side of the island. First, we count and pray, then we start to teach and spread hope."

A month later they were on an estate in which the master lived abroad, leaving an overseer in charge of the workers. Anne noticed a rum bottle clutched in the overseer's filthy hand as he approached John. Dressed not much better than the slaves, he spoke roughly to John and eyed Anne with a look that made her skin crawl.

John stood in front of his wife. "Sir, I expect no trouble, but if necessary, we can return with a constable to help with this task. Please ask your workers to form a line and answer our questions." John spoke with authority and the overseer backed away and called to the people to line up.

Sometimes the plantations offered a table under a shade tree for John and Anne to record the information. John pulled the wagon under a shade tree, while Anne and he sat on the wagon, the ledger resting between them to record the data. Midway through the day John halted the line and drove Anne to a secluded spot where she might relieve herself. She stepped out of the bushes, smoothing out her skirt and smiled.

"Thank you for everything you notice and care about. I would not have wanted to go to any outbuilding on this property. They might have allowed you to visit the loo reserved for the whites, but I feel sure even it might reek of that ghastly man." She covered her mouth, ashamed she had called even this awful man an unkind name.

"Indeed, there is no better word to describe him, but I can think of some worse I've heard."

They returned to find the workers seated on the ground waiting a turn to record their name. Since some folks did not know their age, John and Anne guessed as best they could. Anne wondered if the absentee owner had any idea his people needed better food, clothing, and care. The gaunt faces and resigned looks lingered, locked in her memory. She could not do everything, so she found herself looking ahead to plans for what she could do. This assignment of recording the statistics was not yet helping to ease the injustices humanity had heaped on these souls for whom Christ died.

Over the next eight months it took to complete the records of over 31,060 men, women, and children, Anne never got over the intense awareness of her privilege of freedom. John frequently asked her if she wanted to talk about the heaviness troubling her heart. Sometimes she said no, and he left it alone. Sometimes she spoke of her desire to do more because she had so much, and they had so little. She was a free black, an educated free black, and married to a white man—a wonderful and understanding man who loved her.

Of course, by the time they finished their work, some names had to be marked as deceased, or newborns added to the list. Authorities considered newborn enslaved as well. But the vital information, having the names and ages of slaves, would diminish the temptation to break the law by importing more.

On one estate, John believed it was time to mention what he had longed to ask over the long months of meeting each of the men in charge. "If you would grant permission, my wife and I would like to return on a Sunday and offer classes in how to read the Bible. Would you be willing for us to instruct them?"

The owner looked away as he replied, "Many say once you teach a slave to read the Bible, then they read the newspaper, become discontented, rebel and burn the country." Then looking straight at John, he continued, "But I know change to our way of life looms ahead. I myself am not influenced by religious principles, but if you can bring them under the fear of God, you might be doing them and me a service."

Anne resisted shouting. John shook the man's hand, "We will return in a week. I believe you will see the authority of God can prevail where the whip fails. Thank you, and God bless you."

One day after they had completed their task, Anne stood across the road from the nearby rum shop and it was as if she had slipped into a dream. Time stood still. The girl sitting on the steps looked like Amelia, the nine-year-old girl whom Anne had befriended when she lived in St. John's nearly 18 years earlier. Stunned at the uncanny resemblance, Anne lingered and watched. Eventually an older, harder version of the girl came outside and cuffed the girl on her head. Anne could not help herself. She called out, "No. No, please."

The woman had gained some weight, her blond hair looked in need of a wash, but Anne knew at once it was a grown-up Amelia. She looked across at Anne, then pushed the girl inside the rum shop, and crossing the street stood with her feet askance. "Still around are ya?" Then the woman's hardened countenance softened as she touched Anne's abundance of curly black hair shimmering with red in the sun. Anne wore a hat, but it did not hide her beautiful hair. "You were gone away so long, me mam dead now, and I took her place here."

"Oh, Amelia. I saw the girl and for a moment I thought it was you. Is she a younger sister?"

Amelia looked down and then raised her eyes to look at this helper from years before. Anne had fallen into her habit of asking too many questions too fast for those whose lives were riddled with gaps and deep holes.

"She is mine!" Hands on her hips, the defiant response was a disappointment to Anne. She had feared Amelia might say the child was hers. She knew not to ask if she were married, and not to continue to probe. Without thinking Anne asked, "What is her name?"

Amelia's eyes shimmered with unshed tears. She inhaled and her brief glare turned softer. "Amelia Anne. She is mine, but when she was born, I wished she might be something like you and not my own mum. I never forgot your kindness."

Her tears overflowed and now Anne was crying, too. Just then an unkempt, burly, red-faced man flung open the rum shop door and bellowed like a cow tied up too long.

"Amelia, wha' you doing out there?" His hands curled into fists as he shouted, "Come here now, woman."

Anne watched as Amelia cringed. "Sorry, will you come back someday? Early. Come early, before he is awake!"

With his remark, Amelia sprinted across the road and walked into the rum shop, the swinging half-door shutting off Anne's view.

She told herself to walk on, to put one foot in front of the other, to continue to the market to shop for John's supper. Yet, her feet seemed glued to the spot and she watched as young Amelia Anne briefly stuck her head out the door before she was snatched back inside.

Resolve strengthened her will. There were many like Amelia Anne waiting for someone to care …waiting for someone to stop them before they fell into a life from which women seldom escaped. Yes, she would be back. And it would be early, and she would be careful. The man appeared to be mean and wouldn't think twice before shoving Anne out on the street. Was he the father of little Amelia Anne?

Anne wondered how old Amelia had been when her mother died and who had taken care of her. Thinking about all that must have ensued in the past to bring Amelia to this point in her life was not helpful. Amelia must be about 26 now, with a daughter who had been born when Amelia was still a girl herself.

Anne walked with purpose. St. John's needed a Refuge as much as English Harbour had needed one. There were not the abundance of soldiers and sailors here, but there were evil men such as the brute who had called her a coarse name some moments earlier.

When she reached home, she wrote a letter to Lady Grey describing the need in town for a refuge such as the one established in English

Harbour. That night she poured out the troubling events of the day to John. She wanted them to begin to teach on the plantations, but she also longed to begin a haven for the children whose lives were destroyed by evil right here in St. John's.

"I will go with you next time you visit Amelia. This man, who is possibly the child's father, might see you as a threat to his life. No dog could protect you as well as Tippet did. He served us well. I know you miss him since he died. You have a husband to protect you, but we also need another dog. My next assignment is obtaining another guardian dog for you."

Sometimes Anne contemplated how different her life would be if she had not met John, if she had failed to walk away from the challenging but familiar life she had grown up with and remained single. She also wondered if Elizabeth would have married Charles if she herself had not first taken the step to marry a white man. John added such security, but even more he challenged her to trust God with her aspirations. He gave her joy.

John did return with Anne early the next morning. He walked across the street and looked inside the rum hall. Several men looked as though they needed sleep or maybe had spent the evening slouched in a chair and draped across a table. John caught the eye of the woman likely to be Amelia, motioned to her, and noticed as she glanced at a child curled up on a quilt on the floor. Confident the woman understood who he was, John said not a word but joined Anne outside. The door to the rum hall swung open with a gentle push and Amelia gave a tentative smile to Anne as she crossed the road.

"I was unsure you would return after Sam spoke so rudely to you yesterday. I'm sorry."

"No need to apologize for him, Amelia. I want to help you if I can. I want to help Amelia Anne, too. Please tell me what you need."

Silent tears dripped from Amelia's anguished face. "I need for Amelia Anne to escape from the life I grew up in. I need to give her safety from the men who frequent the tavern, and if I am honest, I want to protect her from Sam. I fear when he gambles and is overcome by the rum, he might trade Amelia Anne for money to stay in a game."

Anne knew she must be careful with her questions, but she had to probe with one fact she must know. "Is Sam the father of Amelia Anne?"

Amelia lifted her head and wiped at the tears dropping from her chin. "The father is not Sam. I am unsure who it was, but I didn't know Sam back then."

Anne cringed at the thought of *back then*. Whatever that meant, she did not desire to fully understand.

Looking to John, he nodded, knowing what Anne would ask next. "Would you want … be willing … for me to take Amelia Anne? I have plans to begin a haven for girls in need, eventually a home for women in desperate situations. She would be safe."

At first Amelia responded by shaking her head no, and then she dropped her shoulders and looked pleadingly at both Anne and John.

"Yes, please. Though she is all in life I love, I do not want her to have my same life. I can't protect her … I can only love her and let her go."

John stepped into the conversation.

"I know you trust Anne, but you can trust me as well. We are trying to secure a refuge for girls and maybe even for other women in need of protection and security."

"Yes," she whispered, "There are so many who need help. I see them every day. God bless you for caring. Give me a week with my daughter and then come for her. Come for her early in the morning. You must keep her far away from Sam. Perhaps I can come and see her?"

Anne gave a slight smile and nodded.

A week later Amelia Anne left her mother and the only life she had ever known. Anne delivered her to her cousin, Elizabeth Lynch, who had already taken a few girls in need of a haven.

Over the next couple of years, Anne, with John's help, administered the Women's Refuge in St. John's and the Society for the Diseased and Destitute Slaves. Elizabeth Lynch's home and refuge enlarged to help 32 women and girls. The years passed swiftly, and by 1821 the Dockyard determined that even with reduced personnel, they wanted John Gilbert back. The authorities appointed John as Naval Storekeeper, offering him a larger home that served as a location to meet for church.

Anne and John, pleased with their return to English Harbour, once again, served alongside Elizabeth and Charles on Sundays. Anne assisted with teaching in the school in Bethesda, as well as aiding the Women's Refuge. The schools grew so large there was precious little time to devote to tea on the veranda, but the sisters spent hours accomplishing what they loved best—teaching.

# 32

# Sinking of the "Maria"

*1826*

As John walked home, he dreaded the sorrow he would shortly impart to Anne. How could he ever bring this news to her? As a couple, they shared mutual hopes and individual struggles, discussing their hearts and minds with each other. Anne never could hide her emotions. They reflected on her face as images dancing on still water. He knew when she was happy, and he knew when she was discouraged. Through the years, the difficulties arising from attempting to work with some who judged her as inferior often proved a major cause for discouragement.

Anne struggled to remain gracious, knowing several of the missionary wives discussed her behind her back. Many of the Methodist missionaries sent to Antigua still viewed John and Anne's marriage with disdain, though they had married nearly 28 years before.

The Methodist mission in Antigua had recently increased to five missionary families. Though John Gilbert preached occasionally, they excluded him from most of their joint planning meetings. Anne suspected they would have accepted her and included John if she were white.

The Jones family arrived in Antigua two years earlier. Anne shared with John how Mrs. Jones ignored her, after asking her how she could be so forward as to marry a white man! After that, Anne avoided Mrs. Jones. Recently, the annual Methodist Missionary Conference in St. Kitts failed to invite John, and Anne knew he experienced dismay because of this apparent rejection.

As John approached their home on March 3, 1826, Anne immediately noticed his ashen face right away.

"John, sit down. What is the matter? Is it Elizabeth?"

Sinking into the chair beside Anne, he shook his head in answer to her question and tears prevented his attempt to explain.

"Please, John. You're frightening me. Tell me what's wrong."

As she handed John a handkerchief, he wiped his blotched cheeks. "My darling wife, a tragedy has occurred with the Methodist missionaries."

Sympathetically Anne interjected. "Excluding you from the annual missionary retreat was a tragedy, and they were wrong not to invite you."

"Stop, Anne! If they'd included me, you would now be a widow!"

During their years together he rarely displayed such a sharp response, and Anne was stunned. "Whatever can you mean? John, what has happened?"

Struggling to choke out the words, John said, "They're dead, Anne. Twenty-one souls drowned within sight of Antigua, within the distance of hearing the church bells ring. The entire Methodist missionary family were on the mail packet boat, returning to Antigua from the island of Montserrat."

A cold chill fell on Anne, and she began to tremble. "The children, John? The babies? All lost?" Anne gasped. Though some of their parents had been impolite to Anne, she adored the little missionary children. They were too young and innocent for their parents' prejudices to have influenced them.

John held her as he continued the story. "Only Mrs. Jones survived to tell the story, and it is unsure if she will recover. They found her holding on the battered hull of the sinking boat, three days after it broke apart on the shoals and rocks outside the harbor."

Now Anne began to weep, her mind conflicted as she wondered how many times she had asked God to forgive her unkind thoughts about some of the people who had died this terrible death. She clung to John, realizing only weeks ago she wished the missionaries had invited him to attend this very conference. "How did it happen?"

"You know the reef outside the harbor, near what they call Sandy Island? The shoals running near the entrance to St. John's can be dangerous, and some say there are times when only seven feet of water lies between the boat and the shoals." He stopped, pausing to drink as Anne handed him a glass of water. "The group of missionaries traveled on a small vessel from St. Kitts as far as Montserrat. Fearing the smaller boat looked unsafe, they waited for the larger ship to bring them back to Antigua. They chose the *Maria,* and when it was almost home the boat hit the rocks and broke apart. The boat they did not take arrived safely three days ago."

Remembering her anger at the mean-spirited decision to keep John from joining the excursion, Anne was now unable to grasp the meaning of it all. "How, John, how?" She pled.

"Many drowned almost immediately, washed away by the waves. A wave tore Mrs. Jones' child from her arms, but she and her husband held onto the wreckage for days. Burned by the sun, parched, and battered by waves, Mr. Jones died in his wife's arms. She felt him slip away hours before a passing boat found her."

Anne fought to come to grips with the memories of her own shameful attitudes. "Oh, John, there were times I had wished they had never come to Antigua. I tried to understand their attitude, their rejection of you, and their rude behavior toward me. Never did I imagine they would all have such a tragic end. Tell me you know I did not want this, *not this, John!*"

He grabbed her hands, lifted her chin, and stared into her blue eyes overflowing with tears. "Of course, I know you did not wish them dead. Nor did I, even though I knew the sting of their rejection and prejudice."

Anne loved the way this man kept her focus clear. "John, I am so ashamed of my own feelings toward them. Yes, they failed to treat me in a Christ-like manner, but I failed to forgive their attitude of superiority."

He wiped her tears once more. "Now we can be grateful they excluded me. God spared my life because they judged me unworthy, yet what a bitter end to our differences. Think of their families in England. We must pray as they eventually hear the news. We must ask God to grant us grace to attend the funeral and pray for Mrs. Jones' recovery. Dear Anne, this will not be easy but our heavenly Father will help us endure."

When all around them appeared bleak, John helped Anne see hope. "May God send us people with strong spirits who come to replace these men and their families. I would choose you again as my husband, even knowing the hurts our union has endured from uncharitable hearts. They traveled across the sea to share Christ, yet failed to show kindness to you."

The couple entered their home with arms entwined. Anne kissed John's cheek, nodding as she let go of him. He knew she would put the kettle on to heat because his predictable, loveable wife would believe a cup of tea might help a little. It might.

# 33
# The Summons

*1827*

Charles and Elizabeth stayed involved for more than 20 years in the numerous schools they established on the southern side of the island. On this evening they finished their walk home. No longer young, they were weary from instructing slaves on a nearby plantation for much of their afternoon. They became alarmed to see the constable awaiting them on their veranda, impatiently drumming his fingers on the railing. Elizabeth looked to Charles and gripped his arm. She feared his presence meant tragic news about someone in her large family.

Charles spoke first. "Good afternoon, Constable, may I help you?" The constable rudely ignored Charles. He looked at Elizabeth and sneered, "You are Mrs. Elizabeth Thwaites?" Elizabeth gripped Charles's arm even tighter and moved to gain support by edging closer to him.

"Yes, officer. May we sit down?" Not waiting for his answer, she approached the small veranda chairs and collapsed into the closest one. The constable whipped a paper from his jacket pocket, and without another word, he dropped it in Elizabeth's lap.

Stunned, she heard him call back as he descended the steps. "Elizabeth Thwaites, you are summoned to appear before the Antigua House of Assembly next week. Make certain you present yourself." Without waiting for an answer, he strode away.

Dazed, Elizabeth examined the document. Charles sat down next to her and broke the silence. "Why ever would they summon only you,

Elizabeth? I know we have experienced people who have opposed us, but why send this to you alone?"

"I can't imagine. I should have offered the constable tea, Charles."

Charles laughed nervously. "Tea? You would serve tea to a dog who bites your hand?

"We will have some tea and bread with cheese, and then I need to rest, Charles." Elizabeth opened the door and flung her large straw hat on a rack, donned her work apron, and went to work.

Later that evening Charles heard a quick rapping at their back door. A rumpled Joseph Phillips, the Moravian who served with Elizabeth in the Society for the Diseased and Destitute Slaves, stood alone. Shaken and pale, Phillips came into the lantern light.

Elizabeth entered the room and gasped. Seldom did anyone but family come to the back door. Elizabeth had let her hair down and had been preparing for bed.

She clutched her wrapper tighter about her. "Come in, Mr. Phillips. Is your family all right?" Something was very wrong. Why would Mr. Phillips come now, after dark, and why come to the back door?

Reaching into his pocket, he withdrew a paper resembling the one delivered to her earlier. Elizabeth sat down. "What is it, Mr. Phillips? Why would the Assembly summon us?"

By now, Charles had pulled out a chair for Mr. Phillips, and he collapsed as if carrying a heavy load. "I believe they fear us. The planters view us as abolitionists and rebels because we are sympathetic to the plight of the slaves. I am afraid they want to make scapegoats of us. We have awakened a sleeping lion, and they mean to devour us because we started the Society for the Slaves.

Shaking her head Elizabeth asked in a whisper, "But why me, Mr. Phillips. Why me?"

"I think they will question you as the secretary, asking who we distributed the funds to. The constable who handed me the summons snarled, "Trying to make the planters look bad are you? Now it will be you and the uppity coloured woman who will look bad." Fear was evident on his face as he looked at Elizabeth. "They aim to stop those who are helping the slaves. I don't know what they will do to us!"

Charles spoke up before Elizabeth had a chance. "They have come at you attempting to pry back the Lord's protecting hand, Mr. Phillips. God will give us strength and courage to do what is right."

Elizabeth added, "God is my refuge and strength, a very present help in trouble. Yes, we will trust in the Almighty to give us answers. Thank you for coming, Mr. Phillips. We will pray for a sense of peace for all of us. Good night."

Charles and Elizabeth appeared before the House of Assembly the following week. The Assemblymen looked at Elizabeth with scornful, condemning expressions. Charles sat beside her and held her hand.

The court officer announced, "Elizabeth Thwaites, please rise and face the Assembly." Elizabeth rose with the genuine smile that had always melted Charles's heart, but seemed to infuriate these men.

"We are here to investigate charges against you, Mrs. Thwaites. You have been responsible for a campaign subscription that started in England to distribute funds to slaves. Do you deny this charge?"

Elizabeth attempted her smile again. "Yes, I have been responsible for distributing funds sent by friends in England for slaves in need of help."

"You will, therefore, submit all the names of slaves to whom you distributed food, clothing, or funds."

Astonished by this request, she asked abruptly. "What will you do with the names of the slaves we helped? Will you punish them for accepting the small gifts sent to them from concerned friends abroad?"

The head of the Assembly raised his voice. "You are not before this meeting to question us, Mrs. Thwaites! You will give us those names as well as the names of the plantations where the slaves live."

"Sir, I cannot give you those names." Elizabeth glanced at Charles, and he reassured her with a look of approval.

"I am not at liberty to reveal which estates, the proprietors, the slaves, or what sort of aid was given. Caring individuals entrusted me, and I will not betray their trust. I cannot."

Now the man was almost yelling. "Before you entered this Assembly, we met with Mr. Phillips, and we voted to hold him in jail for a year because he is withholding the information we requested. He is an abolitionist and a danger to the security of our island. What are we supposed to do with a woman?"

Stunned at the news that Mr. Phillips had been remanded to jail, Elizabeth trembled but replied with courage. "Sir, I can tell you in general what good we have done for those slaves in great need. We have distributed clothing, and food, and sometimes a little money to help them buy medicine. I can give you no more. I will respectfully submit I cannot cause any censure to come to those slaves we attempted to help."

The man's cheeks flushed as he looked to the other members of the Assembly. The service Elizabeth had done over the years protected her with some measure. He was in an awkward position. These men indeed feared what their wives might say if they committed this woman to jail.

The magistrate threatened, "You are dismissed, but know you are being watched."

Elizabeth and Charles walked from the Assemblymen. As the door shut, Elizabeth began to cry as Charles quoted, "For the needy shall not always be forgotten."

"Elizabeth, I am so proud of you. I do not know what I would have done if they had committed you to jail. I could not have borne the anguish. Tomorrow we will go to see Mrs. Phillips. But tonight, I will remind you what we said before we met with these men. '*We commit ourselves to Him who judgeth righteously; He is able to deliver us.*' We will rest in the truth of scripture tonight. We are under divine direction, and my dear, you were as Daniel in the lions' den."

Mr. Phillips had served as the secretary of the Moravian Church. The next day as they visited his wife, she assured them the church had promised to take care of her family during her husband's sentence.

When one of Mrs. Phillips' children clung to her skirt, she picked him up and began to rock him. "You know the planters are irate because my husband decided not only to choose a coloured woman as his wife, but also chose to be the only white man in the Moravian Church. He has been unafraid to sound forth his views on slavery, which further enraged them. God will provide for us, and God will protect my husband."

Months later Charles placed the *Glasgow Courier* on Elizabeth's lap as she sat knitting. "I thought they decided to stop harassing you once they sentenced Mr. Phillips to jail as their scapegoat. But I see the British press is supporting the pro-slavery segment and is attacking not only Mr. Phillips's character but yours as well, my dear wife." He flattened the paper and pointed to the article. "These folks across the sea want to create a scandal surrounding you because you refused to assist the Antigua Assembly."

Elizabeth set her knitting aside and picked up the paper.

> In Joseph Phillips's capacity as the second secretary to the deluding society entitled 'The Society for the Relief of Old Worn-out and Diseased Slaves,' the Assembly of Antigua, in the name of the colony he had unjustly attacked and basely calumniated, has been sentenced to a year in jail. Time, space, and circumstances compel me to quit this tool of anti-colonial faction and rancor, and his bosom crony, Mrs. Thwaites.

Few things caused Elizabeth to display a temper. "What slander! How can they write this?" Uncharacteristically for her, she retorted in anger. "I have never been a 'bosom crony' of Mr. Phillips!" Then she nervously laughed until her laughter turned to tears.

Charles picked up the paper and read further.

> By tools such as Mary Prince and Joseph Phillips, Pringle and the band of which Pringle is the tool and the organ, mislead and irritate this country, browbeat the government, and trample upon, as they are permitted to trample upon, our most transmarine possessions, the value of which I am bound to show to your Lordship and the public.

"I am sad they print such drivel. *Transmarine Possessions*. Sounds as if they are talking about catching fish, not selling living souls into slavery."

"Oh, Charles, even the Methodists are backing down on opposing slavery, and I think they have become rather spineless since Wesley died. I am disappointed in them. They have compromised their view on slavery. When Wesley wrote *Thoughts Upon Slavery,* it was a vigorous abolitionist paper. Since many Methodists are still slaveholders, they can't support our movement."

A week later Charles watched Elizabeth throw the newspaper down with such a force she tipped over her teacup. She rose and walked over to her husband. The spilled tea went unnoticed as she wrapped her arms around his waist.

"My darling, if the news is disturbing, you should not read it. Can you tell me what this is about?"

"Charles, you should read it for yourself, it will disturb you as well. The newspaper printed an article by a woman who strongly dislikes Methodists and has an even worse opinion about abolition. She thinks nothing of demeaning coloureds and free blacks. Knowing the paper chose to print her opinions and observations disappoints me. I am going to work in the garden and pull weeds to release my anger, and then we will discuss this woman and her views."

Elizabeth walked out the door with her basket, leaving Charles to clean up the spilled tea.

A short while later, returning from the garden with a basket of yams, Elizabeth hummed a hymn. Charles knew she had calmed herself with music as she often did when working through a problem.

Charles patted the chair next to him. "Please dear, sit down. It will help if we talk about this offensive article." He handed his wife a freshly brewed cup of bush tea.

She welcomed the fragrant aroma of lemongrass. "I see you've added soursop leaves to calm your agitated wife. I'm sorry, Charles, but if I can reread the article calmly, I may acknowledge there are bits of truth mixed with this woman's false accusations."

Charles agreed. "I read it twice, trying to understand if there could be any truth in it."

Elizabeth frowned. "She wrote that the Methodist teachers use *parrot-style teaching.* I suppose we do at times teach them rote, maybe just repeating truths without being sure they grasp the meaning of what they memorize. We can work on doing this better."

She picked up the newspaper.

> Methodists encourage slaves to attend chapel services, and it is a hopeless method of instruction. The sermons could be preached in Arabic and be as efficacious as preaching in English.

Elizabeth declared, "What she wrote is painful to read. She argues we do not teach morals or civilization. How can she write such things?"

"She writes it because of her church's position—since the state church stands opposed to abolition and freedom for the slaves. The plantation owners maintain the view the coloureds or any blacks lack the character to work independently of a master. They argue the slaves are better off than the working population of England, and indeed, some are. The woman wrote that *slave owners supply every possible need a slave could have*."

"Indeed, every need but freedom!" Elizabeth said forcefully. "My father was a kind master, but I also know some treat their slaves no better than animals. She calls the slaves *savages, impenetrably dull, with no feelings of modesty or shame*."

Setting the paper aside, Elizabeth brought her clenched fists up to her chest. "I am overcome by rather savage thoughts arising in my heart towards this writer."

Charles rose from his chair and knelt before his wife. "She never met you or your family. I do not know any British woman as well-read as you or Anne, or any as modest. And no one who has met you could *possibly* call you dull."

"But Charles, I do see her point in saying the Methodist Chapels place too much emphasis on avoiding dancing and fancy dress. Sometimes focusing on the principles of Christ is *not* taught. I know within our chapels there are those slaves who live life on the Sabbath unlike the way they live the rest of the week. That much is true. We must strive not to teach rules of conduct to please the church, but teach a transformed life, devoted to pleasing God alone."

"Her criticism of Methodists is correct in saying they teach that favor with God comes from obeying a system. However, we understand the thing pleasing to God is a faith coming from knowing Jesus came to die for our sins and placing our trust in Him alone. Many slaves grow up believing the only way to please their owner is following the master's rules. Many do not understand living by faith. We are guilty of this."

Elizabeth wearied from the many hours spent traveling to teach the slaves, so it was especially difficult to hear criticism of their efforts to educate the enslaved. She shrugged. "I know some plantations allow us to instruct the children because they believe we tell slaves to be obedient to their master. We do teach obedience, but we also believe a day will come when the law will bring freedom to the slaves." Elizabeth began to straighten the books on the table and puffed an enormous breath. "This bigoted woman accuses anyone black of having a *dislike of every species of knowledge*. These last few years, we discovered many slaves crave knowledge, and they are indeed as capable of learning as whites or anyone else!"

Striking the newspaper on the table, Elizabeth said, "She points out the state church has not sent out teachers. Indeed, they fear teaching might promote discontent among the slaves. The state church is content for the slaves to remain ignorant. Her description of all the slaves she has met as *contented and happy* is false. Then she quoted Thomas Gray's writings, where he said *ignorance is bliss*. We prove such a statement wrong with every student who learns to read and chooses to seek knowledge. Charles, I am trying to extend grace to this ignorant woman."

Charles realized the plantation owners did not know about their slaves reading and absorbing the Bible, the complete Bible. He chuckled, remembering the many times he had purposefully forgotten his Bible. He left it behind after teaching the slaves. When he was first told to instruct the slaves from a radically abridged version of God's Word, he became angry—a Bible where most of the Old Testament was missing, and only including about half of the New Testament in their version of a *slave Bible*.

"What are you finding so humorous, Charles?" Elizabeth asked as her husband suppressed a grin.

"I remembered how much the slaves appreciate the stories of deliverance—Moses and other Old Testament heroes of the faith. They are thankful my forgetfulness means I often leave behind my Bible—my unabridged Bible—for them to discover and read. I suppose if any of them had started a rebellion, I would feel differently about my intentional absentmindedness. I know some slaves understand a great deal more scripture than their owners. I always leave my marker at Galatians 3:28 hoping they will read where God says there is neither Jew nor Greek, bond nor free."

Her husband rose from kneeling at her feet, rubbed his knees, and placed his hands on her head. "How I praise God for the gift of a wife with so much wisdom, and a woman who extends grace to arrogant white writers with no grasp of the severity of life for slaves. God granted me a quest to share knowledge where He allows us to go. By God's grace, we have prepared many for independence."

Wanting to erase the angry thoughts the woman's article produced, Elizabeth crumpled the newspaper. "When I remember my father working to the point of exhaustion for years, I can't imagine her writing such false statements. This woman said, 'most of the slaves, if given freedom, would never work.' This fills me with resentment. Freedom came to Father before birth. But in her view, because he was one-fourth black, she could be critical of him as well. Charles, help me not to let this woman's false beliefs allow bitterness to creep into my heart."

Both couples continued teaching many slaves. The Sunday schools grew, and the Women's Refuge continued to serve countless women and children. But both the Thwaites and the Gilberts were beginning to feel the many years of their tireless sacrifice.

# 34

# *Great Loss*

*1833*

Anne sat by Elizabeth's bedside, caressing her hand. Sixty-year-old Elizabeth had been feverish for two weeks, growing steadily weaker. Charles sat with her until he finally yielded to Anne's advice that he must rest. When Dr. Percival came offering little encouragement, Anne struggled to remain hopeful. The doctor listened to Elizabeth's lungs with the latest invention from France, a long wooden tube allowing him to hear sounds in the chest. He closed his eyes and shook his head. Though hard to see hope disappear from the patient's family, he convinced himself they needed honesty.

"I hear sounds that indicate fluid in her lungs. You can bathe her in cool water to try to reduce her fever, give her bush tea to drink, and pray. Her condition does not sound good to me, but she is still somewhat alert, and moving about in the bed, so those signs are positive."

Shaking the doctor's hand, Anne thanked him for coming and sank back into the chair beside Elizabeth's bed. As she stroked her sister's hand, Anne asked softly, "Elizabeth, could you drink some tea?"

As her eyes fluttered open, Elizabeth asked, "Did the doctor say why I am so weak? I am cold and feeling rather shaky."

Anne reached for the teapot, trying to sound cheerful. "Yes, you have had a fever. I have some fresh bush tea right here. Charles is resting. You have slept for hours."

Pouring the tea, she continued soothing her sister. "Elizabeth, as you slept, I wondered how we will celebrate the emancipation ceremonies.

Freedom for all is so close now, but a long hard wait for the slaves here. Together with our husbands, we will be there to join them and raise our voices in praise. Only a year away! What a day it will be, and our vision will come true." Elizabeth did not comment as Anne helped her take a few sips of tea.

Anne continued to think about how they must be together for the celebrations, freedom was so close. The battle had been long, but the long-awaited day was finally in sight. Now with only a year left they needed to prepare as many slaves as possible for independent life, free from the yoke that bound them for centuries. As Elizabeth pushed the cup away and turned her head, Anne pled, "We have work to do, so rest and be well, Elizabeth."

Anne let a barely audible whimper escape, thankful her sister's eyes remained shut, relieved she would not notice the tears on her troubled face.

When Elizabeth's breathing grew more labored, Anne woke Charles and they sang hymns, realizing Elizabeth was slipping away.

Charles cradled his wife in his arms. "Go, my darling. We will be all right by God's grace." He laid her down gently, and with a final breath, Elizabeth's faith became sight.

Just then Esther whom John had brought, slipped into the room. She knelt beside the bed, reciting a Jewish prayer.

Charles ran his fingers over his wife's hair, clearing it from her face. "I never imagined I would face a day without her beside me."

The church could not hold all those touched by Elizabeth's life. Many who loved her stood outside in the gentle rain. They sang hymns with less jubilation than usual. The sermon urged all to seek God's call on their lives.

As they lowered Elizabeth's body in the grave, Anne felt as if half of her joined her sister. For years, the two of them, then the four of them joined forces to be a part of what God wanted to accomplish on their beloved island. Now a trio, John and Anne stood on either side of Charles. Elizabeth, the one to see the bright side of every trial, now silently challenged Anne to keep her role in their work alive.

The trio continued to teach at the school in Bethesda. One day, approaching the classroom, Anne overheard Charles speaking to the empty room as if he were talking with Elizabeth. She turned and waited a few seconds before she approached, singing a song to keep from embarrassing him.

Anne understood. She found herself often thinking, "I must tell Elizabeth ..." before she realized she could never again share as they had in past years. The loss of her sister turned out to be a deeper, more profound loss than when her mother or father had died. Anne continued because of her faith that someday they would all be together again.

They built the school in Bethesda on a hillside where the trade winds blowing through the large, glassless windows provided relief from the heat. Students troubled by oppressive heat found attention a challenge. The summer heat clung to clothes and skin, seeming harsher that year. On an oppressively hot day, only a month after the loss of Elizabeth, Charles walked faster than usual to open the classroom shutters for the awaiting students.

Anne realized John struggled walking up the small hill to the school. He almost reached the colourful crotons planted in a hedge around the building, when he turned and declared, "I am not well, Anne." As he said this, he collapsed onto the pathway. Seeing him, Anne cried, "Charles!" Students ran out and helped carry John inside and laid him on a bench.

"We must get him home, Charles. John has been struggling lately to catch his breath when he exerts himself. I pray it is just the heat, but I need the doctor to see him."

Charles immediately understood the urgency of the situation. John was sweating profusely, and his skin turned pale and clammy. Unbuttoning his friend's shirt, Charles watched John's chest rise and fall, noticing his erratic breathing. "I will go for the doctor, Anne. We will bring a wagon to take him home."

Anne rarely saw apprehension in John's face, but she recognized it now. "John, I am going to take you home. I know this bench must be an uncomfortable bed, but please rest, my dear."

Her husband blinked and then shut his eyes. The children all peered into the schoolroom, and some were crying. Their emotional reactions did not help her own fears. Speaking to the children hanging in the open-air windows, Anne announced, “Please children, Mr. Gilbert needs the air. Go home, and Mr. Thwaites will teach you tomorrow.”

The children left, and Anne stayed with John. She prayed aloud, “Precious Savior, watch over my beloved, grant him relief from whatever has him so ill.”

Charles came with the wagon, blankets laid in its bed. John was able to stand but needed help to climb into the back of the cart and lie down. Anne climbed in beside him and opened her parasol to shield him from the sun to help make him comfortable on the bumpy ride home. After settling John into bed, Charles went for the doctor.

While Charles was gone, John began to sound desperate. “Something heavy is on my chest. Move it before it crushes me!”

“No, my love, there is nothing on you but the sheet. Charles has gone for the doctor. Please, John, do not leave me. You are as necessary to me as breath itself. Please!”

John cried out in pain. Then silence. Anne fell across him as he lay still and quiet. After some tense minutes she heard the wagon pull up outside. Charles called her name as he and the doctor came inside. Anne looked at them and lowered her head. Charles helped her up and took her to the porch while the doctor examined John.

“I am so sorry, Anne.”

Anne softly said, “They are both gone. I thought there was no pain greater than losing Elizabeth, and now John too has left us for heaven. I am not ready to have them both ripped from my life. I need him.”

“I am sorry— it must have been his heart,” said the doctor. “There is nothing more I can do. I can walk back to my office, Charles. You stay with your sister-in-law.”

The finality of his words unlocked the dam holding back Anne’s tears. She sank to a chair and sobbed, rocking back and forth, her arms wrapped about herself. Charles sat beside her and quietly sang one of John’s favorite hymns, Charles Wesley’s *And Can It Be That I Should Gain.* At the end, he rose. “I’ll prepare some tea for you, Anne. Elizabeth always believed it helped. I will stay awhile, until Esther can get here. I’ve sent word to town for her to come.”

The next day Charles came again to help Anne prepare for yet another funeral. John was well loved. The many people who came to the service greeted Anne afterwards, relating instances of his influence on their lives. Later Anne sat on her veranda, pondering what her life might have been if she had refused to marry him. God had blessed them with 35 years of serving together.

Anne determined to continue helping at the Women's Shelter in English Harbour. She moved into a small cottage behind the larger home housing the women. She worked tirelessly, though in her head she could hear Elizabeth gently telling her to rest and take a cup of tea. In the year after John's death, she poured her heart into helping the women who were in greater need than she. The work relieved some of the sadness, and it brought great satisfaction. She thought little of her own needs and health, sometimes heading to her cottage long after dark to drop into bed, exhausted but pleased and comforted.

One evening though, she could not sleep. She cut her hand some days earlier on a metal scrap sticking out from a wall. Though she washed and bandaged the cut, it now throbbed as if it would explode. Her head also throbbed, and she tossed restlessly all evening. She prayed earnestly for mercy—or even for an angel to watch over her.

The following morning, she barely woke enough to hear a rap on her door. Anne tried to sit up, but it was as if lead had filled her body. She managed a raspy, "Come in." Surprised by Esther coming through the small tin and wood door, she managed a smile and shaky laugh, "Oh, you must be the angel I prayed for!"

Esther rushed to her side. "Oh, Anne! You should have called for me sooner!"

"Why?" Anne protested, "I will be fine. I have just overworked myself. Why did you come?"

"I saw one of the shelter ladies at the market," Esther explained. "She confided in me yesterday that you looked unwell, and she was worried. She said you would not rest and asked me to come and look in on you."

"I am fine." Anne protested.

Esther placed a hand on Anne's forehead. "You are feverish and flushed, my dear. How long have you felt ill?"

Anne pulled her hand from under the light cotton blanket. Esther gasped at its swollen appearance and lines of purple staining her arm.

When Anne awoke again, the day was passing. When she opened her eyes, she saw Esther. The setting sun shimmering through the clear windowpane highlighted Esther's dark curls—she indeed looks like my angel, thought Anne. Esther explained the doctor came, cleaned her wound, made a poultice to draw out the infection, and left. But he was worried about her health, for her body was not fighting the infection.

"I am here, Anne," reassured Esther, silencing the protests. "I am not going anywhere until you are well. You welcomed me as a sister years ago, and this is what a sister does."

Esther tried to get Anne to eat a cup of vegetable broth and tea, but she had no appetite. Later in the evening Esther awoke to Anne muttering. Her words made little sense, intermittently calling out to Elizabeth or John. Her skin went from burning hot to cold and clammy, and she started breathing rapidly. Esther stepped outside and shouted for one of the yard boys to run for the doctor. On walking back inside, she saw that Anne's breathing was now shallow and sporadic. Anne reached out her hand.

"Esther," her voice barely a whisper, "I'm going home." All went quiet.

"No, no!" Esther groaned as darkness engulfed her as if the light would never break again. She felt helpless. She could not stop this death. She had lost another sister—the brightest colour she had ever known.

# 35

# Emancipation Dawn

*1834*

As the morning of August 1, 1834 dawned for Charles Thwaites, his heart stretched with a mingling of joy and sorrow. He sorrowed that Elizabeth could not be here to rejoice with him, yet he knew joy for the part she had played in this monumental day. What a band of soldiers they had been—he and Elizabeth, Anne with John. Slavery in the West Indies was now only a horrible wound—a scar that would take years to heal completely.

Hearing the church bells pealing liberation at midnight, he remained in bed praying for a peaceful transition. Over the last year, he developed a habit of speaking to Elizabeth as if she were there in the room with him. He spoke to her now. "Elizabeth darling, do you think the singing and dancing will continue throughout the night? I suppose it is a blessing my hearing is not what it once was. I believe I can go back to sleep, so don't be concerned."

How his heart longed for Elizabeth, imagining what a day of celebration they might have shared. When alone, he often told Elizabeth of his day, talking as though she lingered in the room. Now, once again, he talked to his absent wife. "Dear Elizabeth, you left for heaven a little over a year ago, and not long after John Gilbert joined you. I expected at least Anne and I would celebrate together today, but it was not to be. God took her home to glory two weeks ago. Of course, I suppose you know this."

"You might not approve, Elizabeth, but I decided to remain home from church last Sunday." Then to the silent room he remarked, "I'm sure the believers missed me, wondering if I am well. Mrs. Looby's daughter came to check on me and brought supper." In the dark room he smiled as if she could see the humor in his receiving supper because he was absent from church.

After he dressed the next morning, Charles chose to watch the triumph from his front porch. Feeling too old to join the crowds rejoicing in the streets, he sat enjoying their jubilation. The mingling of the joyous sounds of hymns with added drums and children banging pans made Charles laugh. "Oh, Elizabeth, many generations awaited this day. The sound makes me want to bang a kettle myself. Surely people who do not know me would be surprised to see an old white man rejoicing over all the enslaved on the islands finally granted freedom."

Today, he would sit and read his Bible, pray, and talk a little with the absent Elizabeth. "I feel this thunderous chorus of praise. None of the other islands have gone to full emancipation, only our own Antigua. And you know, they are saying it's because of our training ahead of this time that they were ready to be set free. You and Anne and John—we did it, darling. By God's grace, we helped to loosen the chains holding back the slaves."

Charles paused and glanced towards heaven. "May glorious freedom rain down on all these colourful people we love."

He began reading through the Psalms as he sat on the veranda. Glancing up from his Bible, he noticed an elderly woman nearing his cottage. His eyes had dimmed some with age, but something about her looked familiar. When she called out to him, he recognized the voice of Liza, Elizabeth's elderly stepmother. Charles mentally calculated Liza must be at least 78 years of age. Stylishly dressed, she might have appeared to be younger except for the full head of snowy white hair showing beneath her large, fashionable hat. Recently he heard she had become a great-grandmother.

Charles stood up and helped her climb the porch steps. "Liza, welcome and make yourself comfortable. I am surprised to see you in this throng of revelers. What a day!"

He observed her carefully as she sank into a chair, tears softly falling over her wrinkled face. "Liza, what has happened?" Charles slowly settled into the veranda chair beside Liza, touching her arm.

"Oh, Charles, it is too late. Your Elizabeth should have been here to see all this, not me. Anne should have been here too. I admit I heard of Anne's death two weeks ago, and I have no excuse for not attending her funeral."

She paused. "My children attended Anne's funeral, they all loved her so. They adored Elizabeth as well. They came to visit last Sunday, finally telling me how life was for them during what they refer to as my *absent years*. Anne's death devastated them. Anne and your dear wife mothered *my children* during the years I struggled with the cloud surrounding my mind. I was a stranger to those I should have loved." She gave a rueful smile. "Thanks to my children, though it was painful to hear, I now realize how selfish and blind I was. Barry Hart did not deserve a wife such as me. I never became the mother his children and our children needed. I don't know how Anne and Elizabeth bore the burden of caring for all of us. I wish I had told your wife and Anne I am grateful for all they did for me."

"Both sisters tried to do what they could to help you during those years. They did not fully understand the pressures of the many changes, but they chose to stay and love you anyway." Charles said kindly.

She had removed her hat, and her nervousness showed as she began to shift the hat from hand to hand. "Now, I am not only a grandmother, but blessed to live to see my first great-grandchild born. If only I could be as gentle as Elizabeth and as wise as Anne. I sorrow I can't ask them to forgive me."

Charles choked back his emotions. "Liza, you honor them now. This means a great deal to me to know this."

"After the newest child was born this week, I suggested they name her Elizabeth Anne. My days are numbered, and I believe God has forgiven me. I regret I failed to walk with Him during those years I struggled so desperately to make it through each day."

Wiping the tears from his own eyes, Charles wished Elizabeth could hear this conversation. They had prayed for Liza for years.

She stood as if making an official declaration. "Charles, I told my children I would buy a headstone for both Elizabeth and Anne. I want to show everyone I recognize they both deserve my sincere gratitude for all the years they extended grace to me."

"Thank you, Liza." Charles paused before going on. "Anne and Elizabeth do not need anything written in stone, though it is very thoughtful of you. The thousands of slaves—they are their memorial."

Liza raised her eyes to stare at Charles. "Some called you a fool to marry Elizabeth, saying she was not your equal. I understand now how some failed to grasp the role both Anne and Elizabeth played." She gazed at the multitude of former slaves displaying sheer joy. She quietly added, "Neither Elizabeth nor Anne gave birth, but there is no numbering their children. Now I understand how privileged I was to have them in the lives of my children as well."

Charles took her frail, gnarled hand. "I'm glad you came today. I believe we're never too old to learn how much grace God bestows on us, sometimes through the lives of others. May God grant our island His grace to love and accept each other. Marvelous, limitless grace."

Watching the former slaves dancing in the streets, Charles continued, "We have much to celebrate. I wish Elizabeth and Anne could have lived to see this day."

She stood and Charles helped her down the steps and waved goodbye to this woman who was finally realizing the peace she had missed for all those years.

He walked inside telling Elizabeth all about the visit with her stepmother. He sat for a long while staring at the painting she had created years before, using the Colour Box—the gift her father, Barry, had passed along from his Irish father. He stared at the image of Annie Hart surrounded by her children.

He spoke aloud, but this time to Annie, Elizabeth's mother in heaven. "I wish I had known you, Annie Clearkley Hart. I would have told you what a fine job you and Barry did with your girls and your sons as well. Becoming part of the Hart family was an honor. God used them to make a difference among countless people. He created your family from all the wonderful colours Elizabeth captured in this painting of you and your beautiful children. God allowed me to share in your colourful family through Elizabeth."

Charles gazed at the family in the painting. "What a glorious day. Though we did not watch it together, you saw it by faith many years ago." Charles turned to start the kettle for tea. Tea just might help.

# Author's Notes

Pushing our way through thick brush and climbing over mounds of rubble, our family encountered an unexpected sight. We had spent a lazy afternoon exploring the scattered ruins of Bridgetown, an old colonial trading town on the West Indies island of Antigua where we lived. We hoped to find pottery shards or other interesting artifacts. Established in 1675 and once the principal English settlement on the island, Bridgetown boasted an Anglican Church and Methodist chapel, built in 1803. Shipping and commerce eventually moved to today's capital, St. John's. The years saw the town's decline and by the mid-1800s, it had fallen into ruin, hastened by a destructive earthquake in 1843. As we searched for traces of habitation 310 years after Bridgetown's founding, we found few signs, with most of the remains having been bulldozed to prepare the land for farming.

The sight we stumbled upon, overgrown with vegetation and partially covered in earth, was the polished marble top of a burial vault! Exploring the dense undergrowth further, other vaults and gravestones came to light. We discovered the graveyard of the colonial Anglican Church. As we read the inscriptions on some of the headstones, one especially held our interest, the one on the vault we had first seen:

> HERE LYE THE REMAINS
> Of John Frye Esq:
> One of his Majesty's council of this island
> A man too worthy
> In his life and manners
> To be lost to remembrance
> He left this world 6th March, 1747

The parchment rubbing that we made from that gravestone 30 years ago is one of my most treasured possessions. I have tried to picture what life must have been like for this gentleman in that time and place. I have found no mention of him in my research. Perhaps from my Welsh ancestry, I have always had an interest in British history. Living in Antigua for 38 years gave me a wonderful opportunity to become familiar with this former colony and its past—good and grave.

Years later I came across the story of two amazing women—sisters—who lived in Antigua shortly after the time of John Frye. I have always been fascinated by stories of women who defy the odds and do the challenging things in life that many of us who are timid would avoid. These women's lives so captivated me I determined that their story should not be lost to remembrance, unlike John Fry's. The period of their lives involved great social change. Wars ravaged Europe and the Caribbean; the Industrial Revolution dawned and flourished; slavery, that devastating social ill, was coming to an end, and with it, the end of an entire culture in the Caribbean islands. These two mixed-race sisters, Anne and Elizabeth Hart, were not only in the middle of the change, they also chose to hasten the change by defying the social norms of their day—not through protest or agitation, but through the love and compassion shaped by their Christian character.

Sadly, most of what we know about Anne and Elizabeth comes down to us as dry historical facts. Both sisters burned most of their personal journals and papers before their deaths. I discovered though, that their recorded accomplishments and activities, as well as their remaining writings, created a strong outline for a clear picture of their lives. The outline simply begged to be colored in, as if the girls were saying to me, "There was so much more to our lives—so much that has never been told." With my own set of colors and imagination, I have attempted to paint this picture for you. For them.

To say that these women were unusual would be an understatement. In a culture where persons of mixed race were second-class citizens at best, and more likely slaves, their accomplishments in the face of that culture were nothing less than astounding. Their parents blessed them with an enriched childhood, providing a stark difference to many other free black children.

Though not illegal, the stigma and social consequences of mixed-race marriages made them rare and risky. That both sisters married white men demonstrates their strength of character in facing these consequences. Accounts written in the 1800s record fierce opposition to the marriage between John Gilbert and Anne. He was threatened with being committed to the insane asylum and with being court martialed if he chose to marry her. He did lose his job for a time as a result. His office door was painted half black and half white, and his sign thrown into the sea. I can imagine the opposition only strengthened their love and resolve to demonstrate to their small world (a ten by twelve-mile island) that their godly love was strong enough to overcome the antagonism. Seven years later Elizabeth Hart and Charles Thwaites followed the example of Anne and John with another Hart sister's mixed marriage.

In painting the Hart sisters' picture, I have tried to be accurate and stay within the historical lines as much as possible. It helped that my husband and children are explorers, and we visited many of the ruins of plantations and other locations that are a part of their story. I read as many books and records as I could find regarding the colonial culture and history of that period, the island, and the Hart family. As with most historical research, I came across numerous gaps and contradictions. Dates of births and deaths and spelling of names varied from book to book. Often narratives of events disagreed. To make a readable story and avoid confusion where facts were contradictory or unclear, I had to be a bit creative in spots. I hope the following notes may help you understand the background and explain some of the liberties I have taken.

- The sisters' marriages, their work in establishing schools for slaves and Sunday schools, and their work with shelters for women and children are well-documented. Many believe that their education of slaves in Antigua was instrumental in preparing them for full freedom. Antigua was the only British Caribbean island in which, in 1834, the slaves received full emancipation immediately instead of going through stages as occurred on other islands.

- The few writings that survive demonstrate how very articulate and well educated the sisters were. Their father, Barry, wrote columns for the newspaper and later their brother Gratianus became involved with a local newspaper. Anne and Elizabeth were asked to collaborate on a written history of the Methodist Church in Antigua. The letter Elizabeth wrote regarding slavery is one of the few actual documents preserved. This letter was republished and circulated as an antislavery tract. She associated with mainstream British pro emancipation circles. The poem included is also her actual writing.
- In 1809 the two sisters established the first Sunday school in the West Indies, and in 1815 they founded the Female Refuge Society.
- John Gilbert's background is recorded history. I could not identify the brave clergymen who performed the marriage for each sister. Rev. McDonald lived with the Harts, and he died about the time Anne and John married, so I made him the pastor who officiated their wedding.
- Barry's father, John Hart, married twice. John's first wife lived only a year on Antigua. Barry was his son from his housekeeper-slave Fanny Conyers, and Gratianus, Barry's half-brother, was from John Hart's second wife, Elizabeth. In his will John left money to Protestant schools in Ireland and funds to support Barry and his mother, Fanny. Barry inherited two plantations, Harts and Royals, along with their slaves. All reports indicate he was a sympathetic and reluctant owner of slaves. Barry sold both Harts and Royals in 1801 and worked in Trinidad for a time. Records for 1833 indicate the two former Hart plantations possessed 120 slaves. No records indicate how many slaves Barry owned in 1801.
- During this time period families often named a child after the parent. Anne Clearkley named her first daughter Anne. In some cases, I felt it would be too confusing to keep the actual names. I needed Anne's name to be distinctive from her daughter's, so I had Barry call his first wife "Annie."

- This family included multiple Elizabeths, so I shortened the name of Barry's second wife to Liza. I could not find records giving Liza's last name.
- Anne Clearkley and her sister went to England to attend university. The sister's name was Elizabeth, which I changed to Margaret. She was engaged to a Charles Matthews, who drowned when his ship sank enroute to Antigua. Again, for clarity I changed his name to Stephen Matthews since Charles Hart was Barry's youngest son by Annie. Lydia, Annie's sister did serve as the Hart children's tutor for a time.
- None of the research indicates how Liza coped with having such a large family. I imagined a post-partum depression could have occurred. Barry Hart did have as many as fourteen or fifteen children. Historical accounts name Anne and Elizabeth as educators for Barry's large family.
- I chose to make Anne the first child for Barry and Annie, but it appears there was a son named John born first. Two different dates were given for the death of Barry's first wife, Annie. Some gave dates as early as 1780, others as late as 1785. I chose the date that made Anne 16 and Elizabeth 13 when their mother, Annie, died. Although many storms blew through Antigua, the connection between a storm and Annie's death came from my imagination.
- By the mid-1600s 70 percent of the population of the neighboring island of Montserrat were indentured Irish. The Irish O'Rourke girl in my story came from my imagination, as did the Jewish character, Esther. Records of the time period indicate two Jewish men imprisoned about the time Esther joins the Harts. I enjoyed the wonderful Irish lilt that remains with folks I met from Montserrat.
- Thomas Coke did meet George Washington, and he baptized both Anne and Elizabeth in 1785.
- Doctor Ramsey's history is true, but there is no record he met Barry Hart. Ramsey did influence William Wilberforce. Wilberforce might well have read letters that Elizabeth wrote which circulated among abolitionists.

- Attacks on missionaries on other islands and disturbances in Saint Domingue (Haiti) are factual.
- Many of the names I found in historical accounts were the same as the names of people we met during our residence in Antigua. I used names that remain today, but those names blended with my imagination.
- The mail-packet ship *Maria* sinking in 1826 is factual, and all but one missionary died. Mrs. Jones survived, left the island, and remarried.
- The pro-slavery letter causing Elizabeth distress was an actual news article written by a woman living on a plantation during that time.
- Curaçao is called the mother of the Carib-Jewish community (Sephardic Jews), and in 1785 40 percent of Curaçao's white population was Jewish. The history of cocoa is linked with the Jews in Curaçao.
- Anne did inherit two slaves left to her by Mr. Blizard when she was 16. I do not know their names or when she granted their freedom.
- In 1827 Mr. Phillips and Elizabeth were brought before the House of Assembly. He subsequently spent a year in jail. He was the solitary white man in the Moravian church.
- Elizabeth Thwaites died a year before emancipation, and John Gilbert died shortly after Elizabeth. Anne died two weeks before emancipation, which took place on August 1, 1834. Charles lived several more years and records indicate he remarried and had a son. We knew of the Thwaites family living in Antigua in the 1970s, and they operated a photographic developing studio.
- Mrs. Bethune helped financially and indeed sent goods to Anne and Elizabeth. I do not know that Mrs. Bethune ever met Anne Gilman. Her husband, Ephraim, was a ship owner from Alexandria, Virginia, whose ships traded in the West Indies. I had some fun including Anne Gilman and Malvina Amanda Gilman sending gifts to Antigua. Malvina, born in 1810, Anne Gilman's daughter, was my great-great grandmother.

- Barry Hart purchased land from a Mr. Nanton on the corner of Tanner and Temple Streets in St. John's for a Methodist chapel. The Methodists paid him thirty pounds for the property.
- The island authorities set up an internal postal system in March 1841 between St. John's and English Harbour, with Mr. Scotland as the postmaster. From 1858, Great Britain postage stamps were made available for use in Antigua.
- I found my own treasure of a single blue glass bead many years ago on the site of Bridgetown.
- The information about the existence of a slave Bible is documented.
- The French had warships in the Caribbean and, for a short time, occupied neighboring islands surrounding Antigua on all sides. Throughout the European wars many of the Caribbean islands changed hands more than once. Antigua is one of the only islands that did not have years of being French, Portuguese, or Dutch. Some of the neighboring islands changed possession as many as 14 times. Antigua's stability was likely because England chose to heavily fortify the island as a Naval base to protect British interests in the Caribbean in the 1740s. Antigua became one of the most heavily fortified places in the world and remains as the only continuously working Georgian Dockyard anywhere. In the 1950s, the Naval Dockyard in Antigua was renamed Nelson's Dockyard.
- Today Nelson's Dockyard is a UNESCO World Heritage site, and their many historical reports helped with my research. Information about the King's Negroes, the Middle Ground, the hospital for Negroes on Middle Ground, and the bum boat women all came from the UNESCO reports.
- One UNESCO report said: "The most archivally visible African persons are the men enslaved by the Royal Navy. Collectively known as the "King's Negroes," these men formed the core of the workforce at the Dockyard. Most of these men, like Shadwell the Sailmaker, Colin the Sawyer, and Bashee the Shipwright, were highly skilled artisans. Based on archival evidence, boys as young as 13 were purchased directly from slave ships and handed over to

a white master craftsman to train them. During this time the Royal Navy required annual updates on their progress towards craft mastery as well as ability to read and write. While required to be in the yard during the day, each man built a small house and garden plot on the Royal Navy land outside the Dockyard to where they would retire in the evening. In this space, these men could live their own lives, have families, and develop a home."

Though this is a novel, the history connected with the Hart sisters is both inspirational and relevant to today. The diligence of these sisters touched countless lives, with an impact that continues. I also think credit belongs to John Gilbert and Charles Thwaites for resisting the prejudices of the times. They were men to match the determination and resolve of their wives.

If you enjoyed my historical novel, I would love to hear from you. You can contact me at my email: palomarkid@hotmail.com, my website: BarbaraWaiteBooks.com, or on Facebook at facebook.com/barbara.waite.56. Please consider leaving a review on any online bookstore you frequent. This is a valuable encouragement and only needs to be brief. It is usually unnecessary to have purchased from that distributor. Thank You.

# Acknowledgments

*"We make a living by what we get, but we make a life by what we give." —Winston Churchill*

I accomplished writing *The Colour Box* with the help of treasured friends and family who were the midwives assisting the birth of this story. They gave countless hours and energy, cheered me on, and made this story a reality. I cannot thank them adequately; I will forever be grateful for the blessing of each of these who gave much.

My husband, Curt, encouraged me when I was ready to give up and has been my first go-to source for questions of content and grammar.

My adult children eagerly assisted with research since they lived on the island of Antigua all the years they were growing up. Dan helped much with all the work that went into the cover. He even ordered a vintage colour box from England to be a part of the background. Our daughter, Carin, read through countless revisions of the manuscript; she herself is a gifted writer. Our middle son, Christopher, has always been a mimic and he helped write the dialect which greatly enhanced my efforts. Joshua was a great help with research and story line.

Janet has been my collaborator through all three books I have written. She has always been there to encourage and improve my efforts. Janet's sister, Judy, gave superb editing advise, as well as Jan Flickinger. The credit for the amazing cover goes to Janet, my son Dan, and Diane King. My team's ability to create a perfect cover from vintage paintings has been awesome. The background painting is from *Green Castle Estate Antigua* by Nicholas Pocock from the Beinecke Lesser Antilles Collection of Hamilton College. The painting by Augustino Brunias, (c.1770-1796) of the two sisters is in the public domain, and titled *Free Women of Color*. It is in the Brooklyn Museum collection.

I am grateful for amazing help from friends who read through the entire book, helping with grammar and wording. My deep gratitude to Suzy E., Helen, Eileen, Lynda, Masako, Delila, and Mary M. for all the hours spent helping with word choices. Gayle and Janet P. read through the manuscript as well. The gals in my Creative Writing group read through many of the beginning chapters adding their input, thanks to Mary, Joni, Jan, Sandy and Pat.

Thank you to each who helped me create this story, gratitude also to those who read and enjoyed. Praise to The Lord who gave me the privilege and joy of living on Antigua for 38 years. It has been a glorious experience to imagine what Antigua was like in the 1700-1800s.

Made in the USA
Monee, IL
16 April 2021

64738642R00164